WHY BLACK LIVES MATTER (TOO)

A Revolutionary Call to Action

Mary Canty Merrill, Ph.D.

authorHOUSE

AuthorHouse™
1663 Liberty Drive
Bloomington, IN 47403
www.authorhouse.com
Phone: 1 (800) 839-8640

© 2016 Mary Canty Merrill, Ph.D. All rights reserved.

No part of this book may be reproduced, stored in a retrieval system, or transmitted by any means without the written permission of the author.

Published by AuthorHouse   05/10/2016

ISBN: 978-1-5246-0120-1 (sc)
ISBN: 978-1-5246-0119-5 (e)

Library of Congress Control Number: 2016905795

Print information available on the last page.

Any people depicted in stock imagery provided by Thinkstock are models, and such images are being used for illustrative purposes only.
Certain stock imagery © Thinkstock.

This book is printed on acid-free paper.

Because of the dynamic nature of the Internet, any web addresses or links contained in this book may have changed since publication and may no longer be valid. The views expressed in this work are solely those of the author and do not necessarily reflect the views of the publisher, and the publisher hereby disclaims any responsibility for them.

Contents

Dedication ix
Editor's Note xi
Foreword xiii
Acknowledgements xv
Prologue xix

Chapter 1   The Roots of Our Struggle 1
    The History of Slavery in America 3
    The Psychological and Physiological Impact of Slavery,
    Racism and Discrimination 10
    The Plight of Black America 16

Chapter 2   Racism in America 37
    Understanding Racism and Prejudice 39
    The Sociopathology of Racism 40
    The Concept of White Supremacy 42
    Understanding White Privilege 44
    Racial Microaggressions and Marginality 46
    The Myth of Reverse Racism 50

Chapter 3   Institutionalized Racism 53
    Structural Racism 55
    Inequities in Our Criminal Justice System 56

Chapter 4   The Rise of the Black Lives Matter Movement 71
    A Death in Ferguson, Missouri Sparks a Movement 73
    Why We Say Black Lives Matter 74
    Misconceptions about the Black Lives Matter Movement 74
    The Problem with the Slogan "All Lives Matter" 75

Chapter 5 Voices for Equality on Why Black Lives Matter 77

A Call to New Orleans 81
A Walk through History 87
We, As Ourselves, Will Save Us All 94
When I Learned to See 97
One White Woman's Perspective 102
A New rEvolution is Emerging 106
A Conversation with My Students: Dismantling White Fragility and White Privilege in the Historical Narrative 111
The Luxury of Colorblindness 116
An Opened Mind 120
Confronting White Privilege 125
Let's Never Return to "The Good Old Days" 129
Why I Teach My White Child That Black Lives Matter 134
#BLM Supporters Must Recalibrate So the Movement Remains Relevant 138
Why Do Black Lives Matter? 143
We Hold These Truths to be Self-Evident 146
Why Black Lives Have Always Mattered to Me – And the Result 152
Shifting the Paradigm 158
Why Black Lives Matter 163
Being Black Does Not Mean Being Less Than 168
What Black Lives Matter Means to Me 171
Not for Your Convenience, Nor for Your Service 175
When Others Suffer, I Suffer 179
Little Activists Need Information, Too 183
Black Lives Matter... Of Course They Do! 186
Mamma 191
Smacked in My White Face 196
A Sleeping Giant Has Awakened 201

Hoodie 205
White Child on a Bus 209
I Am Not A Racist... Am I? 213
Dear White People: It's Not Always About Us 219
Coffee Makes You Black 223
Living in a Dystopian World 228
Black Lives Matter, and There's Nothing Debatable
About It 233
Taming the Beast of White Privilege 236
We Have to Say Black Lives Matter... Because in America,
They Don't 241
Thoughts of a Recovering Racist 244
A Love Letter to Black America from Her Native Sister 247
What's Going On in America? 252
Why Black Labeling Matters, Too! 255
How Did We Get Here, and What Will We Do About It? 258
Vigilant At the Gate: Black Lives Matter, Too 260
Black Mental Health Matters (Too)! 264
Say Her Name: Blackness at the Margins and
the Erasure of Women in the Movement 267
Why Do Black Lives Matter At All? 270
Removing the Stain of Racism 273
Fair Treatment of All 278
The Evolution of a Cacophony: Why Black Lives Matter 282

Chapter 6   A Call to Action 287
What White People Can Do to Help Dismantle Racism 289

Epilogue   We Are Still Here 305
In Memory 309
Works Cited 313
About the Author and Editor 325

Dedication

For the **Voices for Equality** Community:
Warriors committed to the good fight to protect human dignity
and help make this world a better place

Editor's Note

The Black Lives Matter movement evolved as a protest against police brutality. This book is a contribution that extends beyond police brutality to revolutionize the national conversation about racial injustice and inequality and advocate for freedom and justice for all. We are not the Black Lives Matter movement. We are the **Voices for Equality**.

The African symbol above, which you will see throughout this book, represents **strength** and **courage**.

Foreword

Evil triumphs each time we refuse to stand up for what's right. Despite any criticism or controversy that I may incite in speaking truth to encourage others to think, do and be differently, I will not be deterred. I refuse to slink back and silence my voice knowing that another human being is suffering or in distress. Either I'm a force for good, or I'm nothing at all.

If I can't speak and own my truth, I'm no good to myself or to anyone else. The essence of the Black Lives Matter movement is to affirm Black lives. However, when a movement counters the dominant narrative with unapologetic truth, it is misunderstood and misinterpreted. I chose this book title to reiterate that the statement "Black Lives Matter" is not an anti-white proposition. Inherent in the statement is an unspoken, but implied, *too*. Hence the title, *Why Black Lives Matter (Too)*.

Recognizing that the fight for social justice and equality is bigger than any one person, and that that there is room for diverse talents and expertise of anyone who is committed to freedom, I chose to lead a collaborative effort in the form of this multi-contributor anthology. Although we attempted to maintain consistency in grammar, spelling, and stylistic elements, in some instances certain writing components have been kept intact to preserve the authentic voices of the writers. Chapters in this book address a range of hot button issues and racial disparities that disproportionately impact the Black community. This project is not about perfection, but about sharing honest and heart-felt stories in the best way that we collectively know how to provoke thought and inspire change.

All proceeds from this book will benefit **The Sentencing Project**, a national non-profit organization engaged in research and advocacy on criminal justice issues and dedicated to changing the way Americans think about crime and punishment. The Sentencing Project is a leader in bringing national attention to disturbing trends and inequities in our criminal justice system with the publication of groundbreaking research, aggressive media campaigns and strategic advocacy for policy reform. Our gift will help the organization work for a fair and effective U.S. criminal justice system by promoting reforms in sentencing policy, addressing unjust racial disparities and practices, and advocating for alternatives to incarceration.

Sometimes people hold a core belief that is so strong that when presented with evidence to contradict that belief, they cannot accept it because it would create cognitive dissonance, a very discomforting feeling. And because they feel it is so important to protect this core belief, they will go to any length to rationalize, ignore and deny anything that doesn't align with it. The book that you hold in your hands may or may not fit within your current core beliefs. If it doesn't, it can potentially be life changing. I challenge you to confront your discomfort and use these words to examine your own views on racial justice and equality—in a refreshing way.

Mary Canty Merrill, Ph.D.

Acknowledgements

Fighting for social justice and equality is hard work. It taxes the mind, body and soul. Disappointments, betrayals, and losses... they all come to weigh us down and conspire to create a type of paralysis if we allow them to linger too long. Sometimes, it's our perspective that will make a remarkable difference... lifting us from the mulligrubs and saving us from ourselves.

Several months ago, a member of Voices for Equality, a Facebook Community that I created and co-facilitate, shared with me this quote by Robert Louis Stevenson, which continues to resonate in my heart, mind and soul today: ***"Don't judge each day by the harvest you reap but by the seeds that you plant."*** I would like to acknowledge the following contributing authors, who so graciously planted a seed by lending their time, intellect, passion, energy, financial contribution and voice to this project. Thank you for your unwavering commitment. Thank you for having the courage to rise up and speak out against social injustice and inequality. Thank you for your ongoing encouragement and support. And most importantly, thank you for helping to win a victory for humanity!

Our contributing authors are:

Tamera CJ Baggett	Aine Dee
Laurie Baker	Dawn A. Dennis, Ph.D.
TaNesha Barnes	Sevgi Fernandez
Mirthell Bazemore	Kellie Fitzgerald
Cat Chapin-Bishop	MarySue Foster
Jodi Crane, Ph.D.	Susan Foster

Shaay Gallagher-Starr
Joella Glaude
Sandi Gordon
Kjerstin Gould
Susan Oldberg Hinton
Erin Hooton
Steven Jarose
Christie Kendzior
Susan M. Kuhn
Nicole Lattery
Matthew Lecki
Teresa C. Lewis
Candace Lilyquist
Emma Kate Lomax
Autumn Lubin
Natalie Manuel
Jennifer Watley Maxell
Auburn McCanta
Don Miller

Jared Lucas Nathanson
Linda Neff
Leslie Nelson
Kevin Odom
Kendra Penland
Michelle Rashid
Rhonda Lee Richoux
Bee Schrull
Judy Shepard
Dan Spencer
Valerie Stephens
Susanne Sulby
Erin Conyers Tierney
Muthu (Jordan) Weerasinghe
Crystal Combs White
Rebecca Wiggins
Anthony Wiley
Denise M. Wisdom

A special word of gratitude goes to our very talented Ian Frank for donating his time and talents to our cover design. Ian is an awe-inspiring photojournalist and the owner of **Ian Frank Gallery** in Atlanta, Georgia. To view other aspects of Ian's work, please visit his website at: http://ianfrankgallery.tumblr.com/.

Prologue

By Mirthell Bazemore

I would like to express my appreciation to Dr. Mary Canty Merrill for publishing this book bringing awareness to the importance of the Black Lives Matter movement, and for allowing me to share my insights surrounding the plight of Black America.

I was born on Juneteenth—June 19, 1964. Juneteenth or June 19, 1865, is the date when the last slaves in America were informed of their freedom. Although the rumors of freedom were widespread prior to this date, actual emancipation did not come until General Gordon Granger rode into Galveston, Texas and issued General Order No. 3, on June 19th, almost two and a half years after President Abraham Lincoln signed the Emancipation Proclamation. Though Texas and Oklahoma are the only states to have made Juneteenth a legal holiday, more than 200 cities in the United States have annual observances. Some cities sponsor week-long celebrations, culminating on June 19th, while others hold shorter celebrations. In my birth year, the Civil Rights Act of 1964 (Pub.L. 88–352, 78 Stat. 241, enacted July 2, 1964) was a landmark piece of civil rights legislation in the United States that outlawed discrimination based on race, color, religion, sex or national origin.

Growing up in Oakland, California in the mid-sixties, seventies and eighties taught me the value of Black pride, self-love and love for my people. In my youth, I regularly walked past the Black Panther Headquarters located in East Oakland and saw a group of young educated African Americans making a difference and cleaning up the streets in the Black community. So why in the 1990s did we, as a people, change? Is there someone to blame for this social breakdown? How did our brothers go from referring to Black women as their sisters to calling them bitches? How did we go from being some of the best-dressed people with a sense of pride to walking around with pants hanging off our behinds—mostly likely not even knowing or understanding the true meaning of this trend? How did the N-word, a term used to demoralize us become our term of endearment towards one another? Is this not the same as a pig eating its own vomit? As disgusting as it sounds, such is the perception of those who take part in these behaviors and choose to use this derogatory word in their daily vernacular.

African Americans (descendants of Africans) are creative, constructive, hardworking, spiritual and natural born leaders. It's in our bloodline. We are the descendants of great kings and queens who are written in the Bible and in the history books that have not been altered. But today, all I see is a group of displaced followers. Why are we now the oppressed? You only oppress that which is a threat!

> *We then that are strong ought to bear the infirmities of the weak, and not to please ourselves (Romans 15:1).*

African Americans are the largest racial minority, approximately 16.3 percent of the U.S. population, yet how many of us are educated? Entrepreneurs? Owners of corporations? And what amount of wealth do we bring to this racially divided country? Athletes, entertainers, and business professionals all have an obligation (yes, an obligation!) to lift our brothers and sisters to a higher standard, and lead us down an honorable path. It is OUR responsibility to generate jobs, shelter the homeless, and make sure that there are funds for scholarships to support underprivileged students.

We are riding a constantly and rapidly moving train and at no time or under any circumstances can we afford to become comfortable with the "I got mine, now you get yours" mentality. No thriving culture fails to build interdependent connections. Peaceful cultures are more effective when working together for the common good. Historical figures like Harriet Tubman and Dr. Martin Luther King, Jr. have proven time and again that it takes a vision of building a community and working together. It also takes a desire to give back with no strings attached.

We often hear the saying "It is better to give than to receive." Why is it better? And who is it better for? And how does it benefit us? First, it's better because it strengthens our community. Second, it demonstrates our unity as a people. Third, it creates business opportunities for the next generation, which gives us hope. Shall I go on?

Let's stop looking for the receiving up front because it will be our children and our children's children who will benefit from the seeds that we plant today. Giving back can be a simple word of advice, mentoring, financial gifts or labor. When we hold back on our talents, gifts and contributions because we don't want our brother or sister to get ahead of us, we are merely another crab in the bucket who will continue to struggle. We African Americans are known for embracing the "crab in the bucket" syndrome—"If I can't get ahead, neither can you; so I will do everything in my power to keep you from climbing." This way of thinking not only holds back one individual, it holds us back collectively.

People treat us the way we treat ourselves. We must, as a race, love and respect one another, work together and lift one another up. This is a powerful way of showing the world that Black lives really do matter!

> *And ye shall know the truth, and the truth shall make you free (John 8:32).*

Sadly, we have not received financial retribution for the injustices we endured during 400 years of slavery and racial discrimination. We have not asked for our land back, but what we do ask for is equal protection under the law. After the election of our nation's first Black President, we are seeing and experiencing more overt forms of racism than we have since the Civil Rights movement of the 1960s. We are in the throes of a very painful period. Over the last decade, countless Black lives have been lost as a result of police brutality and cold-blooded murder. This is simply unacceptable and inexcusable. Black people expect the same respect and treatment from our law enforcement officers and justice system that are afforded white civilians. The United States Justice Department has a responsibility to ensure that rogue cops and other justice officials are held accountable for unlawful shootings and executions that plague the Black community. If we are going to live peacefully and thrive as one nation under God, we must first see ourselves as *one nation*.

Mirthell Bazemore is a native Californian. Nurturing an extraordinary gift and love of writing, she launched her career by publishing her fictional novels in 2006. Since 2008, and as an affiliate of AuthorHouse

Publishing, she has been helping and encouraging others to embrace their creativity, even providing a nationwide network and marketing platform to assist other authors and writers in expressing their voice. In addition to helping others philanthropically, the delight of her fan base is her greatest joy. With books suited for film, television, and theater, Mirthell's career continues to be full of possibilities while… "Making a Difference, One Book at a Time." She can be reached at: mirtiebazemore@yahoo.com.

Chapter 1

The Roots of Our Struggle

In the confrontation between the stream and the rock, the stream always wins, not through strength but by perseverance.
– H. Jackson Brown

The History of Slavery in America

FROM AFRICA TO THE SHORES OF AMERICA

The history of slavery is central to the history of America. The trans-Atlantic Slave Trade was the largest forced migration in world history. Some 20 million Africans were traded for raw materials, chained together, and packed 300-400 deep as human cargo in the bowels of ships to make a grueling 6-8-week journey, known as the Middle Passage. Facing nightmarish conditions and an unknown future, at least 2 million Africans died during the voyage. Many chose to die by suicide rather than endure slavery. Others died from widespread disease. Still others were killed by their captors for resisting enslavement.

The key concept of slavery is that of ownership. A slave is a person who is the legal property of and wholly subject to another. Slave traders captured as many as 12 million Africans as human cargo and forced them into labor on plantations in North America, South America, and the Caribbean. To claim that Africans sold their own brothers and sisters into slavery whitewashes history by ignoring or minimizing the role of Europeans in the slave trade.

Ever since the first African arrived on the shores of America shackled in chains, stripped of their humanity, sold on the auction block to the highest bidder, and shipped off to a plantation to endure a life of exploitation, forced labor and torture under the watchful eye and unpredictable impulses of a brutal white slave master, the recurring message has been: *Black lives don't matter*. Slavery can rightfully be called the "original sin" because to the dominant culture, there was absolutely nothing sacred about Black life.

Mary Canty Merrill, Ph.D.

SLAVERY AND CAPITALISM

Blacks were snatched from African freedom and forced into slavery, and slavery played a significant role in the making of America. Slavery created great wealth that translated into tremendous political power. Many people want to classify slavery as an ancient institution, but anyone who is honest about American history will admit that the evolution and modernization of the United States was a direct result of chattel slavery. In his book *The Half Has Never Been Told*, Edward Baptist reveals that "... the expansion of slavery in the first eight decades after American independence drove the evolution and modernization of the United States. In the span of a single lifetime, the South grew from a narrow coastal strip of worn-out tobacco plantations to a continental cotton empire, and the United States grew into a modern, industrial, and capitalist economy."

The economic benefit overshadowed the inhumanity of slavery. Slavery lasted as long as it did because it was profitable. There's a close relationship between slavery and capitalism, and thus capitalism and racism. Racism was created to justify slavery and support capitalism.

RACISM AFTER SLAVERY

The concepts of *race* and *racism* are modern inventions born of the dominant ideology within the context of the African slave trade in the 1500s and 1600s, which lasted more than 400 years. The only way that we can combat racism is to understand its origin and nature.

Racism stems from ignorance. Racism exists when one group dominates, excludes, oppresses, or seeks to annihilate another group based on the idea that some hereditary difference, such as skin color, makes them inferior to their oppressors. While the Civil War abolished slavery, it did not abolish racism. Racism was used as a structural tool by the white ruling class to continue oppressing Blacks economically as sharecroppers and low-wage laborers.

Racism is more than a Black-White dichotomy. It reflects the original binary of America—the need to define, through a process of elimination, who is white and who is non-white. This racialization assigns individuals to a specific category and then assigns social meaning to that category in ways that shape individual, cultural and institutional identity. This meaning is built into our social processes and expressed in daily lived experiences. Today, the racist ideology (aka white supremacy) that originated during slavery is deeply woven into the fabric of our capitalistic society and used to divide races by category: *superior* and *inferior*. This means that racism is still very much alive in our contemporary structures and institutions, intertwined with systems of oppression, and devastating to people of color.

Indentured Servitude versus Chattel Slavery

As the conversation about reparations as a means of justice for slavery in the U.S. continues, I recently engaged in a debate with a white male who pushed the narrative of "white slaves" as he shared a social media image promoting Irish slavery. In fact, the Irish were *not* slaves, but indentured servants. Indentured servitude was a system of labor in which people worked for a pre-determined number of years to pay for their passage to the New World. This individual's intention was to use the white slaves myth as a derailment tactic to claim a shared heritage of victimization, absolve himself and his ancestors from any involvement in racial oppression—past and present—shut down any discussion about the legacy of Black slavery in America, and dismiss the unsavory fact that racism is still a pervasive problem in this country. This type of flawed rhetoric diminishes the Black experience, justifies the oppression of African Americans and fuels racial tensions. Consequently, I would have been remiss to let this man—or anyone who thinks like him—off the hook so easily.

Indentured servitude was *bonded* labor, slavery was *forced* labor. Indentured servants: (1) chose to come to the colonies; (2) signed over their rights in a contract; (3) willingly worked for 4-7 years to pay for their passage; (4) received freedom after a period of time; and (5) owned property. And—most interestingly—the Irish rose in society to eventually become African slave owners themselves. In stark contrast to indentured servants, slaves: (1) were forced from Africa and enslaved in the U.S. against their will; (2) were owned and not paid for their labor; (3) did not receive freedom, unless they were no longer alive; (4) were separated from family; (5) were stripped of their language and culture; (6) were bought and sold as property; (7) had no rights; (8) were forbidden to own property; and (9) were often born into slavery and relegated to a lifetime of servitude.

Chattel slavery drove racism, which continues to be very prevalent in our 21st century society. Irish slavery is nothing but a convenient myth aimed at marginalizing America's shameful history surrounding the African slave trade. Indentured servitude was voluntary; chattel slavery was not. Indentured servitude does not equate to racialized chattel slavery. No white person in this country has ever been subject to the government-sanctioned horrid and dehumanizing conditions that African slaves endured. To indicate otherwise is to whitewash history in service to white supremacist ideologies.

No Blacks Allowed—Especially After Dark

While much as been written about the history of segregation in the U.S., in 2005 I was introduced to the hidden history of "sundown towns", a continuation of the long and troubled history of U.S. race relations in the form of segregation that perpetuated all-white communities through discriminatory laws, threats and violence. According to James W. Loewen (2005), the creation of thousands of these whites-only towns began sometime around the end of Reconstruction in 1890 and continued until the fair-housing legislation of the late 1960s. These sundown towns were known by signs posted at their city limits that read, "Nigger, don't let the sun go down on you in [name of town]." Even today some towns still remain all white. Loewen argues that during this approximate 70-year period, it is very likely that a majority of all incorporated places in the U.S. banned African Americans. Because of the misleading census figures, Loewen found it challenging to determine the exact number of sundown towns, but estimates anywhere between 3,000 and 15,000 independent towns in the U.S. went sundown between 1890 and 1930.

To achieve this ethnic cleansing, white mobs used threats and violence to drive African Americans from these towns. Legal ordinances were passed that banned renting or selling Blacks homes or hiring them for jobs. Sometimes, the threat of violence was sufficient in expelling Blacks from towns. At other times, mass spectacle lynchings were used as a tactic whereby all whites participated in this community event. These events, announced beforehand, drew hundreds—and sometimes thousands—of spectators. In the aftermath, it was typical for no one to be brought to justice for these public murders. Even more devastating was the fact that white spectators sold fingers and other bits of the victim's flesh as souvenirs and made post card photos to send to friends and relatives across the country. Such events convinced African Americans that they were not safe in these communities, and prompted them to flee.

For decades, white communities have formally or informally excluded African Americans and other people of color. Some towns that historically excluded Jews, Mexicans, Asians and other ethnic groups no longer exclude them today, yet African Americans continue to be banned from these communities. Today, many residents of sundown towns assume that the town itself or the surrounding area is all-white because of the dominant white population. However, Loewen's (2005) research confirms that these towns were purposely established as all-white.

Sundown towns form a foundation of America's history, but they are not included in our contemporary discourse on race relations. This is perhaps because we were taught to believe that racism was largely limited to the south, so racism is most often viewed as a Southern problem. However, these sundown towns were not relegated to the south but spread throughout the country, especially in the Midwest and West. While it's illegal for sundown towns to exist on paper today and many former sundown towns no longer boast this status, it's disturbing to know that such towns very likely still exist and play a significant role in the racial divide and the exclusion of African Americans.

Loewen (2005) speaks of the paradox of exclusivity whereby residents of elite suburbs are far less likely than independent towns (or working-class suburbs) to admit that their communities exclude Blacks—or at did so until recent years. We can see this exclusion play out today to the degree that neighborhoods are ranked more prestigious to the extent that they exclude African Americans. This exclusivity denotes high-level social status or "good breeding" and is one of the reasons why whites in such communities have done little to combat racial segregation, and have instead fostered it.

Here is the ethical paradox: living in an exclusive area is good on one hand, because it symbolizes having achieved prestige and success. On the other hand, exclusion is bad when it conveys a negative connotation about the elite when they exclude Blacks and other people of color from their communities. To compensate for this cognitive dissonance, the upper class will develop *soclexia*, a condition that Loewen (2005) refers to as "a motivated blindness to the workings of social structure." They want to deny admission to Blacks and at the same time, deny that their neighborhood is intentionally all-white. They also want to avoid the social responsibility for the racial composition of their community by maintaining that Blacks do not have the financial means to move into their neighborhood because of economics. This reinforces the notion that in America, it is perfectly acceptable to exclude on the basis of socioeconomic status.

Equal Rights for Blacks Are Still Not Equal

In 1857, the U.S. Supreme Court in the case of Dred Scott (a slave hoping to be granted freedom) had this to say: The Black man *"had no rights that a white man was bound to respect"* meaning that Blacks were not and never could become citizens of the United States. The truth of the matter is this: the U.S. Constitution cannot fail Blacks, because it was drafted, debated and approved by slave owners and exploiters who regarded us as inferior and did not consider us citizens; so it was never written with us in mind. Despite the thirteenth Amendment, when we consider ongoing racism, disparities, discrimination and bigotry that are imposed upon us, we can unequivocally say that America is *still* a white private club that excludes full membership to Blacks.

When reading the opening lines of the Declaration of Independence—all men were created equal—one would think that America does not live by a double standard. However, American rhetoric and laws have been hypocritical since the founding of this country. For its entire history, Black Americans have faced prejudice, racism, discrimination, oppression and a justice system that treats us differently than white citizens. The civil rights of Blacks are routinely ignored and violated by law enforcement. Because the laws were not written for Blacks, we have never had and still do not have any protection from maltreatment by our governing authorities. This lack of protection erodes our integrity as a community and subjects us to aggressive sociopathic attitudes and behaviors.

Racism is deeply embedded in America's culture, politics and education and there is nothing to indicate that racism in this country has ceased to be a problem for Blacks. The remnants of centuries of racism and oppression continue to linger today, affecting millions of Americans. Such is the plight of Black Americans today.

The Psychological and Physiological Impact of Slavery, Racism and Discrimination

"Being a Negro in America means trying to smile when you want to cry, it means trying to hold on to

physical life amid psychological death. It means the pain of watching your children grow up with clouds of inferiority in their mental skies. It means having your legs cut off, and then being condemned for being a cripple. It means seeing your mother and father spiritually murdered by the slings and arrows of daily exploitation, and then being hated for being a[n] orphan." – Martin Luther King, Jr., 1967

After at least 12 generations, chattel slavery had a damaging psychological and physiological impact that reverberates today. African slaves lived with the constant threat of separation, so slavery not only prevented healthy family formation, enslaved people also could not legally marry. This forced many men and women to enter into relationships and consider themselves husbands and wives, knowing that their union was not legally protected by state laws. Moreover, some enslaved fathers had a different owner than the mother and children, so they lived on separate plantations. These are just some of the key factors that destroyed Black families and made creating and nurturing a stable and secure nuclear family challenging at best.

A series of surveys in recent years reveal that most whites think that discrimination against whites is a bigger problem than bigotry against Blacks, which tells us that white people's limited awareness of racial disparities in this country is pervasive. For example, the majority of white people say that racism exists everywhere—except around them. A 2015 *Huffington Post* survey shows that three out of four white Americans believe that racism is a "somewhat serious" national problem, compared to nine out of 10 Blacks—that's 68 percent of Black respondents, compared to 31 percent of whites. Additionally, most white respondents say that racism is not an issue in their community, so they do not feel compelled to act on it—despite acknowledging it as a national problem. Sadly, a majority of whites have no sense of the depth of anger and rage over racism that is suppressed by African Americans, and have no idea which straw will finally break the camel's back.

INHERITED TRAUMA AND SELF-DESTRUCTIVE BEHAVIOR

Slaves were dehumanized; treated as a commodity; stripped of their language, culture, dignity, and freedom; and suffered physical, mental and emotional abuse causing irreparable damage. Slavery in America is not without consequences. Its negative impact is immense. Despite being abolished over 150 years ago, the legacy of slavery continues to reverberate throughout the Black community today. The end of slavery was merely the beginning of the Black quest for freedom, justice and equality.

Trauma has long played a vital role in the African American community. So what is trauma? *Trauma* is a deeply distressing usually violent experience caused by an outside force. This injury can be experienced on multiple levels and upset our emotional balance and well-being. If the trauma is severe enough it can also distort our values, beliefs, attitudes and world view. The result is dysfunctional behaviors which can produce further unwanted repercussions. This pattern is exponentially magnified whenever an individual repeatedly experiences additional trauma, especially at the hands of another human being.

While improvements have been made in terms of Black status, the underclass continues to grow and the trauma from the racism inherent in a system that dehumanized Blacks is still widely felt today and has been impossible to dismantle. The emotional legacy from centuries of chattel slavery continues to impact us in terms of our values, beliefs, cultural norms, self-esteem, self-perception, self-efficacy, attitudes, relationships, behaviors, lifestyle choices, parenting styles, and in how we project our identity. We must understand the multi-generational effects of slavery and far-fetching racism if we ever hope to be emancipated from its aftermath, break its multigenerational bond, and cast off the shadow of the past.

Self-Hatred

> *"I freed a thousand slaves. I could have freed a thousand more if only they knew they were slaves."*
> – Harriet Tubman

Russell, Wilson and Hall (2013) believe that Black identity begins with self-hatred. Studies reveal evidence of self-hatred in children as young as three years old. Further studies show that by adolescence Black teens have defined stereotypes about skin color. This is also the time when prejudice among Blacks most commonly occurs and has the most negative effect on the psyche. These teens then evolve into adulthood carrying with them traumatic experiences and skewed perceptions of their own community. As a result, Black people are easily influenced by the warped standards of beauty characterized by society and portrayed in the media.

White people excel at stirring internal confusion and self-hatred in Black people. However, Blacks are descendents of African kings and queens. So we must not allow anyone to make us feel inferior or that our lives do not matter. We must be vigilant and our silence broken so that the value of every Black life is reinforced... because Black lives matter, too!

Chattel slavery was a brutal practice of human bondage and exploitation. We rarely examine our history to understand how African Americans adapted their behaviors over centuries to survive the traumatic effects of slavery. African Americans are the only race of people who were kidnapped from their homeland and forced into slavery for nearly three centuries. Therefore, it should not be surprising that the psychological and psychosocial consequences of the descendents are still prevalent today. There is also no denying the multi-generational trauma and widespread stigmatization associated with the entire Black race. Every Black person, regardless of their skin tone—dark, medium or light—learns from an early age that their Blackness renders them different from and less valued than their counterparts in mainstream society. Knowing this exacerbates the inherited trauma and self-destructive behavior that are the legacies of slavery. Breaking this cycle and healing and reclaiming our humanity after years of mental, emotional and physical abuse takes time and will require much effort from us all.

Individual responses to trauma may range from constructive adaptation to psychological dysfunction—mentally diffusing any perceived threats, avoiding and escaping them, or tackling them directly at the risk of being labeled as aggressive or altogether ostracized by the white community. African Americans have traditionally and continue to tap into religious resources and insights in an attempt to lessen the sting of racism, discrimination and oppression. Slave spirituals, Gospel music and other religious music serve as a comforting reminder that there is a better life waiting beyond the troubles of this world. Either way, skills and strategies in dealing with the suffocating experience of racism and countering internalized messages from exploitation, discrimination and oppression become a crucial aspect of African Americans' survival as we venture daily into a white-dominated world and be damned for a skin color over which we have no control.

Our Heritage is Our Strength

> *"When you show a mental slave freedom, they are more likely to turn and attack you for disturbing their paradise: Liberation is their chains, and liberators their enemies."*
> — 'Alik Shahadah

Dr. Joy Leary DeGruy (2005), who developed the theory and popularized the concept of *post-traumatic slave syndrome*, addresses the residual impacts of generations of slavery and elicits a discourse on how African Americans can leverage the strengths that we have amassed in the past to help us heal in the present. DeGruy refers to African Americans as a strong and resilient people. We have a long history of enduring and persevering through the worst kinds of trials and tribulations. In the face of adversity, inherited trauma and our current condition, still we rise.

African Americans are an industrious people, having built communities under seemingly impossible circumstances and extreme conditions. We have the ability to care for one another with fewer resources and an uncompromising attitude and approach during the most desperate times than even the poorest whites.

African Americans are a creative people. In the midst of slavery and oppression we have established a distinctive culture sated with new names, language, customs, behaviors, art, music, activities, foods and fashions.

African Americans are a noble people. Notwithstanding incessant oppressive conditions, we have repeatedly proven that while we don't forget, we can forgive the wrongs leveled against us and courageously fight for justice and equality without being crippled by hatred and revenge.

African Americans are a loving and hopeful people. We possess a fundamental dignity that undergirds our love and respect for humanity. It is a testament to our strength of character, our backbone and our spirit that we still have the wherewithal to hope and dream. This is why we can hold fast the profession of our faith without wavering, and cling to the assurance that we will draw from and build upon our collective strengths to heal ourselves and our communities.

The Plight of Black America

Internalized Racism and Oppression

In his controversial article, *The Plight of Black America*, Jonathan Zhao posits, "The greatest obstacle to the advancement of black Americans isn't racism or past injustices but rather the black community itself. Instead of paving a road to prosperity, the self-defeating economic policies advocated for by the black community are shackles of poverty and disillusionment, miring blacks in a cycle of underachievement and social immobility... Lastly, and perhaps paramount to all other cultural issues, is the pervasive sense of crippling victimhood...blaming problems on past injustices and racism.... While racism certainly exists and past injustices like slavery were undoubtedly evil and a blight on American history, using those two excuses as a crutch keeps the black community stuck in the past and prevents it from moving forward in a constructive manner."

While Zhao presents a rather straightforward diagnosis, it reeks of right-wing attitudes and ideologies about the Black community. What Zhao, who just so happens to be Asian, cannot relate to or fully comprehend, is the *depth* of trauma experienced by Blacks and how it has shaped our current condition. Zhao is a glaring example of conservatives' refusal to challenge their own ignorant assumptions or make sweeping changes to overcome systemic and systematic racism. If the problems in the Black community were so easy to fix, they would have been remedied by now. Dr. James P. Comer, Professor of Psychiatry at the Yale Child Study Center speaks on the legacy of slavery that was passed down to African Americans:

> *"The slave family existed only to serve the master and in order to survive physically, psychologically and socially the slave family had to develop a system which made survival possible under degrading conditions. The slave society prepared the young to accept exploitation and abuse, to ignore the absence of dignity and respect for themselves as blacks. The social, emotional and psychological price of this adjustment is well known."*

Mental slavery continues to have a psychological grip in which many Blacks remain trapped in a web of misinformation about themselves, their history and the world. Mental slavery is more sinister than physical slavery because these chains are invisible and transferred across generations that perpetuate dysfunction. Many Blacks still struggle with feelings of inferiority, incapability and worthlessness, which impede their growth and development on various levels—psychologically, emotionally, physically and spiritually—and cultivate dependent and passive behaviors.

Consequently, they are more apt to complain about their condition and dismiss every possible opportunity to be agents of change and devise strategies to transform their reality by emancipating themselves from slavery and achieving their full potential—propelling themselves deeper into the throes of oppression.

Does the Black community have a lot of healing to do? Absolutely! The chains have been physically removed, but the psychological chains are still binding. Our ancestors had no psychological assistance or mental health interventions to help them overcome the greatest crime against humanity. This is what has set us back as a people. Yet, no other race of people possesses the powerful resilience of Blacks in the face of adversity. Therefore, to say that the Black community is using slavery and injustices as a crutch is a dismissal of our stamina, a blatant disregard for the level of trauma that we have experienced as a race of people, and an insult to our very humanity. No, we cannot forget that our African ancestors endured 300 years of chattel slavery—suffering unrelenting inhumane treatment in the form of psychological, emotional, and physical abuse—at the hands of white slave masters. We also cannot forget the maltreatment that Blacks continue to be subjected to today relative to denial of privilege and true freedom at the hands of white America. Little wonder why African Americans exhibit self-destructive and maladaptive behaviors as we persist in the struggle to strengthen our communities, despite ongoing oppression.

Racial discrimination is an all-consuming life experience for Blacks, and studies have shown that being part of an oppressed group diminishes self-esteem. I don't think that white people fully understand the impact on Black lives or the feelings and emotions that it precipitates—anger, rage, frustration, depression, embarrassment, bitterness and a host of other negative feelings and emotions that, in turn, provoke strong reactions to white America. Unfortunately, these feelings and emotions are also turned inward as internalized oppression.

Black people discriminate against one another based on skin tone, facial features and hair texture. This color complex involves light-skinned Blacks rejecting dark-skinned Blacks. This behavior stems from life during slavery when Blacks held the ideology—which became embedded in their psyche—that whites are superior. Generally, light-skinned slaves were given indoor assignments while dark-skinned slaves were relegated to grueling field work. Light-skinned Blacks were taught to believe that they were better than their dark-skinned counterparts. This "whiter is better" favoritism and separation created a rift that continues to plague and be a barrier to progress in the Black community.

Despite any obstacles that the Black community imposes upon itself, there is no denying the racism, discrimination and oppression inflicted by whites on the Black community. For example, the deliberate disenfranchisement of the Black underclass is a systemic and systematic tactic by the government to avoid making any notable structural or social changes. African Americans face poor conditions as a result of discrimination and exploitation. They are stereotyped; segregated in impoverished communities; denied jobs; racially profiled, harassed, and brutalized by police; and convicted of crimes, often culminating in maximum sentences when compared to their white counterparts.

Many of the behaviors displayed within the Black community today were used as a means of survival during slavery and passed down through generations to survive and thrive. Many Blacks have become frustrated or disheartened to the point of throwing in the towel. Slavery lasted for nearly three centuries, and Blacks continue to encounter various forms of oppression today. Therefore, it can logically be expected that progress will require dedicated time and intentional effort. We must continue to bring dysfunctional beliefs, attitudes, assumptions and behaviors to light, examine them, and replace them, as necessary, to promote and maximize our advancement and provide hope for future generations.

Poverty

In the U.S. single mothers and ethnic minorities are the public face of, and African Americans are disproportionately affected by poverty. Stereotypes about the poor and ethnic minorities reflect each other with intersecting depictions including laziness, sexual promiscuity, irresponsible parenting, lack of interest in education and disregard for the law. This integration is especially noticeable for certain subgroups of the poverty-stricken, such as welfare recipients and the urban poor (Gans, 1995; Henry, Reyna, and Weiner, 2004).

Over the past couple of years, we have witnessed scenes of civil unrest playing out in racially segregated high-poverty inner-city neighborhoods such as Ferguson, Missouri and Baltimore, Maryland as a result of violent encounters between unarmed Black men and law enforcement officers. While the media has provided pervasive coverage, there's one glaring element that has been left out of the conversation: concentrated racial poverty. In *Architecture of Segregation*, Paul A. Jargowsky makes a stark and inescapable point: *"These neighborhoods are not the value-free outcome of the impartial workings of the housing market. Rather, in large measure, they are the inevitable and predictable consequences of deliberate policy choices."* Jargowsky goes on to examine key trends surrounding the population and characteristics of neighborhoods inflicted by extreme deprivation:

- The number of people living in high-poverty neighborhoods has almost doubled since 2000—increasing from 7.2 million to 13.8 million—and these increases were well underway before the Great Recession of 2008.

- Poverty has become more concentrated, and more than one in four poor African Americans live in neighborhoods of extreme poverty, compared to one in thirteen of poor whites.

- The fastest growth in concentration of poverty among African Americans (12.6 percent) was not in the largest cities, but metropolitan areas comprising 500,000 to 1 million residents.

- A poor Black person is over three times more likely to reside in a neighborhood with a poverty rate of 40 percent or more than a poor white person.

Data from a five-year (2009-2013) American Community Survey reveal that more than a third of all poor African Americans in metropolitan Chicago live in high-poverty census tracts (where the poverty rate is above 40 percent). That number has worsened since 2000. And it's about 10 times higher than for poor whites.

In a *Washington Post* article entitled *Black poverty differs from white poverty*, Emily Badger (2015) points out that the poverty affecting African Americans differs from the poverty affecting poor whites, because it is isolated and concentrated—occupying the entire neighborhood. A poor Black family is more likely than a poor white family to live in a neighborhood where many other families are poor. This is a condition sociologists refer to as the "double burden" of poverty.

Badger (2015) further states that 29.5 percent of poor African Americans in St. Louis live in concentrated poverty compared to 1.6 percent of poor whites. In most major metropolitan areas, poor whites are spread out, whereas poor African Americans are not. Concentrated poverty is growing worse and several factors drive this phenomenon: systemic discrimination, modern zoning laws that block the poor from wealthier communities, and concentrated public housing policies.

Pervasive poverty, the lack of opportunity, and increasing hopelessness of ghetto life set in motion a social-psychological dynamic that produces a culture of segregation, which makes it impossible to build healthy self-esteem and nurture the values and ideals of achievement associated with the larger society. This interconnection between poverty and segregation concentrates a variety of detrimental social and economical characteristics that create an environment where Black male unemployment, female welfare dependency, drug abuse, teenage pregnancy, single parenthood and crime are considered the norm and reinforces negative stereotypes about and perpetuates unfavorable attitudes toward the Black community.

The circumstances of Black Americans have ebbed and flowed since the Civil Rights movement of the 1960s. The struggle produced unprecedented improvement in the lives of most Blacks, but even with these gains the socioeconomic gap between Blacks and whites persisted through the 1970s and 1980s. Along with the deepening class divisions were brewing racial tensions, often as a result of police brutality. It was not until the 1990s inspired by government policy and economic growth that we began to see significant economic gains for African Americans.

Fast-forward to the Great Recession of 2008 when much of the gains amassed in the 1990s were obliterated. Wealth inequality has increased along racial lines since the 2008 recession. Between 2007 and 2010, African Americans lost 31 percent of their wealth, compared to 11 percent for their white counterparts. According to the Pew Research Center, by 2011, Black families had lost 53 percent of their wealth. In 2013, the wealth of white households was 13 times that of Black households. Lost homes, lost jobs and lost retirement savings make it difficult for many Blacks to ever imagine struggling to regain the socioeconomic status they once held. It's unfortunate that people reading the news and consuming media coverage are not getting a complete picture or understanding of the astounding poverty existing in the Black community and the driving forces that created a Ferguson or Baltimore.

HEALTH CARE

There are a number of health issues that plague the Black community as a result of depression, poor diets, smoking, obesity and sedentary lifestyles. Health care disparities increase disease differences between Black and white Americans. Following are some daunting health care statistics.

- According to the American Diabetes Association, diabetes is one of the most serious health problems in the African American community—and is a growing epidemic. It is reported that 13.2 percent of African Americans aged 20 years and older have diagnosed diabetes. African Americans are 1.7 times more likely to have diabetes than whites, and more likely to suffer from complications such as blindness, amputations and kidney disease.

- Partners Healthcare Asthma Center tells us that Blacks are three times more likely to die from asthma than whites.

- Various studies reveal that sarcoidosis—an inflammatory lung disease—is more prevalent among African Americans than whites. Sarcoidosis is estimated to occur in 40 of every 100,000 African Americans, compared to only 5 of every 100,000 white Americans. Also noteworthy is the fact that Black women are two times more likely to contract the disease than Black men.

- Despite improvements in health care across races, African Americans continue to suffer the greatest burden for the most common types of cancer. According to the National Cancer Institute, Blacks have the shortest survival time and highest death rate for most cancers of any racial group in the U.S. Black men have a 40 percent higher death rate from cancer than white men, while Black women have a 20 percent higher cancer death rate than white women. For all cancers combined, the death rate among African Americans is 25 percent higher than for whites. In addition, while white women have the highest incidence of breast cancer, Black women are most likely to die from the disease. Moreover, Black women are more likely to be diagnosed with cervical cancer. Black men are 50 percent more likely to get cancer—despite lower tobacco exposure—than white men.

- The American Heart Association tells us that heart disease is the number one killer for all Americans, and stroke is also a leading cause of death—and the risk is higher for African Americans, which is the highest in the world. Black Americans 35-54 years of age die from strokes at a rate 4 times higher than whites. More than 40 percent of African Americans have high blood pressure. African Americans also develop high blood pressure at an earlier age and at more severe levels than whites.

- The National Stroke Association reports that African Americans are more impacted by stroke than any other racial groups. The rate of first stroke among African Americans is almost double that of whites and African Americans are twice as likely as whites to die from strokes.

- The Center for Disease Control and Prevention reports that African Americans are the most affected by HIV than any other racial/ethnic group. African Americans comprise 12 percent of the U.S. population, but were 44 percent of the new HIV diagnoses in 2014—73 percent were men and 26 percent were women.

- A special report by the State of Obesity reveals that more than 75 percent of African Americans are either overweight or obese (69 percent of men and 82 percent of women), compared with 67.2 percent of whites (71.4 percent of men and 63.2 percent of women). African American adults are 1.5 times more likely to be obese, compared with their white counterparts. Approximately 47.8 percent of African Americans are obese (37.1 percent of men and 56.6 percent of women) compared with 32.6 percent of whites (32.4 percent of men and 32.8 percent of women).

Although all humans have the same physiology which makes them vulnerable to the same illnesses and respond to the same medications and it is natural for diseases and treatment responses to vary by person, there are unique issues of disparity—racial and ethnic disparities in health care, socioeconomic status, education, housing and overall standard of living among them—that disproportionately affect African Americans. Because poor people have limited or no access to quality health care and Black people tend to have more aggressive forms of disease, they bear a heavier burden than the general population.

MENTAL ILLNESS

Another health issue that I'd like to highlight is depression. Depression is a mood disorder that causes an overwhelming and persistent feeling of sadness. However, some depressed people do not feel sad at all—instead, they may feel lifeless, empty, and apathetic, and some may even feel angry, aggressive, and restless. Whatever the symptoms, depression is different from normal sadness in that it engulfs an individual's day-to-day life and interferes with their ability to work, study, eat, sleep, and engage in enjoyable activities. These feelings of helplessness, hopelessness, and worthlessness are intense and unrelenting, with little, if any, relief. Depression distorts how we view ourselves, others and our environment.

While depression is not the only type of mental illness, I emphasize it because of its pervasiveness among African Americans. Mental Health America reveals that 63 percent of African Americans perceive depression as a personal weakness, and only 31 percent perceive it as a health problem. Even more disturbing is that African Americans are more likely to perceive depression as a normal state of being. This is probably due in part to the fact that Blacks have always been required to be strong regardless of what is happening in their lives—even enslavement and oppression. These myths and faulty notions account for the high rate of depression and low rate of treatment among African Americans.

Many Blacks, particularly Black women, suffer from higher rates of depression than our white female or Black male counterparts—whether we choose to name it or not. Because of an intense, longstanding stigma (or negative attributes) around mental illness in the Black community, we will go out of our way to hide or ignore it and label it stress, anger, frustration, disappointment, exhaustion, or some other dis-ease. And it has us self-medicating by eating, drinking, smoking, drugging, social media-ing, Internet surfing, televisioning, spending, styling, churching, sexing, nagging, meddling, cursing, lying, gossiping, stealing, fighting, cowering, excusing, rationalizing, running, under-achieving, hating, twerking, partying, gambling, over sleeping and engaging a host of other destructive activities in an attempt to minimize or alleviate our pain.

The stigmas that surround mental illness can be attributed to private and public shame and is the primary reason that many do not seek help for their condition. Mental Health America reports that Black adults are 20 percent more likely to report serious psychological distress than whites, and Black adults living below poverty are two-three times more likely to report serious psychological distress than those living above poverty. Also, while Black teens are less likely to die from suicide than white teens, Black teens are more likely to attempt suicide (8.2 percent compared to 6.3 percent of whites).

Despite these very telling statistics, many Blacks refuse to seek help because of negative cultural sanctions, myths and stereotypes, which can lead to further complications. Stigma can lead to blatant, subtle or unintentional negative attitudes and discrimination towards those who suffer from mental illness. These issues are multiplied for Blacks who are already subjected to white prejudice, discrimination and oppression.

Regardless what we choose to call depression or how we choose to compensate for it, the condition is still depression and can be destructive when not effectively treated. Once we name it, we can confront it. And professional mental health treatment can make a remarkable difference in terms of improving our overall quality of life. There is no shame in admitting and seeking professional assistance for depression.

EDUCATION

Cook (2015) points out that the U.S. education system is "still separate and unequal." Although high-quality care environments have been shown to have a lasting positive impact on a child's education, Black children are more likely than white children to be enrolled in low-quality day care. There are similar inequities in formal education. Black students are more likely to be held back than their white counterparts. According to the U.S. Department of Education, 12 percent of Black students are held back in ninth grade compared to just 4 percent of white students. When all grade levels are combined, Black students are three times more likely to be held back than their white peers. Notwithstanding these dire statistics, mounting research shows that holding a child back does not benefit them academically or socially, and in fact contributes to their tendency to eventually drop out of school altogether before earning a high school diploma. Sixteen percent of Black students drop out of high school compared with 8 percent of white students. Only 68 percent of African American students graduate from high school. This rate is about 10 to 15 percent less than the graduation rate among white students. This means fewer Blacks are eligible for college enrollment at the outset.

Cook (2015) further argues that Black children are much more likely to live in low-income households, lack sufficient food and receive long-term welfare support than white children. Additionally, Black children are less likely to live in a household where at least one parent has secure employment; Black children have the highest rate of any race of children living in homeless shelters; and Black children are more likely to live in unsafe neighborhoods.

Further data shows that Black children are also more likely to suffer traumatic experiences that negatively impact their childhood, such as witnessing domestic violence, neglect, violent crimes, sexual abuse, or the death of a parent. The maltreatment rate among Black children is 14.2 per 1,000 compared to 8 per 1,000 for white children (Cook, 2015). Moreover, when children suffer from hunger, neglect, and a home environment rife with substance abuse it impacts their ability to concentrate at school.

When a child is living in poverty, it's easy to understand how the lack of funds for school supplies, lack of computer and/or Internet access will impede their ability to complete homework assignments. The factors of race, poverty and family structures are associated with a broad range of other problems: lower academic achievement, behavioral problems, grade retention, high-risk sexual behavior, higher risk of obesity and illness and a greater risk of interpersonal and self-destructive violence. These and other behaviors continue through adulthood and create a vicious cycle that is difficult for many to escape.

Nationwide, only 59 percent of all first-time full-time college students graduate in six years, according to the National Center for Education Statistics. The rate for Black students is significantly lower at 39.5 percent. A 2014 U.S. Department of Education report highlights a large racial gap in college graduation rates. At public colleges and universities, 39.7 percent of Black students earned their undergraduate degrees within six years from the same institution in which they enrolled compared to 60.2 percent of white students. At private colleges and universities, the graduation rate for Black students was 44.5 percent compared to 68.1 percent for white students. There also exists a significant gender gap in graduation rates among African Americans. At public colleges and universities, 43.3 percent of Black women earned their degrees within six years compared to 34.2 percent of Black men. At private colleges and universities, the graduation rate for Black women was 48.5 percent compared to 39.2 percent for Black men.

These troubling statistics underscore the disadvantages that Black students bring to the education arena. When these challenges are not effectively addressed and corrected in the K-12 classroom, at-risk children fall through the cracks, and the education gap increases, leading directly to a cycle of incarceration in increasingly high numbers—known as the "school-to-prison pipeline."

Black enrollment could further decline if the Supreme Court rules in favor of Abigail Fisher, a white woman who claimed she was rejected from the University of Texas at Austin based on her race. The Justices appeared skeptical of any benefits relative to race-conscious admissions when hearing the case on December 9, 2015. Justice Antonin Scalia, now deceased, made comments that have been interpreted as embracing the idea that underprepared Black students would perform better in "lesser colleges" instead of struggling to thrive at the University of Texas at Austin.

The low number of Black students attending selective colleges threatens to increase segregation and fuel tensions on campuses and partially explains the large gap in the proportion of whites versus their Black counterparts who hold college degrees. Black students who have above-average SAT scores attend college at the same rate—90 percent—as their white counterparts. However, once enrolled, white students are more likely to graduate, partially because they attend more elite colleges and universities that have better resources and higher overall graduation rates.

UNEMPLOYMENT

While the economy is showing signs of improvement, Black unemployment remains high. Wilson (2015) emphasizes that unemployment among Blacks was 9.5 percent during the second quarter of 2015 compared to only 4.6 percent for whites. This gap is slightly larger than the one that existed 15 years ago, or even before the recession. Many people cite education as a major cause of this disparity. White Americans obtain a college degree at a rate of 41 percent compared to 22 percent of Blacks. However, Wilson argues that educational differences cannot fully explain this unemployment gap. Economic Policy Institute research shows that among whites who did not complete high school, the unemployment rate is 6.9 percent compared to African Americans at almost two-and-a-half times that rate at 16.6 percent. And a gap persists even among those African Americans who have completed a bachelor's degree or higher, with an unemployment rate of 4.1 percent compared to 2.4 percent for their white peers with the same level of education.

For every level of education attained by African Americans, their unemployment rates are similar to or higher than those of less educated whites. For example, white Americans who obtained only a high school education have a very similar unemployment rate as Blacks who have completed at least a bachelor's degree—4.6 percent compared to 4.1 percent. These findings suggest a racial disparity whereby African Americans at each level of education have the same or higher unemployment rates than less educated whites.

Also, despite rising college attendance among Black students, they are still less likely to attend prestigious schools, make valuable connections and gain career advantages as their white counterparts. Although the data show that even though Blacks are successful in attending and completing college, they are less likely than their white peers to be gainfully employed. This suggests that less education isn't the whole problem, so attempts in bolstering educational attainment figures among African Americans will not completely solve the problem.

The jobless rate for African American males is more than double that of white males. Social scientists and economists cite a number of reasons for high unemployment among Black males: lack of training and education, loss of public-sector jobs, unequal access to social networks, high incarceration rates (six times that of white men, according to a 2010 Pew Research Center study), and outright discrimination. Finding gainful employment is difficult for Black males in a system that is stacked against them.

This brings us to more daunting statistics from a Gallup poll conducted by Witters and Liu (2015) which reveals that young Black males in the U.S. have lower well-being than young non-Black males, and this difference is wider than that found among those between the ages of 35 and 64. As a group, young Black males have lower graduation rates, higher unemployment rates, higher incarceration rates and less access to health care than other racial, gender and age groups in the U.S. These well-being issues underscore the difficulties that young Black males encounter with law enforcement and in the criminal justice system.

As is evident from the aforementioned statistics, African Americans face social and economic inequality that includes greater exposure to racism, discrimination, violence and poverty—all resulting in lower health status. Addressing these disparities requires removing obstacles that make affordable and quality health care accessible and ensuring that communities have safe and accessible places for people to be physically active.

CRIME

The media have relentlessly fanned the flames of racial hatred, while engaging in an ongoing pattern of misinformation and suppression of facts regarding the perpetrators and victims of crime. Inevitably, when someone broaches the subject of police brutality against Blacks, there's the counter-argument about Black-on-Black crime. According to the U.S. Department of Justice, when whites commit violence, they choose fellow whites as victims 82.4 percent of the time. Also, FBI homicide data reveals that a white person is almost six times more likely to be killed by another white person than by a Black person.

According to the Prison Policy Initiative, for all races, most murders are committed by members of the same race because criminal violence usually occurs within one's own community. Blacks represent 13 percent of the U.S. population, but 40 percent of the U.S. incarcerated population. Whites make up 64 percent of the population, and 39 percent of the prison population—direct evidence of institutional racism.

Farbota (2016) argues that there exists a conservative narrative espousing that the disproportionate incarceration of Blacks is not a result of systemic racism, but shortcomings in the Black community. The narrative also indicates that Black people commit more crimes than white people, a fact used to justify that Blacks have a natural propensity for criminal activity and a culture of violence is the reason for the plight of Blacks in America. Blacks are incarcerated five times as frequently as whites, but it does not mean that Blacks commit five times more crimes. Here's the reason:

1. If a Black and white person commit a crime, the Black person is more likely to be arrested as a result. This is partially because Blacks are more heavily policed.

2. When Blacks are arrested, they are convicted more often than whites arrested for the same crime.

3. Once convicted, Blacks are more likely to be incarcerated, compared to whites convicted of the same crime.

In addition to racial disparities as a source of differential incarceration rates, poverty, lack of education and career opportunities and geography are all likely contributing factors. These factors exacerbate the effects of systemic racism and perpetuate the vicious cycle of poverty, incarceration, and unemployment plaguing the Black community. Despite the precise factors that fuel the incarceration gap, in addition to a number of interacting elements, racism is a significant factor.

These are revolutionary times. Black Americans are confronted with the fierce urgency of *now*. If we ever hope to experience a new way of being, it is incumbent upon us to shift from a place of comfort and complacency and rise up to revolt against antiquated systems of exploitation and oppression and overcome the crippling legacy of racism, inequality and injustice.

Chapter 2

Racism in America

When you dismiss my humanity, you dismiss your own.
When you disrespect my humanity, you disrespect your own.
When you devalue my humanity, you devalue your own.
– Mary Canty Merrill, Ph.D.

Understanding Racism and Prejudice

In using the term *racism* in this book, we refer not only to the prejudices and discriminatory actions of white racists, but also to the institutional discrimination and the recurring ways that white people—consciously and unconsciously—dominate Blacks in virtually every major aspect of our society. Racism is often viewed as a flaw in individual personalities, but racism transcends being merely a personal attitude. It is deeply embedded in, maintained and enforced by our legal, educational, political, economical, religious, cultural and military institutions. Racism is an institutionalized configuration of personal attitudes. Racism manifests itself everywhere we turn, so virtually any encounter that Blacks have with whites in our social institutions and public spaces can prompt a confrontation with racism.

At the heart of prejudice lie ignorance and fear. *Prejudice* is a "pre-judgment" that arises from ignorance. All human beings tend to pre-judge others on the basis of limited knowledge and understanding of their racial, cultural, social, economical, political, religious and other notable differences. Given the scope of this book, let's focus on how Whites use prejudice as a primary means of sustaining institutionalized racism.

Considering the structure of American society, most white people have virtually no conceptual idea or first-hand experience of the lives of Blacks and other people of color. This is because segregation and separation are norms that prevent people of diverse racial/ethnic backgrounds from interacting with one another in meaningful ways to gain understanding and insight. This perpetuates ignorance and fear, which give rise to prejudice and racism. Political, media, academic, corporate and other elites play an important role in perpetuating racism because of their stake in maintaining white group dominance.

Prejudice is a mental framework driven by people defending their positional privilege. Whenever they feel that their privilege is threatened, they will become fearful and react. Fear extends deeper than ignorance and lies at the root of prejudice, privilege and power. Ever since the 16th century onward, racism has become affirmative action for white people.

Even when claims of prejudice are supported with factual evidence, they are often dismissed or hotly debated. The old adage applies here: "A person convinced against their will is of the same opinion still." Fear will make a person benefitting from privilege safeguard their position of social advantage and strike back, but it will not convince them to change their mind. To be sure, old-fashioned racism has not been extinguished. Racism still exists in subtle and blatant forms; and contrary to what many people choose to believe, we are *not* living in a post-racial America.

The Sociopathology of Racism

Racism and hostility are not inborn, but learned behaviors. When a person does something and knows that it's wrong, they are not ignorant but well aware of what they're doing. They know better, but they don't care. Whether for money, fame, followers, or beliefs, they think what they're doing is okay. They actually believe that the ends justify the means.

A sociopath is a person who lacks a sense of moral responsibility or social conscience, has a lack of remorse or shame, lacks sincerity, demonstrates antisocial behavior, is irresponsible, has shallow emotions, thinks irrationally, is manipulative and cunning to gain approval or profit, exhibits dangerous and violent behaviors and lack of impulse control, lacks the capacity to love, has a grandiose sense of self, and will change their image in any way possible to avoid prosecution. Despite the fact that the sociopath shows a pervasive and blatant disregard for the feelings and rights of others, he or she is often intelligent, exhibits superficial charm, and is extremely convincing, so is therefore likely to have many followers.

Sociopathy is not a mental health diagnosis nor does it refer to individuals with a mental illness. To speak of racism as a mental illness would insult those who genuinely struggle with mental health issues and foster white denial and ableism, when white supremacy is not ableism. White supremacy is taught and reinforced through institutionalized racism. Since whiteness deems what is accurate, valuable and socially acceptable, whites can employ these and other destructive behaviors to police, oppress, and control Black people. We can effectively say that sociopathy is a *social disease* comprising a collection of learned emotions and behaviors passed down from generation to generation. Sociopathy, then, is not a mental illness, but a status quo perpetuated by white supremacy.

Consider George Zimmerman, the self-appointed neighborhood watchman who fatally shot Trayvon Martin, a 17-year-old Black teen in Sanford, Florida on February 26, 2012. Zimmerman's anti-Black attitudes and assumptions were directly connected to his suspicions of the unarmed teen who was returning home from a trip to the store, carrying only a bag of Skittles and a bottle of tea. Zimmerman's grandiose sense of self, irrational thinking, shallow emotions, lack of impulse control, deep-seated hatred, and disregard for Black life precipitated and supported his violent behavior. Even after the murder, Zimmerman continued to display a lack of remorse and a blatant disregard for Trayvon Martin's rights, as well as the feelings of Martin's family. In Zimmerman's mind, Black life was not valuable, so he felt that it was okay to dehumanize the teen and accept zero responsibility for his murder. Zimmerman was so convinced that he had done the right thing that he went so far as to brag about the shooting death on Twitter saying, "We all know how it ended for the last moron who hit me." Despite the backlash from that tweet and being acquitted of the murder, numerous media outlets have continued to highlight Zimmerman's ongoing patterns of self-grandiosity, manipulation, irrational thinking, lack of empathy and impulse control, and denial of responsibility.

The sociopath's sense of entitlement rules their mind and behavior. And because they lack a moral anchor and social conscience, they ultimately destroy those close to them—without any feelings of guilt, shame or remorse. When we refer to these types of individuals as ignorant, not only are we giving them a free pass and letting them off the hook by not owning and taking responsibility for their maladaptive behaviors, we are coddling and excusing behaviors that are much more sinister than ignorance. No, this is not ignorance. This is full-blown sociopathy, and it is a by-product of white privilege.

The Concept of White Supremacy

White supremacy is an historically-based, institutionally replicated system of exploitation and oppression of people of color for the purpose of maintaining and defending a system of wealth, power and privilege. The development of the class structure in the U.S. is intricately woven with the development of white supremacy, so whites are elevated above Blacks, even when they share similar class positions.

Fear mongering and hate baiting is the soul of white supremacy and violence lies at its heart. White supremacy can be likened to a cult. A *cult* is a social group that amasses power by instilling fear and obedience. Cults assume many forms: religious, satanic, mystical, political, racist, terrorist, human potential, and commercial, to name a few. From a psychological perspective, a cult attempts to maintain dependency, uses mind control by eradicating individualistic and critical thinking, and exploits members to advance the self-proclaimed and omniscient leader's goals.

Humans are social animals. Regardless of demographic (gender, race, ethnicity, age, ability, sexual orientation, familial status, economic status, education or profession) people join cults because it speaks to some unmet psychological need by providing a sense of affiliation, identity and security. White supremacy can be considered a racist cult in that it demands followers to: isolate themselves from family and friends; judge and condemn those who look, believe, think, and act differently than whites do; adhere to strict and unquestioning obedience; communicate in coded language; engage in ritualistic practices; and pledge allegiance at any cost, with dire exit consequences. These are very clear warning signs that individuals who agree to follow these ideologies are headed for trouble.

Deeply rooted beliefs about race and the value of Black lives create hostility for those who fall outside of the realm of whiteness. Racism and white supremacy are so pervasive that we do not have to do anything to consciously participate in it. It's in the air that we breathe; it's in our social institutions; it's deeply embedded in our thoughts, ideas and behaviors. If we are not actively challenging privilege, power and oppression, we are colluding with it.

Being in the dominant group provides freedom and privileges that people of color can only hope for. What many white people believe is that living a life of privilege is so powerful that everyone is living their experience. They don't have the same ongoing concerns about race issues as people of color, so we're the ones who have to adapt.

Oppression not only affects the oppressed, but also the oppressor. There are psychological, social, economical and spiritual costs related to oppression. White America will never see progress unless they come to terms with their ancestral demons of white supremacy.

Having said this, as the racial demographic of the U.S. shifts, we are experiencing a disintegration of whiteness and what it means to be American. It will be interesting to see what the unfolding mainstream will look like, how whites will fit into the new structure and what it will mean to white people when whiteness is no longer the norm.

Understanding White Privilege

Privilege is a right or advantage specifically granted to an individual or group, and withheld from another. White privilege—unearned and largely unacknowledged—is a historically-based, institutionally perpetuated system of preferential treatment of white people based solely on their skin color and/or European descent. It is also an exemption from racial oppression, again based on skin color. From this perspective, white privilege and racial oppression are two sides of the same coin.

White people have white privilege even when disabled. *"When you're accustomed to privilege, equality feels like oppression."* I've seen this quote floating around on Facebook, and it rings true. Why is it so difficult for white people to acknowledge their privilege? When people say you have privilege they are not saying that you don't have any problems. They are saying that you **do not have the specific problems that arise from the oppression of institutionalized racism**. This is not a difficult concept once you open your mind to understanding it.

White privilege is difficult to discern by those who were born with access to power and resources. Peggy McIntosh, anti-racism activist, Associate Director of the Wellesley Centers for Women and a speaker and the founder and Co-Director of the National S.E.E.D. Project on Inclusive Curriculum says, "I was taught to see racism only in individual acts of meanness, not in invisible systems conferring dominance on my group." She proceeded to work on herself by identifying some effects of white privilege in her daily life by outlining conditions that attach themselves to her skin-color privilege. She further noted that her African American friends, acquaintances and coworkers with whom she frequently interact cannot rely on most of these conditions. McIntosh lists forty-six examples of white privilege in her 1988 essay, *White Privilege and Male Privilege: A Personal Account of Coming to See Correspondences Through Work in Women's Studies.* After reading McIntosh's essay, it's impossible to deny that whiteness in America affords certain people privileges that other racial groups are consistently denied. Many of our deeply-embedded social ills are perpetuated by white privilege. This elitism must be acknowledged and tackled by whites themselves in order for social progress to be made. When white people begin to view privilege and oppression as *their* issue, and render it unacceptable, neither privilege nor oppression will have much of a future.

Racial Microaggressions and Marginality

Racism is alive and well in 21st century America. Yet, most white Americans do not perceive racial discrimination as a deeply-entrenched or widespread problem. Those that do acknowledge that racism exists do not believe it's a significant problem. The majority of whites tend to view racism as a concept monopolized by extreme bigots who don't represent the white majority. This makes it easier for whites to either deny that racism still exists or downplay it as an insignificant issue. Moreover, it renders white people immune to many of the challenges consistently faced by people of color. White privilege affords the benefit for whites to remain ignorant of the world around them.

Denial has a way of keeping many white people distracted from reality, and therefore, stuck. If you're hearing pervasive outcries against racism and you continue to insist that we live in a post-racial society, you are in denial and a significant part of the problem.

Here's an example: I'm working with a client who claims to be the best leader since sliced bread. Yet, there's widespread anger and discontentment among employees as the department races to hell on a fast bicycle. Despite how great the exec thinks he/she is, the staff thinks the person sucks, and performance, productivity and morale are at an all-time low. Needless to say, there's a clear disconnect in perceptions that must be addressed if there's any hope for improvement across the board.

Covert racism is no less insidious than overt racism. Much like bad medicine: whether you drink it from the bottle or take it with a spoon, it's still toxic and produces adverse effects. If you're one of those people swimming in the sea of denial, this is an opportunity for you to ask some thought-provoking questions about your values, beliefs, assumptions, attitudes and perceptions... and why they continue to create and perpetuate division.

The reality is there is no respite from the racism that Black Americans face every day of their lives. The psychological warfare games that Black people must play just to survive are astonishing. When Blacks wake up each day, we have a range of issues to deal with before we ever leave home. *Will I encounter a police who may pull me over for the slightest offense, or worse, kill me? Will my white colleagues harass me because I don't fit within their cultural norm? Will the person who interviews me for the job find some way to discriminate against me so that I'm not hired? Or if I am hired, will my hiring be attributed to affirmative action, rather than my skills and expertise? Will I have to carefully measure my words in the meeting, so I'm not perceived as a threat? Will my child get expelled from school because of some zero tolerance policy? Will I be followed around a store like a common criminal while I'm trying to shop? Will I be denied a bank loan simply because of my skin color? Will I have access to quality medical resources and care? Will I be steered away from a particular community because Blacks are not wanted in the neighborhood?* Oftentimes, the tension between conforming to white standards and struggling to maintain personal integrity and Black identity is overwhelming. No amount of hard work, achievement, money or success can protect Black people from the hatred and destruction that white America directs at us each and every day in one way or another. The pain, frustration and rage over this pervasive and persistent racial stereotyping, prejudice, discrimination and oppression can be all-consuming.

Surprisingly, many people have never heard of the term *microaggression*, let alone understand its meaning. The term was coined in 1970 by psychiatrist and Harvard University professor Dr. Chester M. Pierce to describe insults and dismissals he regularly witnessed inflicted on African Americans by non-Black Americans. Racial microaggressions are brief and commonplace daily verbal, behavioral or environmental indignities. Whether they are intentional or unintentional, they communicate hostile, derogatory, or negative racial slights and insults that have an unpleasant psychological impact on the targeted recipient.

Here are a few examples of microaggressions:

- Senator Joe Biden when Senator Barack Obama announced his presidential run: "I mean you got the first mainstream African American who is articulate and bright and clean and a nice-looking guy. I mean, that's a storybook man." (Hidden message: He represents his people well.)

- A white female in an elevator clutches her purse more tightly when a Black man steps in. (Hidden message: Blacks are criminals.)

- A Black woman moderates a meeting and one of the white participants says, "Wow! You are so articulate! (Hidden message: You do not sound Black.)

The recent surge in the popularity of this term is attributed, in part, to a 2007 academic article published by Derald W. Sue, a Columbia University psychology professor. We have been socialized in a society where there exist biases about Blacks and other people of color that have been passed down through generations. It is not the old-fashioned overt racism that is most harmful to people of color, but the contemporary forms known as *microaggressions*. According to Sue (2011):

> "The characteristics of these forms of bias are invisible, unintentional, and subtle, generally outside the level of conscious awareness. Racial microaggressions create psychological dilemmas for the perpetrator and recipient because they represent a clash of racial realities. Also, microagressions create a hostile and invalidating climate for marginalized groups, saps their spiritual and psychic energies, and their cumulative nature can result in depression, frustration, anger, rage, loss of self-esteem, anxiety, [and other psychological and emotional conditions]."

Sue (2011) outlines additional disparities associated with bigotry and microaggressions:

White European males make up only 31 percent of the U.S. population, yet they:

- occupy 80 percent of tenured positions in higher education;
- hold 65 percent of elected offices;
- occupy 89 percent of the U.S. House of Representatives;
- occupy 93 percent of the U.S. Senate;
- occupy 92 percent of the Forbes 400 Executive CEO level positions;
- are 90 percent of public school superintendents;
- are 99.9 percent of athletic team owners;

- are 97.73 percent of U.S. Presidents; and
- have eight times as much political power as women of color.

The above statistics underscore the fact that white men are persons of privilege and we do not live in a racially reflective democracy. Nationally and politically, chauvinistic ideologies trend toward patriarchy and sexism underscoring the notion that white males are inherently superior to people of color and where white men have more power than white women—with women of color occupying the lowest level of society. America's toxic system of patriarchy continues to demonstrate that white men are more interested in making the rules, controlling others and perpetuating white supremacist ideologies than engaging in self-examination to confront their fear and resentment. As the U.S. approaches a profound demographic tipping point and witnesses a growing revolution against racism, discrimination and oppression, only time will tell whether this is the dawning of a post-racial age and the end of the white male ruling class.

The Myth of Reverse Racism

Reverse racism is a term created and used by white people to deny their privilege. It's a term that refers to the anger and hostile behavior of people of color toward whites because of the privileges that they possess. Let's debunk this myth once and for all. **There is no such thing as reverse racism.** White people often use this term whenever people of color call out racism and discrimination. While people of color can have certain beliefs, perceptions and ideas about white people, racism is far more complex and goes much deeper than that.

In order to be racist, an individual must possess two traits. The first is privilege—a structural social advantage, which whites benefit from even when disadvantaged in others ways. White privilege is bestowed upon individuals at birth, it is considered normal and it cannot be given away.

- Whenever you use yourself and your experiences as a reference point for everyone else, you are invoking and validating your white privilege.

- Whenever you shift the focus back to yourself—even when the conversation is not about you, you are invoking and validating your white privilege.

- Whenever you disconnect yourself from the realities of people of color, you are invoking and validating your white privilege.

- Whenever you attempt to control what people of color know about their histories, you are invoking and validating your white privilege.

- Whenever you think that people of color come to the table having been dealt the same cards as you, you are invoking and validating your white privilege.

- Whenever you believe that you are the only person in the picture and people of color are not worth mentioning, you are invoking and validating your white privilege.

The second trait required in order to be racist is power—whites have access to opportunities and resources not afforded to Blacks and other people of color. The power that racism bears depends upon how it is rooted in institutions and whether or not racist acts boast institutional support.

Despite the fact that the Emancipation Proclamation freed slaves and the 14th Amendment gave Blacks the right to vote, institutional racism has never been dismantled. Racism, at its core, is a system in which whites benefit from the oppression of others, whether they intend to or not. Every racial group in America does not have equal opportunity, status, power or privilege. While they may experience poverty, police brutality and other social issues, it's not on the same scale of the Black experience. Throughout history, white people have never been enslaved, colonized, forced to segregate or otherwise oppressed by people of color. White people do not face housing or job discrimination, police brutality or mass incarceration because of their race. White people do not face officially sanctioned discrimination and oppression by people of color. In order to be racist, one must possess privilege and a structural, institutional or social advantage. Even when disadvantaged in other ways, white people possess racial privilege and benefit from advantages structurally, institutionally and socially that allow them to leverage more power and influence than people of color. This represents an imbalance of power that is deeply embedded within the very fabric of American society.

Please do not delude yourself. You are always a PART OF the system and thus able to thrive in our society, because privilege and power permeate every aspect of your life. The real question here is: are you PARTICIPATING IN the system in a way that reinforces your privilege or challenges the status quo?

Chapter 3

Institutionalized Racism

No one can be perfectly free till all are free;
no one can be perfectly moral till all are moral;
no one can be perfectly happy till all are happy.
– Herbert Spencer

Structural Racism

In the United States, structural racism is the normalization of a range of dynamics—cultural, historical, interpersonal and institutional—that routinely provide advantage to whites while producing adverse outcomes for people of color. Structural racism is a system of hierarchy and equity that is characterized by white supremacy at the expense of racially oppressed people of color. Structural racism encompasses the entire system of white supremacy and is infused and diffused in every aspect of and within the entire fabric of our society.

Institutional racism emerges from structural racism and occurs within and between institutions. It is the unfair policies, inequitable opportunities and discriminatory treatment based on race produced and perpetuated by institutions (political, educational, religious, etc.) that advantage whites while oppressing people of color because of their race.

Structural racism perpetuates injustice and inequality. A recent example is the Flint, Michigan water crisis. On January 16, 2016, President Obama signed an order declaring a state of emergency in response to a government-created health crisis resulting from contaminated water.

In April 2014, Flint's water supply was switched from Lake Huron to a new regional water system in a mandated cost-cutting measure. While waiting for the system to become accessible, the city pumped water to the residents from the Flint River. The corroded pipes permitted lead to leak into the water supply, and has since induced lead poisoning and created developmental disorders in children.

Flint is a poor city devastated by deindustrialization compounded by the Great Recession and has a Black population of almost 57 percent. The U.S. Census Bureau labels it the second poorest city in the nation (after Youngstown, Ohio) with more than 40 percent of its residents living below the federal poverty line. The median income for Flint residents between 2009 and 2013 was $24,834 annually, compared to the state's median income of $48,411.

Despite mounting evidence to indicate otherwise, the emergency City Manager and Governor continued to insist that the water was safe and denied and even went so far as going to court to contest the evidence and fight efforts to switch the water supply back to Detroit. It was not until October 2015 that the Governor acknowledged the contaminated water supply, and several months later declared a state of emergency and requested federal assistance.

Thanks to Michigan government's transgressions, a predominately Black population, and systemic and systematic neglect, this avoidable disaster clearly illustrates structural racism—the most profound and pervasive form of racism. It also further emphasizes why it's necessary for us to say that Black lives matter.

Inequities in Our Criminal Justice System

Racial Profiling

The American Civil Liberties Union defines *racial profiling* as "the discriminatory practice by law enforcement officials of targeting individuals for suspicion of crime based on the individual's race, ethnicity, religion or national origin. Racial profiling is a longstanding and deeply troubling problem, despite claims that the United States has entered a "post-racial" era. Racial profiling is a violation of human rights, is unconstitutional, socially corrupting and counter-productive."

The U.S. Department of Justice tells us, *"Racial profiling at its core concerns the invidious use of race or ethnicity as a criterion in conducting stops, searches and other law enforcement investigative procedures. It is premised on the erroneous assumption that any particular individual of one race or ethnicity is more likely to engage in misconduct than any particular individual of another race or ethnicity...Racial profiling in law enforcement is not merely wrong, but also ineffective. Race-based assumptions in law enforcement perpetuate negative racial stereotypes that are harmful to our rich and diverse democracy, and materially impair our efforts to maintain a fair and just society."*

Despite this statement by the Department of Justice, racial profiling is a significant problem in the U.S. Let's take a look at some alarming statistics:

- A February 2009 study by the Criminal Justice Statistical Analysis Center reveals that Black motorists were 1.64 times more likely to be stopped than whites.

- A 2002 Minnesota study found that statewide, African American, Hispanic, and Native American drivers were stopped and searched more often than whites, yet contraband was found more frequently in the cars of white drivers.

- After passing the 2003 Illinois Traffic Stops Statistics Act, the state revealed that the number of consent searches after traffic stops of African American and Hispanic motorists was more than double that of whites, but whites were twice as likely to have contraband.

- A 2005 Texas study revealed a disproportionate number of traffic stops and searches of African Americans and Hispanics, although law enforcement authorities were more likely to find contraband on white drivers.

- On the night of June 14, 2008 in Newark, New Jersey, two youth ages 15 and 13 were riding in a car driven by their football coach, Kelvin Lamar James—all three were African American. Police officers stopped their car in the rain, pulled the three out, and held them at gunpoint while searching the car. James stated that the search violated his rights, and one officer replied in abusive language that the three didn't have rights and the police "had no rules." The car search produced nothing more than football equipment.

- In New York City between 2005 and mid-2008, approximately 80 percent of traffic stops made were of Blacks and Latinos, who comprise 25 percent and 28 percent of the city's total population, respectively. During this same time period, only about 10 percent of stops were of whites, who comprise 44 percent of the city's population.

- Between 2005 and mid-2008, Blacks comprised 85 percent of individuals frisked by the New York Police Department, compared to only 8 percent of whites.

- Between 2005 and mid-2008, an extraordinary number of NYPD stops resulted in the use of physical force against a disproportionate number of Blacks and Latinos—24 percent, compared to 17 percent of whites.

- Per 10,000 residents in Los Angeles, the Black stop rate was 3,400 stops higher than the white stop rate from July 2003 to June 2004. When stopped, Blacks were 127 percent more likely to be frisked than whites. When frisked, Blacks were 42.3 percent less likely to be found with a weapon than whites, yet 29 percent of Blacks were more likely to be arrested.

- Research studies reveal that police officers perceive Black boys as violent, and older than they actually are (12-year-old Tamir Rice, who was fatally shot by Cleveland, Ohio police on November 22, 2014 while playing with a toy gun, comes to mind here). Thus, police are much more likely to use excessive force when Blacks are dehumanized while suspected of wrongdoing.

The issues facing the Black community are so much deeper than reforms in law enforcement. Every aspect of Black life is impacted in some way, shape or form by systemic racism that permeates our daily existence.

Racial profiling continues to be a significant problem and people of color are disproportionately policed, incarcerated and sentenced to death at significantly higher rates than their white counterparts. Check out these chilling statistics:

- The Center for American Progress (2012) reveals that while people of color make up about 30 percent of the U.S. population, they account for more than 60 percent of those imprisoned. One in every 15 African American men is incarcerated compared to one in every 106 white men.

- According to the Sentencing Project, for Black males in their thirties, one in every 10 is in jail or prison on any given day. One in three Black men can expect to be imprisoned in their lifetime. Black men represent over 40 percent of the prison population. African Americans are twice as likely to be arrested and almost four times as likely to experience force during police encounters.

- According to Unlocking America, if African Americans and Hispanics were incarcerated at the same rate of whites, today's prison and jail populations would decline by approximately 50 percent.

- Thirty-five percent of Black children grades 7-12 have been suspended or expelled at some point in their school careers compared to 20 percent of Hispanics and 15 percent of whites.

- In school, students of color face harsher punishments than their white classmates, leading to a higher number of incarcerated youth of color. Black and Hispanic students represent more than 70 percent of those involved in school-related arrests and law enforcement referrals, with Blacks making up two-fifths of confined youth today.

- African American youth have a higher rate of juvenile incarceration and are more likely to be sentenced to adult prison. According to the Sentencing Project, although African American juvenile youth are about 16 percent of the youth population, 37 percent of their cases are transferred to criminal court.

- The Center on Juvenile and Criminal Justice reports that nationwide, African Americans represent 26 percent of juvenile arrests, 44 percent of youth who are detained, 46 percent of the youth who are judicially waived to criminal court, and 58 percent of the youth admitted to state prisons.

- The number of incarcerated women has increased by 800 percent over the past three decades, and women of color are disproportionately represented. African American women are three times more likely than white women to be incarcerated. One in 100 African American women is in prison.

- Although the Human Rights Watch tells us that people of color are no more likely to use or sell illegal drugs than whites, the war on drugs has been waged primarily in communities of color, and people of color are more likely to receive harsher punishments. African Americans comprise 14 percent of regular drug users, but are 37 percent of those arrested for drug offenses. From 1980 to 2007 about one in three of the 25.4 million adults arrested for illegal drugs was African American.

- Five times as many whites are using drugs as African Americans, yet African Americans are sent to prison for drug offenses at 10 times the rate of whites. African Americans represent 12 percent of monthly drug users, but comprise 32 percent of persons arrested for drug possession.

- In 2002, Blacks constituted more than 80 percent of the people sentenced under the federal crack cocaine laws and served substantially more time in prison for drug offenses than did whites, despite the fact that more than 2/3 of crack cocaine users in the U.S. are white or Hispanic.

- According to the Sentencing Project, African Americans serve virtually as much time in prison for a drug offense (58.7 months) as whites do for a violent offense (61.7 months).

- The U.S. Sentencing Commission reports that in the federal system, Black offenders receive 10 percent longer sentences than white offenders for the same crimes. The Sentencing Project reports that Blacks are 21 percent more likely to receive mandatory-minimum sentences than white defendants and are 20 percent more likely to be sentenced to prison.

- Voter laws that prohibit people with felony convictions to vote disproportionately affect men of color. An estimated 5.3 million Americans are denied the right to vote based on a previous felony conviction. Thus, 13 percent of African American men are denied the right to vote. These voting policies have led 11 states to deny the right to vote to more than 10 percent of their African American population.

- Studies show that people of color, particularly, Black men and women, face wage disparities following release from prison. While there is no evidence of racial divergence in wages prior to incarceration, following the release from prison wages grow at a 21 percent slower rate for Black inmates compared to their white counterparts.

Goffman (2014) identifies a number of persuasive tactics used by police to gain cooperation from relatives and friends to pressure them to "give up" a wanted Black suspect—whether or not the person has actually committed a crime. This includes: threats of arrest, eviction, or loss of child custody; injury to the family member or friend and/or their property; denigrating the suspect to weaken relationship bonds; moral appeals indicating that it may not only be best for the suspect to be taken into custody, but best for the entire family; promises of confidentiality—which may or may not be honored; and interrogation. Most often, when family members and friends come under intense police pressure, they will eventually cave.

Lawful and legitimate policing means that law enforcement personnel comply with constitutional, legal and professional standards. Yet, according to the American Civil Liberties Union (ACLU), a major barrier to eradicating the discriminatory practice of racial profiling is the unwillingness of the federal government to pass legislation that prohibits profiling at all levels of law enforcement including local, state and national.

Skin color and racial stereotyping are not justifiable reasons for criminal suspicion, and using it as a legitimate basis for targeting people of color puts them in extremely vulnerable positions. Racial profiling is not only unconstitutional, but a type of social corruption that intentionally exploits and unfairly victimizes people of color—particularly Blacks, violates human rights and affects the lives of millions of American citizens. Despite any claims that we live in a post-racial society, it is clearly evident that racial profiling continues to be a persistent, pervasive and deeply troubling problem in this country.

Police Brutality

The consequences of racial profiling are clearly evident: strained relationships and racial tensions between law enforcement officers and minorities, especially Blacks. Law enforcement justifies their profiling with the hypothesis that stopping more Blacks will increase their likelihood of finding criminals, since criminals are more likely to be Black. However, according to law professor, David A. Harris, this hypothesis has been repeatedly proven wrong. Harris found that racial profiling actually renders police less accurate in catching criminal activity, because it wastes resources on false positives among people the police would never otherwise stop (a Black university professor on his way to work), and the focus on race diverts attention from the clues that actually suggest criminal activity.

If America is truthful with herself, there's a stark fact that none of us can ignore: U.S. law enforcement has always been an enemy of Black people (check out our long-standing history) in that it was created, to a large extent, as a means of monitoring, controlling and punishing us. For Black males, getting pulled over by the police is probably the most daunting and horrifying experience that they will ever encounter—even if they are innocent of having committed any wrongdoing.

A recent report by The Counted, a database created by *The Guardian*, reveals that despite making up only 2 percent of the total U.S. population, Black males between the ages of 15 and 34 comprised more than 15 percent of all deaths logged in 2015 involving the use of deadly force by police. The rate of police-involved deaths among Black males was five times higher than for white men in the same age group. Non-white Americans comprise less than 38 percent of the total U.S. population, yet almost half of all people killed by police are minorities, and minorities make up more *unarmed* people killed by police. [Note: The Counted was created in response to widespread concern about the federal government's failure to maintain a comprehensive record of people killed by police. Officials at the U. S. Department of Justice have since begun testing a database that attempts to do so, directly drawing on The Counted's data and methodology.]

MASS INCARCERATION

> *"The United States imprisons a larger percentage of its Black population than South Africa did at the height of apartheid. In Washington D.C., our nation's capital, it is estimated that three out of four young Black men (and nearly all those in the poorest neighborhoods) can expect to serve time in prison."* – The New Jim Crow

In recent years, the U.S. has celebrated the 50th anniversaries of the March on Washington, the Civil Rights Act and several other landmark achievements considered pivotal relative to African American progress. Yet, despite these accomplishments, African American men continue to face high levels of unemployment and incarceration as they did a century ago.

The War on Drugs and the War on Crime have taken millions of young Black males from families, schools and work, relegated them to jails and prisons, and returned them to society with felony convictions. This often means continuous cycling through the criminal justice system and a dismal future filled with disadvantages and restrictions that will play a significant role in fostering social injustice and inequality.

Historically, poor Black communities have not been able to turn to the police for protection because the police were either uninterested or absent altogether. Today, Blacks in poor communities—especially Black males—face an additional barrier: the inability to turn to police largely due to legal entanglements that prevent them from doing so. Once an individual has gotten caught up in the criminal justice system, it's virtually impossible for him to escape it. He will always be suspected of wrongdoing and viewed as a dubious criminal, even when he has done nothing wrong. He now knows that the legal system will exploit, arrest, and imprison him for the most minor offense. His life thereby becomes punctuated with legal entrapments—a net that casts itself far and wide—and fearing that he can and will be taken into custody at any time and for any reason, he learns to avoid the cops, the courts and the legal system at virtually any cost. This is why it's not uncommon to see a Black man, at the slightest provocation, running for his life from the police—even when he has not committed a recent crime.

A University of Chicago study by Neal and Rick (2014) reveals that the rise in incarceration rates among Black males, combined with a significant increase in unemployment since the Great Recession, have left most Black men in a position that is no better than the one they occupied a few years after the Civil Rights Act. The data reveals that more than 10 percent of Black men in their 30s will be incarcerated at some point in any given year, compared to approximately 2 percent for white males in the same age group. The study attributes the devastating impact of mass incarceration on the African American community—at least in part—to more punitive criminal-justice policies. Black men in their prime working years, especially those without a high school education, are much more likely to be incarcerated than their white peers.

According to writer, journalist and educator Ta-Nehisi Coates (2015), America's incarceration rates doubled from the mid-1970s to the mid-1980s from approximately 150 people per 100,000 to about 300 per 100,000. It doubled again from the mid-1980s to the mid-1990s, reaching a historic high of 767 people per 100,000 before registering a moderate decline to 707 people per 100,000 in 2012. America's jail and prison population has increased sevenfold since 1970 from 300,000 to 2.2 million people. America currently accounts for less than 5 percent of the world's population, and 25 percent of the incarcerated population.

Recently, researchers at the University of Sheffield have identified "troubling" patterns in court decisions involving Blacks in South Carolina. Blacks receive consistently harsher criminal penalties during sentencing than their white counterparts. Of particular note is that this pattern of disparity appears to affect Black offenders who have limited criminal histories or have committed less severe crimes. Not only were Black people with a less criminal background more likely to be jailed, custodial sentences increased by 43 percent for those with no prior criminal history.

There is nothing new about mass incarceration. It is merely a continuation of a long history of racist and discriminatory practices in our criminal (in)justice system. There is something very wrong with a society in which prisons are its largest form of public housing. Reading these dire statistics, it doesn't take one long to recognize that mass incarceration is a modern day evolution of slavery.

Mary Canty Merrill, Ph.D.

THE U.S. PRISON INDUSTRY: A NEW FORM OF SLAVERY

The prison industry complex is one of the fastest growing industries in the U.S. and backed by Wall Street investors. The Corrections Corporation of America has seen its profits increase by more than 500 percent in the last 20 years and the growth shows no sign of stopping. Today the $5 billion industry houses approximately 2 million inmates in state, federal and private prisons.

Statistics show that the U.S. holds 25 percent of the world's prison population, but only five percent of the world's population. The U.S. has a higher rate of incarceration than any other industrialized nation: a half million more than China, which has a population that's five times greater than the U.S. Ten years ago there were only five private prisons in the country, with a population of 2,000 inmates. Today, there are 100 private prisons, with a population of 62,000 inmates. Based on statistical data, that number is expected to rise to approximately 360,000 in the coming decade.

Private prisons are exploiting inmates for profit. The private contracting of prisoners for work provides incentives to incarcerate people. Corporate stockholders make financial gains off prison labor, so lobby for longer sentences. The Progressive Labor Party likens today's prison industry to Nazi Germany's forced labor and concentration camps. While we may think that we know how the criminal justice system operates, we really don't understand the depth or devastation of it. This is largely because television dramas about crime, police and prosecutors are generally related from law enforcement's point of view.

In her book, *The New Jim Crow: Mass Incarceration in the Age of Colorblindness*, Michelle Alexander reveals that the "War on Drugs", implemented by the Reagan Administration, focused largely on the crack explosion in poor communities of color. However, the crack epidemic waned in the late 1980s, so law enforcement agencies shifted their attention to marijuana. According to the American Civil Liberties Union (ACLU), more than 20,000 people were incarcerated for possessing marijuana.

Alexander further articulates the problem with mass incarceration:

> *"It is far more convenient to imagine that a majority of young African American men in urban areas freely chose a life of crime than to accept the real possibility that their lives were structured in a way that virtually guaranteed their early admission into the system from which they can never escape."*

Prison labor is rooted in slavery. Prisons have been historically linked to forced labor, inhumane conditions, a reproduction of slavery-like conditions, and the needs of the capitalist elite—reinforcing the link between prison, slavery and capitalism. According to the Center on Budget and Policy Priorities (2014), corrections spending is now the third-largest category of spending in most states, behind education and health care. State corrections spending, which more than doubled between 1986 and 2013 (after adjusting for inflation), rose from $20 billion to over $47 billion. Spending rose in every state except Virginia by more than four times in nine states (Arkansas, Colorado, Idaho, North Dakota, Oregon, Pennsylvania, West Virginia, Wisconsin and Wyoming) and by five times in three of those states (Colorado, Idaho and Pennsylvania). Growth in corrections spending has outpaced growth in expenditures in other critical areas of state budgets, such as K-12 and higher education. State spending on higher education—that is, money spent through the state budget, not by students and families through tuition—rose by less than 6 percent between 1986 and 2013, after adjusting for inflation. State support for K-12 education grew by 69 percent over this period—but corrections spending jumped by *141 percent*.

Despite being heavily capitalized, the prison-industrial complex has a number of failings. First, it is not proven to be effective in terms of rehabilitating prisoners, which supports recidivism rates. Second, it has not decreased or bears any relationship to crime rates. Third, it coincides with the escalation of violence among young men in our national history. Finally, it has pursued incarceration patterns that emphasize racist and discriminatory practices. Today, we are experiencing a redistribution of wealth and resources whereby social justice-based reforms suffer in favor of imprisonment and thus, prison spending. The prison-industrial complex boom is not only providing capitalists with imprisoned consumers, but also with cheap and reliable labor through increased incarceration rates.

In light of aforementioned and other criminal justice system statistical data, it is clearly evident that the prison-industrial complex plays a significant role in perpetuating racism and discrimination. The system is adept at exploiting prisoners to maximize profit. These racial disparities not only threaten the Black community but deprive them of their most basic civil rights by denying equal access to housing, education, employment and public benefits, and limiting voting rights. Eliminating these racial disparities must be at the heart of justice and equality efforts in America.

Chapter 4

The Rise of the Black Lives Matter Movement

*Power concedes nothing without a demand.
It never did and it never will.*
– Frederick Douglass

A Death in Ferguson, Missouri Sparks a Movement

In response to the acquittal of George Zimmerman, who fatally shot unarmed Black teen, 17-year-old Trayvon Martin in Sanford, Florida on February 26, 2012, a woman took to Twitter and tweeted, *"Black lives matter."* The Black Lives Matter movement officially started after Darren Wilson, a Ferguson, Missouri cop, fatally shot 18-year-old Michael Brown, an unarmed Black resident on August 9, 2014.

What happened to Michael Brown is a breakdown of the social order. This situation was not caused by "black culture" but is instead a government-driven problem evidenced by a rightfully sick and tired group of people who are painfully aware that societal protections do not apply to them—particularly young Black males.

I am in no way excusing or condoning criminal behavior. People who commit crimes should be held accountable and face the consequences of their actions. At the same time, aggressive policing has become a routine modern-day tactic used to continue controlling and justifying the maltreatment of Blacks. Having said this, it doesn't take a rocket scientist to predict the fallout when a group of people are regularly subjected to widespread discrimination, abuse and oppression—with little hope of ever achieving social equality, justice and economic success.

Since the deaths of Martin and Brown, there's a new generation of mobilized activities on the ground and online to protest police brutality and demand an investigation into and reforms of the systemic racism and inequalities associated with modern-day policing and our criminal justice system when dealing with people of color. The Black Lives Matter movement swiftly caught on around the country and has become a rallying cry for social justice and equality.

Why We Say Black Lives Matter

President Abraham Lincoln signed the Emancipation Proclamation on January 1, 1863 that officially freed most of America's 4 million slaves. Yet, here we are in the 21st century still fighting for racial justice and equality. Africans became Americans under the most oppressive and inhumane conditions. Today, Blacks continue to endure a brutally oppressive system, and we continue to be viewed as uncivilized, inferior and passive people. I have presented a significant amount of statistical data to shed light on racial, class, educational, political, legal and social disparities to support the fact that Black lives have never been and are still not valued in this country. This is why it is necessary for us to say that Black Lives Matter.

Misconceptions about the Black Lives Matter Movement

I'm reminded of an African proverb: *"Until the lion learns to write, every story will glorify the hunter."* While the story of abolition gets short-changed in American history books, Black people's fight against injustice and inequality is not new. There is a long history of Blacks' active resistance to racism from the time Africans were captured and enslaved on ships bound for America. Manisha Sinha (2016), a professor of Afro-American studies at the University of Massachusetts Amherst and author of a new book, *The Slave's Cause* argues that Blacks played a much larger role in bringing about their own liberation than has been previously acknowledged by white slaveholders. From the beginning of 17th century trans-Atlantic slavery, Black thinkers influenced the ideology and strategies of abolitionism. Blacks rebelled, protested, escaped and challenged the status quo to advance the goals of the abolition movement.

Striking in its simplicity, yet painful that the words must be uttered at all in 21st century America, the Black Lives Matter movement—originating in the African American community as a rallying cry against police brutality—has escaped control by the mainstream ruling establishment. While escaping challenge, the movement has been rife with criticism. Some have called the movement a hate group. Others have labeled it anti-white. Still others have dubbed it anti-police. In a September 8, 2015 article in *Cosmopolitan* magazine, Brittney Cooper outlines eleven major misconceptions about the Black Lives Matter movement and proceeds to counter them with facts. Regardless how people may downplay or challenge this movement, there have been Black Lives matter protests in every major U.S. city and solidarity rallies in small towns and abroad to campaign against racist police violence and advocate for the validity of Black lives. All movements experience ups and downs, so we cannot predict the trajectory of any movement. However, we can say that a new generation of activists and revolutionaries is rising up to advance the fight for racial justice and equality and social transformation.

The Problem with the Slogan "All Lives Matter"

Let's turn our attention to the "All Lives Matter" slogan and why it's a problem. It seems that America is more offended by Black Lives Matter than by racism, oppression and police brutality. The truth is we know that white lives matter because we've been supporting white lives throughout history. Whenever whites respond with "All Lives Matter" it tells us that you think there's nothing wrong with a cop taking an innocent Black life or Black people being oppressed and discriminated against. It tells us that you think it's wrong for us to care about our own Black lives.

Saying that Black lives matter is not the same thing as saying that other lives do not matter, or that *only* Black lives matter. It is an acknowledgement that Blacks disproportionately suffer racism and discrimination in the form of police brutality, as well as in our criminal justice system.

We can again use the Flint, Michigan water crisis as a clear example of white privilege and the problem with saying All Lives Matter. Governor Rick Snyder was allowed to lie about the safety of the city's water supply, which has poisoned thousands of Black residents and created developmental disorders in children. Yet, at the time of this writing, he still retains his job and there are no signs of his forced departure. Conversely, Detroit's former young Black Mayor, Kwame Kilpatrick is serving 28 years in prison for misusing city funds and tax crimes. I am in no way excusing or trivializing Kilpatrick's behavior, but aiming to present an unambiguous illustration that having white skin is the ultimate privilege in America.

To say that all lives matter when Black lives continue to be subjected to widespread vitriol is paramount to pouring gasoline on a burning fire. Don't be so quick to assume that Black lives matter means that other lives do not matter—just recognize that in America, white skin reigns, which is why it's necessary for us to say that Black Lives matter, too.

Chapter 5

Voices for Equality on Why Black Lives Matter

They tried to bury me but didn't realize I was a seed.
– Unknown

If the truth be told, I did not set out to engage in social justice work. This calling found me, and I am continuing to identify ways to integrate various aspects into my profession as an Industrial and Organizational Psychologist, because I'm committed to being a voice for the voiceless. What is our knowledge, hard work and financial gain for if we cannot use it to improve the human condition?

We must continue to break the silence of racism whenever we can. Breaking this silence is a survival issue, so I am fully committed to the cause. This means recognizing, confronting and moving beyond our fear to engage in thoughtful and meaningful dialogue to raise consciousness and effectively lead to action and social transformation. History has often lied to us about the Black experience, and few people have been taught to think critically about the issues. Therefore, educating ourselves and others is an essential step in advocating for social justice and equality to bring about social change. I am a Black woman, so find strength in studying and seeking out other Black women who have been catalysts for social change. I also study the lives of White allies—past and present—to increase my knowledge and inform my perspectives.

In addition to reading and studying the truth about American history, I established the Facebook group, *Voices for Equality* in August 2015. What started out as a very small group of individuals connecting online to express concerns and address issues of racism, injustice and inequality has quickly grown to a community of 750 members representing diverse races, ethnicities, generations, backgrounds and life experiences.

We have adopted a dialogue-into-action approach, which means we educate, communicate, and then circulate in our individual communities to promote and advocate for diversity, inclusion, justice and freedom in the drive social change. We confront racism, sexism, classism, heterosexism, ableism and other forms of discrimination (based on race/ethnicity, gender, religion, age, ability, language, education, geographic location, and other demographics). Each of us is committed to open and honest dialogue and participate with the understanding that community growth depends on the inclusion of every individual voice. While we express concerns based on our individual perspectives, we are open to divergent points of view. We also actively pursue opportunities to combat the myths and stereotypes about our own and other groups in an effort to break down the barriers that prohibit our collective understanding, development, cooperation and progress to help win victories for humanity.

In addition to our ongoing efforts, I thought it would be a worthwhile endeavor to write a book explaining why Black lives matter using a cross-cultural lens. So I put out a call to the group to solicit volunteer contributing writers to express, in their own voice, why Black lives matter. The following essays were penned by these contributors who have taken a risk and put themselves on the line to speak out about the issues of racism that we are facing in 21st century America. I appreciate each of them having the courage to speak up about a growing and troubling social problem. These contributing authors represent cross-culturalism in terms of race, ethnicity, gender, and age, and I have reserved this chapter for them to share their own interpretations, impressions, insights, and ideas through original essays regarding why Black lives matter, too.

A Call to New Orleans

By Tamera CJ Baggett

It was August 29, 2005, and I was volunteering at Philadelphia's American Red Cross on the "Bridge" where the emergency communications come in. The televisions were showing the devastating flooding due to the levees breaking in New Orleans. Philadelphia is a national call center, so we were receiving calls from people who were trapped in their attics with no way out and the water rushing in. All we could give them was a location to go to according to their zip code, but they could not get out to go anywhere, this is how systemic racism functions. People of color are trapped in a system that is not serving them.

Their cell phones were dying; they only had a little room left of suffocating hot air at the top of their attics with the water rushing in. As they cried realizing their demise, most hung up, or their phones went dead, while I was on the line. We are all on the line now, when it comes to Black Lives Matter. We must heed the call to right an injustice that has been going on for almost 400 years—since August 20, 1619, when the first Africans were brought to these shores.

I had to go to the Gulf Coast; I could not take another shift listening to people suffering and dying over the phone. I was given a flight number for the next morning. After waiting for 37 years to obtain a higher education degree, I was finally attending Temple University, the semester had just started. I went home to pack and e-mailed my professors. I called my elder sister and she exclaimed, "But what about school?" I told her I had to go. When we are called we must step up. I flew into Houston and drove with others into Baton Rouge.

We were so close, but it felt like we were trapped on the outside of New Orleans. When we first arrived in Baton Rouge, we saw countless rescue volunteers from France, Belgium, England, and Canada. They shared their frustration in trying to get in. Those with helicopters were ready to drop food and water, but they were not allowed to fly over New Orleans. They came and asked us Red Cross volunteers if we would go up with them, thinking perhaps then, they would be allowed to drop supplies in, but to no avail we were all kept out. All local phone service was out. Around New Orleans it was difficult to communicate. Due to power outages, even local news was not available. In the dark, we left town for our assigned location.

A local Red Cross leader told me, "I want you to run triage, focus on what people need." I took that to heart; survivors need to be treated like human beings with respect. I created a spreadsheet of all services, which the community had to offer from vaccinations to clothing and public assistance. I worked with the locals. We came to an understanding, when they would say something dehumanizing, I would cue them by covering my ears with my hands, and they would stop and affectionately call me, "Dam Yankee!"

The beautiful town had a population of about 10,000. There were at least 5,000 of their statesmen from New Orleans seeking shelter there. The majority of the guests were African Americans and a few Asians and Latins. The out-of-state volunteers like the locals were European Americans. They were sincere and really wanted to help, but had little or no prior contact with African Americans before coming to serve. Many volunteers came from all white communities in the Midwest.

The volunteers' hearts were in the right place, but their brains were battered from centuries of social constructs portraying Blacks as menacing. The white volunteers kept trying to run the shelter like a Maximum Security Prison. One morning, volunteers had plastered every window in the front entrance with large Florissant orange posters, stating, "Call your parole officer immediately!" The second I saw them; I rushed to rip them down. The overnight volunteers had been ordered by local sheriff to post them. I asked the volunteers, "Why didn't you just put the posters in the guests' restrooms?" Why would you think this message applies to everyone here? Why post them on the front doors where all the community volunteers are coming in to serve? What message were you sending? The volunteers exclaimed they had to protect the locals. I constantly asked, have you witnessed one incident, where anyone being housed here would give you any concern? The answer was always no. I was perplexed regarding what caused this imagined fear. Being unconscious of 400 years of white supremacy messages is a privilege that we whites share, without even being aware that it is occurring.

Many citizens who had to flee New Orleans indicated that they had good paying jobs, bank accounts and owned their own homes, but everything was under water now. They literally wept about how they felt being treated like criminals. The treatment of the guests were dehumanizing in many ways, but everyone seemed oblivious unless it was pointed it out. Many of the infants had constant diarrhea and the parents were made to stand in long lines several times a day to receive a ration of only three diapers at a time, as their child's current diaper was leaking all over the place. The room where the diapers were kept was stacked to the ceiling with 100s of cases of diapers. There was no valid reason why everyone who had a child in diapers was not just given a case of diapers to be used when needed.

The guests were housed in the gymnasium where the floor was covered with wall-to-wall mattresses and a sea of bodies, which reminded me of the *Middle Passage*. For some, the loss was just too much to endure and they passed away during their sleep, never to face another day in a nation that does not cherish the sacrifices that they and their ancestors made. I witnessed the pain of the guests who had just made it out of the storm with only the clothes on their backs, having to strip off all they had to be burned, if it had made contact with the floodwater. This scene reminded me of their African ancestors, who survived the Middle Passage, and were stripped of their language, culture and heritage.

Volunteers wanted to have patrols over the grounds and lock the guests in at night. What made them want to act like *Paddy Rollers*? There were several tables and chairs set up outside where adult guests would share their narratives, concerns and hopes for the future. The temperature was over a hundred degrees most days. So in the evening as it cooled and the children slept, the adults needed a way to unload their traumas. Some guests were housed in hotels and would come to the University and collapse. They were alone with their children and had no one to hear their cries or their stories. The lack of witnesses to their stories kept them from healing.

Many local volunteers wanted to save the guests, so every Sunday there were countless volunteers with vans to shuttle the guests to church, so they could be saved. People would even set-up and pray outside the shelter for the guests to repent. They blamed the guests for what they had endured. But when a guest needed to shop for a bra in preparation for a job interview, finding a volunteer to take them shopping was difficult even though the guest had money for their purchase. Many things that were said about the guests, I cannot repeat, it makes my soul weep.

Whenever I witnessed implicit racism, I would gently point it out. At first the individuals would deny it, but I would catch them several more times exemplifying the same racist behaviors. I kept calling them out again and again and asking them to see if they could remember what cued their fear. Eventually, they became aware enough to realize what they were doing. At first they were upset. They would be sent home and ultimately defend themselves, claiming it couldn't be racist because it wasn't intentional.

I explained that most person-to-person racism was not intentional, and if it had been it would be considered a Hate Crime. The volunteers then shared the hateful things their community and family had said to them before coming to serve and all the many sacrifices they made to be there. They desperately wanted to be acknowledged for how hard they were trying. Despite their implicit racism, the volunteers gave their all, working 12- to 24-hour shifts daily for weeks – even giving to the guests out of their own pockets.

This experience made me realize that the levees were not the only thing that needed to be rebuilt in America. Our humanity is broken, even those of us who are well-meaning are harmed by centuries of systemic racism and we are often blind to our behaviors. Although rebuilding has started in New Orleans, there are many communities untouched and in need of healing now as we approach the 400th Anniversary of The African Landing Day in 2019. I hope that during

Mary Canty Merrill, Ph.D.

the next three years we can come together to learn the history of African Americans, not just for one month but all year like we do European History. I also hope that we all come to understand that Black Lives Matter, Too as we confront and dismantle systemic racism, which harms not one of us... not some of us... but all of us.

Tamera CJ Baggett is an Intergenerational, Narrative Community Therapist and teaches African American Genealogy and History in Philadelphia at Temple University's Pan African Studies Community Education Program (PASCEP). She can be reached at Tamera.Cheri@gmail.com.

A Walk through History

By Laurie Baker

Take a walk with me, if you will, back through time... an emotional walk through Black American history. American history is so important because we cannot understand our present without understanding our past and its consequences.

Black Lives Matter, TOO, because since the beginning of time, all of humanity has mattered, every single life on earth is precious. However, for centuries the precious lives of people of color have been treated with a callous lack of dignity, humanity, and love. Skin color is a social construct, meaning a mechanism, phenomenon, or category created and developed by society. This social construct caused whites to view people of color differently and even inferior to us. It created a society in which a Black person's life is believed to be dispensable and unworthy of respect.

In America from approximately 1619 to 1865, stolen Africans were inhumanely enslaved for an estimated 246 years, because their skin color wasn't valued by society. Generations after generations of Africans were born into slavery and died never having known a life of freedom. The treatment that people of color endured for almost two and half centuries of enslavement was enough to leave very deep psychological scars. There was even a book written and entitled, *Post Traumatic Slave Syndrome* to help present-day Black Americans overcome these scars.

It's important to learn about the history of death and oppression inflicted upon stolen and enslaved Africans and the effect it's had on all Black Americans, as well as American race relations. You will rarely hear me use the word, "slave" because it's dehumanizing. Stolen Africans and now, Black Americans were never "slaves" but enslaved human beings from Africa.

Black lives did matter when they were ripped from their homeland and heritage in Africa. They mattered tremendously while they were taken through the Middle Passage into slavery, chained in pairs, wrist to wrist or ankle to ankle. Their lives mattered despite the fact that an estimated 2 million died at sea while slavery was in effect. There were various ways to die on "slave" ships. Some died of disease and hunger. Others died from self-starvation or jumping overboard to escape maltreatment and whatever unknown fate awaited them. It also wasn't unusual for "slave" ships to take on too many Africans and throw them overboard due to a lack of supplies. Imagine that... human beings casually thrown overboard as though they were nothing but trash. Sharks regularly followed these "slave" ships and would eat the humans who were thrown overboard. Africans **mattered**... the pain they experienced, the terror, and their lives... all **mattered**. Yet, they failed to matter to the ships' captains and crew.

The lives of enslaved Africans were harsh and brutal for a number of reasons. I believe one of the worst of many reasons is that millions of Black families lived in constant fear of being separated from one another. It happened over and over again when husbands, wives, parents and/or children were "sold" to a new "owner". I cannot even imagine the pain of having my daughter ripped from me, all the while imagining the life she would have to endure and suffer alone, without me. It would be enough to destroy the spirit of the strongest men and women. The families who were separated; the Mothers, Fathers, Husbands, Wives and children they missed and wept over at night, **mattered**! Their grief, their pain, their loss and their tears... all **MATTERED**. Yet, their pain and loss was of no concern to "slave owners."

One savage and despicable reality of slavery is the millions of women and men of color who were raped by and at the will of their "masters" and raped by whomever else their "master" saw fit. Their bodies were treated as nothing but an object of pleasure for sick and twisted "men". Their bodies were used and abused but still, they ***mattered***. They didn't matter to their rapists but their pain, their fear, their shame, their dignity and their right to their bodies **MATTERED** to each of them.

Also heartbreaking are the millions of men and women of color who were beaten into submission. It was common for the strongest among a group to be beaten into submission, a practice called "buck breaking". Every beating, every scream, every cry of pain, every whip of the lash across the back of a person of color, and the painful open wounds... **MATTERED**. But not to those unleashing anger and pain on their victims.

One less physically painful reality of slavery, but mentally and psychologically damaging is that it was illegal for stolen Africans to educate themselves. Many learned to read in secret, but if they were caught they were barbarically beaten and sometimes their fingers and toes were amputated. Their teachers were either: fined, imprisoned or whipped. Their desire to read and become educated certainly mattered. Knowledge is power, so without an education, an entire race of stolen Africans was left powerless at the hands of white Americans. That lack of knowledge and power mattered and it still matters and makes a difference today. Unfortunately, this lack of education and power wasn't a problem for those white people in power. It was actually beneficial to them to perpetuate ignorance in order to retain their supremacy.

America's enslaved Africans were freed during and after the end of the Civil War from 1862 through 1865. Despite their freedom, there was no relief from horrific treatment at the hands of white Americans. According to research, hundreds of thousands of Black Americans died when they were freed, either from disease or starvation. It is believed that between 1862 and 1870, a quarter of the estimated 4 million freed Black Americans died. Heartbreakingly, many ended up in "contraband camps" that were nothing but former "slave pens", where conditions weren't sanitary and food was scarce.

The 13th Amendment, abolishing slavery was ratified on December 6, 1865. On July 8, 1868, the 14th Amendment was put in place granting Africans both American and State Citizenship. On February 3, 1870, the 15th Amendment giving African American men the right to vote was ratified. However, certain laws still prevented Black men in the South from voting until 1965. The first "Civil Rights Act" protecting African American civil rights passed on March 1, 1875. But in 1877 when federal troops were pulled from the South, Blacks lost any government protection they had during the Reconstruction Era.

In 1883, the Supreme Court decided through the consolidation of five civil rights cases that the Civil Rights Act, as well as the 13th and 14th Amendments was unconstitutional. It was decided that the courts were not responsible for protecting Blacks from violence or discrimination from private citizens. The Federal Government's only responsibility now was to uphold Black citizenship and freedom from legal slavery. Blacks lost the right to file murder charges resulting from physical attacks by private citizens.

It was then that the "Black Codes" also known as "Jim Crow Laws" were born in the South and some of its practices adopted throughout America. It was made legal to refuse service to Black Americans. Businesses, schools, and public facilities would be segregated until the Civil Rights Act of 1965 which was ratified on July 2, 1964.

Up until 1964, Black America was treated with merciless hate and violence. It is estimated that close to 4,000 Black men, women and teenagers were lynched by white Americans. They were often raped, beaten, castrated, dragged by vehicles, and dismembered before being lynched. Years ago, I read a story that remains etched in my memory of a woman named Mary Turner. Mary's unborn baby was cut from her stomach and then stomped to death. This is a disturbing and heartbreaking look at the inhumanity and heartless behavior that white men were capable of. I cannot begin to imagine the pain and terror a woman would feel seeing her baby murdered, while she herself is then savagely beaten and murdered. My heart aches for her and all those who suffered so much pain, horror and agony. Heartbreakingly, it goes without saying that Black lives did not matter to white America then and they still do not matter to white America today.

Throughout the Jim Crow Era, Black and white Americans were segregated leading to an unequal distribution of education, wealth and power. Black schools were underfunded and Blacks were unable to work in white establishments, which led to a lack of job opportunities. Black neighborhoods, schools and businesses also suffered due to a practice called "redlining." In the U. S., redlining is carried out through the denial of services and raising prices for people in certain areas based on their race or ethnicity. Redlining led to the underprivileged and underfunding of Black schools and neighborhoods.

Despite their oppression, Blacks were able to build successful and strong communities, but many times they were destroyed by angry, jealous white mobs. These communities mattered to those who built and lived in them; but they obviously didn't matter to those who destroyed them and murdered the citizens of communities like Rosewood, Florida and "Black Wall St." in Kansas.

In Sanford, Florida on February 26, 2012, a 17-year-old Black teenager named Trayvon Martin was murdered on his way home by a self-appointed Hispanic neighborhood watchman named George Zimmerman. Zimmerman thought Trayvon looked "suspicious" so he followed and confronted the teen, shooting and killing him in a struggle. Zimmerman claims that he feared for his life, and was subsequently found innocent of Trayvon Martin's murder citing Florida's "Stand Your Ground" law. Zimmerman was set free after following, confronting and murdering an unarmed Black teen. Where is the justice in this? Why did Trayvon's right to life and *his* fear not matter? Why didn't Trayvon have the right to defend himself in the eyes of the jury? Trayvon's life mattered to him, mattered to his family and to most Americans. Sadly, the racism in America is so deep and ugly and I've seen and heard numerous heartless comments from white Americans that Trayvon was a "thug who got what he deserved." There is no other reason for this lack of humanity than racism.

In Cleveland, Ohio on November 22, 2014, 12-year-old Tamir Rice was shot in a park by a cop within two seconds of approach. The child was given no opportunity to inform the police officer that what he held in his hand was a toy gun. Tamir's life had so little value to this officer that he instinctively shot Tamir within TWO SECONDS. Tamir's life mattered to him, his family and many outraged Americans. Nonetheless, there have been more than a few comments from white Americans blaming the minor and his mother for his death. Tamir's life didn't matter to some Americans and it certainly didn't matter to the officer who murdered him.

There are hundreds, if not thousands, of stories of unarmed Black Americans being killed by law enforcement or while in police custody, and police officers are rarely – if ever – held accountable. There's Eric Garner telling officers he couldn't breathe, Sandra Bland being dragged out of her car after a minor traffic violation, and John Crawford III who was gunned down by police in a Walmart after picking up a BB gun in the store and walking around with it, never having pointed it at anyone.

For the past 397 years in America, Black lives have not mattered to those who hold power and enforce the law. They have not mattered to racist white Americans who were taught to hate and fear Blacks. It's time we work together to change these dynamics. It's time to hold accountable those who do not value the precious lives of Black Americans. I solidly stand with the Black Lives Matter movement, because I believe in justice and equality. I believe that we can learn to respect and appreciate our differences instead of letting them continue to divide us. The time for equality and justice has come and I believe that love and righteousness will triumph over hate and violence.

Laurie Baker lives in Virginia with her biracial family and works in a cancer and blood disorders unit in a children's hospital. She is a 35-year-old American Caucasian woman of Italian, Irish and German descent. She believes passionately in equality for everyone and dreams of a better world for her daughters and for all children of the future. Laurie also has a page on both Facebook and Instagram entitled "Heal the Hate" which advocates against racism and for the Black Lives Matter movement. She can be reached at: Lbaker8059@yahoo.com.

Mary Canty Merrill, Ph.D.

We, As Ourselves, Will Save Us All

By TaNesha Barnes

Black lives are the beautiful, living, contemporary evidence of the origins of humanity. To say Black Lives Matter (too), is not only deeply rooted in the belief of white supremacy, but worse, suggests the internalization of an inferiority complex. Because language matters. Our humanity is not in question and never has been, at least to ourselves, so of course our lives matter. The "too" is even worse. It suggests that somehow the intrinsic value of whiteness is clear and unquestionable as we struggle to prove our own. To whom are we screaming this? Who is the audience we are addressing? Why?

How we approach the next leg of this conversation matters. It matters most importantly to how we shape the minds and understanding of Black people collectively and, most in particularly, our children. The way we do this properly is through correcting the default, the origin, through which we speak about our lives and the position they honestly hold—historically and currently—within American society.

Our energy and words must be reserved for conversations within ourselves and our community. Ownership of the direction of the conversation will serve to eliminate Black pain and struggle as performance for the white gaze. It will allow mental and emotional space for us to dictate the direction and strategy for freedom.

In my early twenties, I owned and operated a business that imported authentic designer bags from warehouses in Italy. I became business partners with an older Jewish woman. At that time I still felt young and inexperienced. No one in my family was an entrepreneur and at that point I had learned everything through trial and error, so it seemed like a good idea. She was very crafty. She had money and connections at her disposal and availed them to me in various ways. She would call me to check in several times a day, as if she were my employer. She created the idea in my mind that she was an essential part of the puzzle. In reality, I spoke Italian. I fronted half the money. I had more business contacts. I closed the deals. And I had the clientele. However, her mind game had me believing that she was essential when, in fact, she was not. When I realized what was happening, I promptly stopped taking her phone calls and continued my business with my own capital. America has been playing the same mind game with Black people for centuries. Leading us to believe that we are indeed in need of a white paternal parenting and as the child of this system, we have to prove our value to the collective American society and continue to educate them that we are indeed layered, diverse and dynamic.

The United States is the only country in history that not only instituted slavery but built its entire economy based on slavery, and arguably still does through the imprisonment of Black bodies. Black labor, ingenuity, skill, intelligence and strength are literally the foundation of the American economy. In reality, the current second largest American export is entertainment. Black culture is the only authentic American cultural creation, and the evidence of the monetary value we generate can be heard in a night club from Florence, Italy to the airwaves of Marrakech, Morocco. Black people in America set the trends. We fill the stadiums. And we win elections...twice. THAT is the reality! And until we restructure our language and point of view to see OURSELVES more clearly, wholly, then we will keep begging for acceptance in a country that we continue to build—while asking for our lives to be seen as equitable to others.

The idea that we, as Black people, are fighting for equity is a fallacy. The enslaved Africans were far superior physically, spiritually, morally and intellectually which allowed them to survive the vicious brutality of America for centuries. Therefore, the subsequent fight for civil rights has been incorrectly labeled a fight for equity. Black people in America have proven themselves far superior, and in that truth lies the core conflict. That truth is the reason why we are killed, the hatred toward our revolutionary political leaders, the disdain for a Serena Williams, and the disrespect of our current President. *To survive AND excel under the American condition of hatred does not make it necessary for Black people to prove their equity to other citizens within the country but essentially the other way around.* The more Black people strive toward "equity" within America the farther away we move from ourselves, and the lower we fall morally, physically, mentally and spiritually. Give America back its god, its terrible non-food, its perverted ideology and its lack of a moral compass and remember who you are my people… we, as ourselves, will save us all.

T. Barnes: Solana's Mama. Lover of Black People. Beauty/Fashion Entrepreneur. Esthetician. Thinker. Speaker. Social Justice Activist. Educator. Global Citizen. She can be reached at: *tbarnes@tbarnesbeauty.com*.

When I Learned to See

By Cat Chapin-Bishop

I owe a moral debt to the Ferguson, Missouri Police Department. Because until they woke me up, I was a race-blind racist.

I didn't mean to be racist; I didn't think I was. But I had grown up in the 1970s, inside a more or less hermetically sealed white bubble, in a safe, affluent Northern suburb, and I'd believed that the Civil Rights gains of the 1960s had "fixed" racism in my country. Certainly, I didn't see very much evidence of racism when I looked around me. Indeed, I didn't see much evidence of race, period: I was white, my neighbors were white, my classmates and my teachers were white, and the only Black and brown faces I saw were on the news or downtown, in the decaying city center where they "just happened" to live—as opposed to the comfortable former farm-community where people who looked like me "just happened" to live.

I had never heard of redlining, had no idea that having laws were on the books to forbid discrimination in housing and lending didn't mean they'd stopped. In my mind, and in the minds of everyone I knew, racism was a matter of hateful *individual* white people, who talked like Archie Bunker. I didn't know anybody who talked like that.

And I certainly had no concept of systemic, as opposed to individual racism. I knew, vaguely, that racial profiling was something that "used to happen," and every so often there would be an outcry from the Black community over a police shooting of an unarmed Black motorist. But the police always had an explanation, and since all of my encounters with police had been positive—like the cop who let me off with a warning the day I was stopped for my first traffic offense, and cried—I assumed that was what policing generally was.

You see, I believed in something called an "isolated incident." I understood that racism still existed—far away, in other parts of the country. When I went to college, and heard my first stories from Black classmates of being stopped for "walking while Black," I was saddened and shocked... but I thought those must have been unusual experiences—"isolated incidents." And anyway, it was Virginia, not my enlightened Northern town. (Everyone knew the South had its problems with race.)

Later, working in rape crisis in the Midwest, I learned that few Black women would call our mostly-white volunteers for help. *Of course*, I thought, wisely. *All that bad history*. History: accusations of rape against Black men by white women, ending in a rope and a tree. I never asked myself whether anything like that history was still going on. But I saw that it was "only natural" that it might be hard—for a while—for Black women to trust us white counselors after a sexual assault. And even after I learned that the ambulances would not serve the Black neighborhoods in town, and after I learned of several women who had been assaulted by cops, and after Black women told me of being threatened by white men who said, "No one would ever believe you, you know," I still believed these were "isolated incidents." No connection to that history I'd learned about in school.

When Trayvon Martin was killed, it was clear to me that he died because George Zimmerman held racist beliefs that led him to gun down a teenager for the crime of being Black in what Zimmerman believed was a white neighborhood. But I still didn't see it. Or rather, I saw it as something that didn't connect to me, to my life, my America. I mean, it was Florida. The South. Guns. "Stand your ground" was a craziness I didn't think had anything to do with me, or my life.

And then *Washington Post* reporter Wesley Lowery was arrested inside a Ferguson McDonald's for no discernible reason other than that he was a reporter covering the protests in the wake of Michael Brown's death. And—oh yeah... he was Black... like Michael Brown.

Some people can tell you where they were when Kennedy was assassinated. Others can tell you what they were doing when they heard the news about the Challenger disaster. I can tell you where I was when I first learned to see. I was staying in a beautiful little cabin on the Maine coast. I'd been away from the news for days, but when I finally booted up my laptop—this was the first story I read. And something inside me finally went, "Wait—*what? What???*"

Wesley Lowery was following the orders of police dressed like an invading army, police who refused to answer his questions, and who gave contradictory commands. These police were nothing like the police who'd stopped me when I was seventeen.

I didn't yet understand why Lowery, unresisting, said he was afraid when he heard the cop tell him to "Stop resisting"—more afraid than he'd been of tear gas and rubber bullets.

Tear gas and rubber bullets? "Wait—*what? What???*"

And I looked again. Finally, after fifty-four years of learned blindness, I actually looked at race and at racism:

- I saw that Michael Brown's body was left where it fell for *four hours* before it was removed;
- I saw that police were driving armored vehicles through the streets of Ferguson, Missouri; and
- I saw that there was no number of Black eyewitnesses whose word would be taken over the word of a single white police officer.

And then I looked some more. I saw Aiyana Stanley-Jones, shot at the age of seven, asleep on her grandmother's couch when a SWAT team broke down the door to serve a warrant. It wasn't even the right address.

And I thought, *"Who sends a SWAT team to serve a warrant?"* And, *"How can it be, they killed a little girl, and no one is going to jail for this?"* And I saw that she lived in Detroit, which is not in the South.

And then I saw John Crawford, shot for picking up a toy gun in a Wal-Mart. In Ohio. In the North. *In an open carry state.*

And I saw Eric Garner (New York) and Tamir Rice (Ohio) and Walter Scott (South Carolina)—but do I seriously think that makes a difference, anymore?

And I finally got it—this may not be the way people who look like me are treated, but it is the way people of color are treated. In my country: North and South.

As I say, I owe a debt to the Ferguson Police Department for teaching me at last that Black Lives Must Matter—even though they never have in the history of America.

I no longer believe in "isolated incidents."

Cat Chapin-Bishop is an English teacher, a Quaker and a Pagan who lives in the Berkshire Foothills of Massachusetts. Her writing can be found online at Quaker Pagan Reflections. She can be reached at: dalgret@fastmail.fm.

Mary Canty Merrill, Ph.D.

One White Woman's Perspective

By Jodi Crane, Ph.D.

I am a white woman in my middle forties living in rural Kentucky. As a child I lived two places in rural Iowa before we moved to Utah where I attended a parochial school. I only remember seeing one Black student there and none in Iowa. In junior high one of my friends had a Black boyfriend. I doubt her parents knew and I'm not sure what they would have thought of their racial differences.

In high school, we moved to a suburb of Dallas, Texas. My public high school's mascot was the Colonel, the school flag was the Confederate flag, the school song was *Dixie* and the cafeteria had a mural of a Southern plantation. A small percentage of Black students attended there. I didn't have any Black friends. Over 25 years later the majority of my high school is Black and Hispanic. Gratefully, the flag has changed, the mural is gone, the song has changed, but the mascot has not.

I attended college and graduate school in three places in Texas. Each place seemed to have even more Black students than the school before, but all were predominantly white. In college my friend had a Black personal trainer. She befriended him and invited him over to our apartment complex pool to swim. He whispered in my ear, "Have you ever kissed a Black man? Have you ever dated a Black man?" I felt appalled, then confused, then embarrassed by my emotions. My answer was no, but I kept quiet.

During my master's program a friend and fellow student was living with her sister and Black brother-in-law. They had parties at their house. I thought nothing of the mix of races in attendance, yet I spent my time there with my white friends.

The entire cohort of my doctoral program was white. As part of a class presentation, a fellow student shared that one of her main childhood playmates in Fort Worth, Texas, was Black. I remember feeling slightly jealous, wishing I had had more diversity in my life.

I have counseled some Black individuals and families. I have been a caregiver to Black children in day care and school settings. I have traveled to more cosmopolitan cities than the town in which I reside. I have visited Caribbean nations with dark-skinned natives. Unfortunately, in all my life experiences Blacks have not been part of my closest circle of companions.

I am married to a white man from San Antonio, Texas. I have Hispanic brother- and sister-in-laws. My husband's grandmother was a Villarreal. My sister was once married to an Asian-American man. Today I have a few Black colleagues who live and work in other places and a small number of Black students in the college classes I teach. One of my daughter's closest friends is biracial. I attend a church that is almost entirely white, except for one biracial child. Most of my interactions with African-Americans that are the closest to me calling them friends are through social media.

These have been my experiences. I only share them to make the point of how limited my racial repertoire is. I wish I had more diversity in my life, yet this has been my involvement or lack thereof. I wish I had more everyday experiences with Blacks as friends. Because of this drawback, even though I value diversity greatly, I feel inadequate to write an essay on why Black lives matter.

However, with a second look, I do have something to contribute.

Once my father preached a sermon where he admitted that his own father had made racist comments. This racism would have occurred sometime during the '50s and '60s in rural Kansas. I remember feeling an initial shock and guilt and then some knowing, given the time and place.

We fear what we don't know. We fear what we've been taught to fear. If, by matter of our time and place, we mainly only know white people and Blacks are mostly portrayed in negative ways through TV, movies, and other media, then we may wrongly fear them. We are likely to make assumptions that are not true.

Our brains are such that we judge and categorize visual stimuli including how others look, the color of their skin. We all do it. This critique does not mean that we must give a value statement to what we see. I know I have been guilty of negative evaluation and fear. If we find ourselves doing so because of our experiences, we can stop and notice it. Then make a point to change that perception. The more we do this we can eventually change our thinking.

I believe every person has value. Every person is worthy. Everyone is connected. As a white person, a person of privilege in American society, it is up to me to educate myself about the unique experiences of my Black brothers and sisters. With education comes appreciation. I care and I care very much. I know racism exists. When others are hurting, I am too. When others aren't free, I am not free either.

Saying "Black Lives Matter" does not mean that white lives don't. This statement should not be threatening to me, but instead should be empowering to me. It is not an either/or proposition. It is not a fight of one against the other. Until we live in a culture of both/and, of cooperation, of seeing strengths in one another, we must focus on those who are marginalized, have been mistreated, and have not been valued. Given American history and present day racial injustices, those people are Black. It is morally right for me to stand up for the rights of my fellow Black Americans. This is why to me, Black Lives Matter.

Dr. Crane is Associate Professor in the School of Professional Counseling at Lindsey Wilson College in Columbia, KY. She is a Licensed Professional Clinical Counselor, National Certified Counselor, and Registered Play Therapist – Supervisor. She is Chair-Elect of the Board of Directors of the Association for Play Therapy. She can be contacted through her website at: www.playcrane.com.

Mary Canty Merrill, Ph.D.

A New rEvolution is Emerging

By Aine Dee

The Black Lives Matter movement represents a critical pivot point in our American personal and cultural history. It has raised awareness of the targeted deaths and abuse of Black people in this country at the hands of our supposed protectors. It is a passionate call for all of us to understand that we will only thrive together—or we will all perish together if we exclude, marginalize, exploit, or harm any group or part of life on this planet.

It doesn't matter what else this movement accomplishes, in my opinion, just as it didn't matter to me if Occupy Wall Street never designed the ultimate solutions to what it was calling out in our society. There are brave and bold humans whose sole/soul purpose in life is to bring to the attention of the unconscious, and call out those benefiting, a gross injustice that cannot continue without harming all of us.

Black Lives Matter has called all of us white folks out. Now what will do about it?

AWAKENING TO WHITE PRIVILEGE

As an educated, comfortable white woman of much privilege and limited engagement with, considering myself as a good person who would never wish anyone harm—this movement began as a harsh, gut-wrenching, heart-breaking wake-up call, exposing to me that I had much unexplored racism and bias.

White Supremacy had been so pervasive in my own life, with so little real diversity to challenge it, and I see the same so clearly now in other white people. It is a tiresome process to move white people like me from the denial (I am not a racist), hurt (how can you not see that I'm a good person?), fragility (you are attacking my character, I don't deserve it, and I can't take it), and the white privilege of avoidance (I quit trying to understand because you're not nice to me).

I enjoy the life I've created *because* structural and systemic racism made sure I didn't have the barriers to: my physical safety and legal protection; my educational, economic, and social opportunities; and my self-image as to what is possible for me and the encouragement so critical to achievement. These barriers are made nearly insurmountable for people of color.

That extreme advantage, the guilt and shame of the deeds of our race, the fear of being the lowest on the economic food chain, and/or the terror of retribution has made it difficult for many white people to face the truth and take responsibility to proactively end the advantages that we now enjoy.

LINEAGE LANDMINES

For the first time in almost 65 years, I had to look at what it means to be part of the white race. While I rejected passionately all cruelty, exploitation, extraction, and injustice, it was sobering to realize that those very behaviors were a part of my lineage.

Those cellular memories I carry in my genes. Therefore, I have an inherited responsibility—not to feel guilty or paralyzed by the shame of it, but to make things better in my lifetime for the future that follows. I have an inherited obligation to allow with empathy and honor with compassion the justifiable anger and rage that is the natural and healthy expression of such racial abuse.

The white race created racism to benefit itself, including the atrocity of slavery and the modern version of killing and incarcerating the targeted and disproportionate number of Black men. Consequently, the white race must proactively dismantle racism or be dismantled. The fear of justifiable retribution is not something every white psyche is willing to acknowledge. It hovers like a numbness and dumbness over the well-intentioned and inflames the aggression of the discontented and greedy.

The emotional landmines on both sides from the genetic, social, and psychological scars of slavery and continued racism are palpable and daunting. It is my hope that we can find a way to detonate them in an intentional, compassionate, and committed manner. Trying to avoid them is keeping them buried in a more lethal and potent form.

WHITE SPIRITUAL PROZAC

In my effort to avoid the dogma, judgments, and separation encouraged by most organized religions of my youth, I took refuge in my white spirituality. It has disturbed me recently to observe that any form of righteous anger or activism around racism is often subdued with words of love and peace.

Passive, non-personal divine love, an avoidance of the manifestation of negative fears, a positive focus to maintain personal vibrational frequency, and the claim that each individual is solely responsible to change their own lives is somehow elevated to mean "enlightenment." While there is certainly truth and value in these beliefs, they are all seriously out of context with the human reality playing out on the planet that requires our proactive countering.

In the context of racism, this type of "enlightenment" is serving white supremacy beautifully. It is the closet thing to the notion of the Anti-Christ that I never believed was credible. While this is an exaggerated indictment of whitewashed spirituality, its emphasis on individual ease, comfort, bliss, alignment, and resonance as the path to enlightenment is surely the Prozac we need to avoid as we step up to change the trajectory of our world.

We need to be the best humans that we can be right now—not the most detached spiritual seekers. We need to get down and dirty with our inner demons, biases, and reactions—where it's real, messy, uncomfortable, and frightening—but also truly enlightening. We need to join the rest of our brothers and sisters and stand up together for the sovereignty and liberation of us all.

rEVOLUTION VERSUS EVOLUTION

"The significant problems we have cannot be solved at the same level of thinking with which we created them" is attributed to Albert Einstein. What that has always meant to me is that we need to be better, more aware, more intimately and authentically connected to ourselves, to our own sense of a higher power, and to others—more evolved than the scarcity mentality that believes that if I don't take from you I will not have enough.

Black Lives Matter to me is the righteous call-out. But I wonder…

Is it the wake-up rumble before the white race evolves beyond this archaic manipulation for the benefit of the few?

Or is it the warning rumble before the rEvolution we all secretly dread?

Or is it the trumpet call before the white race is left behind as obsolete without a second glance?

Mary Canty Merrill, Ph.D.

I am encouraged by the clear voices of Black people who are empowered without white buy-in, permission, or support. There is a new level of personal liberation and sovereignty that is emerging, and perhaps because of this, the emotional confrontation will happen between whites and our own unexplored consciences.

I highly recommend the exploration of your own complicity in upholding white supremacy. It is hard and it hurts—but only for a short while. Then it requires you to ACT as the kind of person you really always wanted to be—a conscious, proactive part of the solution and not a passive part of the problem.

Aine Dee is the CEO, Founder, and rEvolutionary of Wealth Reimagined, Inc. She specializes in mentoring entrepreneurs to evolve how they feel, think and behave around their own self-defined concept of wealth – money, health, and work. After decades of innovative work in small business and community development finance she is recognized as an astute financial, business, and community project strategist. She is also an intuitive observer of human and spiritual inner workings that drive our choices and behaviors. She can be reached at: aine@wealthreimagined.com.

A Conversation with My Students: Dismantling White Fragility and White Privilege in the Historical Narrative

By Dawn A. Dennis, Ph.D.

> *"An educator in a system of oppression is either a revolutionary or an oppressor."*
> – Lerone Bennett, Jr. (1928 -)

"But Professor," a student asked, "Don't all lives matter in history? I mean they all matter to me at least...." And so the course began with fifty students and a twelve-week inquiry into the catch-phrase fallacy that "All Lives Matter," in the early historical narrative of this nation.

At a time when police brutality and violence towards Black Americans has increased in cities across the nation, one of the most significant issues revealed during the last four years is the understanding of the past in this nation. The historical past has produced contentious debate between white supremacists and the mainstream media on one side, that assert that "All Lives Matter," while condemning the actions of Black activists, and the remaining citizens of this nation, who recognize that "Black Lives Matter," in the present and in history.

This brief essay is a conversation about history; or rather the absence of learning history from reputable educators and organic scholars in the community. Thus, the actual understanding of history is the root of the problem in this nation, as there are two conversations about the past that are simultaneously occurring.

The learning of history is not a linear process; rather reading the past is a cyclical process in which events discussed on the first day of my course will be discussed on the last day of the course. History is not dead; we experience history each day. Yet, many white Americans rely upon a linear understanding of the past to influence their opinions regarding current events.

The collective white-cry of "All Lives Matter," to the emergence of the "Black Lives Matter," proclamation following the 2012 murder of Trayvon Martin, represented a linear understanding of history and is the product of white fragility. As Robyn DiAngelo noted, white fragility is the fear of historical accountability, of the reconciliation of the past, of admitting our own complicity and privilege in history.

I asked the students if the decisive slogan "All Lives Matter," can be sustained in the historical narrative; meaning does the economic, social, and political structure of this nation support the claim that "all lives matter." Many students did not know where to begin their research and I asked the class to think about the word, *benefit*, in regard to the creation of laws and institutions in this nation. Who benefited? Who did not benefit?

The use of the "All Lives Matter," phrase reveals white historical amnesia and is grounded in the feelings of white Americans, who are uncomfortable with the words "white supremacy," "white privilege," and "race." Hence, this is one of the many reasons for the inability of many whites to understand the historical meaning of "Black Lives Matter."

The issue of race in the historical narrative has created discomfort and hostility with academia. Discussing white supremacy in a critical-thinking exercise in history either produces a vitriol response by a few colleagues or "OMG, Yes! My professor just said that," from students. Colleagues and institutions view educators that challenge the inaccurate interpretations of history as agitators, anti-white, biased, and racist.

Yet, the comfort of white people is no longer a concern in this nation, and the historical narrative can't be dismissed at the expense of the feelings of whites. The teaching of history should reflect the challenges to and problems of white privilege, as students will not benefit from a regurgitation of history that diminishes the experiences of people of color. One can support Black Lives Matter and dismantle white supremacy during a discussion about the reactionary phrase, "All Lives Matter."

I suggested that students begin with the sources left behind that detail the dynamics of the historical past. What contract, laws, treaty, "truce" for land, freedom, rights, war, societal customs and norms included or supported the concept of "all lives matter"? The Mayflower Compact? The Declaration of Independence? The Constitution of the United States? The chattel property deed of a slaveholder in Mississippi? Any of the Paris treaties and meetings? The treaty of Guadalupe Hidalgo? Any wars? The anti-imperialist meeting in Brussels? Voting rights for women in 1918? Treaties and agreements made during the Cold War era? None. Not one at all. Each example has excluded an ethnic, cultural, and/or racial group in history. Only one group benefitted at all times: white women and white men. Our history clearly demonstrates that all lives have not mattered, especially those belonging to people of color.

The use of language in history does not support the belief that "All Lives Matter." The power of white fragility, white privilege and denial of history is clearly demonstrated by whites who have difficulty understanding the language of white supremacy: the enslavement, oppression and violence directed towards people color on a daily basis. As whites desire to speak of what it means to be "civilized," are we unaware of our historical past, and the language used to secure our privilege in history? Did we forget colonization, imperialism, the Nadir Period, "Jim Crow," our foreign policies in Africa and Latin America?

During this conversation, many students began to suggest specific historical examples to disprove the claim that "All Lives Matter." Several mentioned Christopher Columbus, who described the indigenous as "children of nature," in his early observations. Others mentioned the early chattel slave records in Virginia, whose language dehumanized and reduced Africans to mere property. A few students suggested the 3/5 clause of the United States Constitution, while others questioned laws, such as the Fugitive Slave Act in the 1850s.

The discussion with my students led to a historical inquiry into the "protest" and "rebellion," in early American history. Why the need to protest and rebel if all lives matter? Black Lives Matter sustains the Black Radical Tradition in history, and challenges the authenticity of the all lives matter argument. As history has demonstrated with the American Revolution in the late 1770s, crafting a literary argument to challenge hegemonic control is an essential tool of any revolution. As this nation was founded on a revolution, it is problematic when whites condemn young Black protestors, many of whom are students, for demanding social justice. During the American Revolution, colonists used the penny-press to organize resistance and craft an argument to challenge British control of the colonies in an effort to organize a revolution.

During the 2015 summer uprising in Baltimore, Black youth took control of the media and challenged erroneous perceptions and stereotypes of the community. The media, specifically *CNN*, and *Fox and Friends,* were forced to pay attention to systemic issues within the city. As a product of anti-Black racism during the early colonial period, these stereotypes were sustained during enslavement and the period of Jim Crow in this nation.

During the submission process for the exam project, students shared their research regarding the "All Lives Matter," statement in history. The results were unanimous, as not one student could find evidence in history suggesting that all lives matter. I knew this; but more importantly I needed my students to know this.

Dawn's work as a historian has afforded her valuable opportunities to obtain expertise in the areas of archives, historic preservation, research, and publications. She holds a Ph.D. in History from Claremont Graduate University, with fields of race and ethnicity. Currently, she is a lecturer in history at Cal State University, Los Angeles. She can be reached at: Ddennis3@calstatela.edu.

Mary Canty Merrill, Ph.D.

The Luxury of Colorblindness

By Sevgi Fernandez

It is a luxury to walk through life not having to constantly be aware of your race. As a mixed woman, racial labels have followed me wherever I've gone, and I'm keenly aware that the darker a person's skin, the more this statement is true.

"I am Colorblind" or "I don't see color" are statements you have either heard or have said yourself. I truly believe that the only people who can "choose" to be colorblind are whites. It is a luxury not to have to think about race. In a workshop I held last fall, we watched the documentary, *A Conversation with White People on Race*. Some of the statements, although simple, were profound. For example, a thirty something white man said, "I don't think about being white, I just don't." This was followed by a middle aged white woman who said, "I really did not know I had a racial identity. I had no idea what that meant, how that shaped my outlook on life, my sense of optimism, sense of belonging, sense of safety."

Now, I can all but guarantee that every single Black person on this earth, knows they are Black and is reminded of this fact each and every day. I think Black people are very aware of our racial identity, and we are aware of how our racial identity dictates how safe we are, what type of education we can get, what type of healthcare we receive and what types of jobs we can attain. Race is, of course, not the only factor in any one of these, but it's often the *deciding* factor.

Racism is a social construct developed to oppress. It has evolved over the centuries, but in essence, the process of labeling and stereotyping a person based on the color of their skin to keep them subservient to the dominant white race has remained the same. I'm going to share a pivotal event in my childhood that truly awakened me to the fact that the world saw me in the context of "race" not "person."

> *Standing in line at school, the red-faced white boy in front of me asked, "What are you?" "I'm half Black, half white." I said, feeling a little uncomfortable. The boy then scathingly stated, "Well at least I can respect HALF of you." And he turned to laugh with his friends. At that moment I felt a myriad of emotions jumping rapidly from one to another, shame, embarrassment, humiliation and when I landed on rage, my 12-year-old fist connected with his 16-year-old face. I'm not sure who was more shocked!*

I share this story as a way of illustrating that even as children we are shown that we are different, that we are less than. That certainly wasn't the first time I became aware that my race and my skin color played a part in how people would treat me; and still to this day, as a 43-year-old soldier in the war on racism, I know that the future holds much more of the same.

In order to make sense of the world around us, we run every person through a set of implicit and explicit biases that we have developed over time. Implicit and explicit biases have been a part of history since our inception. We are seeing the implications of these biases throughout the world and here in the United States. It seems to me that as we make more strides in this country towards tolerance, inclusion and equality for all, for example, electing our first Black President and legalizing same sex marriage, we become more divided as a society as race and racism become more prominent.

The effects of this systematic racism are apparent in the African American community across the country, wherever we look. It's in the hopelessness of our youth, in the violence within our communities, and at the hands of the police. It's in the educational system that is set up to fail our children and the healthcare system that is either unattainable or so discriminatory that many fear ever seeking out the care they so desperately need. Rather than educating and nourishing the minds of our young people of color, the system is feeding the school-to-prison pipeline. Therefore, it is unlikely that you will encounter any Black person who says they are "**colorblind.**"

Black people have been systematically oppressed, discriminated against and brutalized *simply* because of their race since they were brought to this country as slaves. The system was set up to deny what should be our *human* rights, and that system is still at play today. We, as people of color, certainly believe that **All Lives Matter**, yet **All** people haven't had the daily struggles that Blacks have faced in this country. Moreover, **All** people aren't being shot, hung and choked to death by police.

These are facts that cannot be denied. The reality is that for the most part, our lives truly don't matter outside of our own communities and as we internalize the racism and oppression, they begin to matter less and less to us.

I do believe there are a growing number of white people who are concerned about this racial divide and social injustice and inequality against people of color. Everyday, I am seeing more whites challenging themselves and asking the hard questions regarding their white privilege and implicit biases. I think the movement from the Black community over the past year specifically, has garnered much-needed attention in mainstream and social media. This has enabled our messages related to the extreme state of racism and inequality in this country to reach whites who otherwise would remain unaware. I am seeing more whites participating in protests and dialogues on the issues, and I work alongside many whom I deeply respect for their courage, commitment, humility, their ability to ask questions, their acknowledgement when they're wrong, and their willingness to learn. It is quite exhilarating and gives me great hope.

Although our country is arguably as polarized as it was 60 years ago, and some may even say 400 years ago, today a revolution is underway. Today people, be they black, white, yellow, red, brown or all of the above, are coming together as one to challenge the machine that is institutionalized racism. Each day that a step is collectively taken, a brick in the foundation of white supremacy that this country was built upon is removed. Until we all have the luxury of being colorblind, the statement and movement **Black Lives Matter** will continue to be necessary and relevant.

Sevgi Fernandez has worked as a diversity coach/consultant for the past decade both independently through her company Diverse World Coaching, and as Senior Vice President of Race and Cultural Diversity at ARMCGlobal. She recently founded an organization, Together We Stand (TWS) which advocates for victims of racism, discrimination and police brutality. Her hope is to develop a TWS youth academy that will educate teens on social justice advocacy, particularly through changing legislation. Sevgi can be reached at: Twstherevolutuon@yahoo.com.

Mary Canty Merrill, Ph.D.

An Opened Mind

By Kellie Fitzgerald

When I was first approached about contributing to this project, my mind immediately went to my own personal experiences. You might find that interesting since I am white so let me explain. In life I have been blessed with friends from seemingly every race, religion and nationality, so I've seen first-hand how those who are "different" are treated. I've had discussions about race with various people and on numerous occasions. Almost uniformly my white colleagues talk about how great the strides against racism and discrimination have been through the years. Equally as often, my Black colleagues will talk about their latest experience with racism. No matter how great the strides against racism and discrimination may be, I know these things still exist. I consider myself lucky to be born in a white body; I am able to look at racism and be alarmed even disgusted at how Black people are still being discriminated against and de-valued as people without fear of suffering these things myself. They have no such luxury.

In case you think my view is incorrect, let me share a personal experience. One day, I went to lunch with a man I was dating and his sister, and they happened to be Black. We went to a lunch spot we each had been to before separately, but never together. The restaurant was not crowded, yet we waited for more than ten minutes to be seated. Once seated, we waited for our server to come and take out order. After another ten minutes I got up, approached the manager and told him about our experience in his restaurant. He was very apologetic and offered free appetizers to compensate us for what he termed "lousy service." When he asked what table I was seated at I pointed at my friends and saw his face drop. Immediately, I realized the reason for our lack-of-service: this manager did not approve of my choice of friends and allowed his racism to infect his entire staff.

Understand that this did not take place in the deep-South in the 1960's where these things were a daily occurrence. This was 1980's San Francisco, a time and place one would not expect to have such an experience. This was my wake-up call. Prior to this incident, I would have told you that we had pretty much abolished discrimination in the U.S. and that people of color were considered equal to whites. I had no clue what my Black friends really lived through on a day-to-day basis.

When the Black Lives Matter movement started, my first thought was "Yes, it's about time someone said this." However, the reactions of many of my white friends and colleagues were very different. They did not understand. Most likely they'd never had an experience like the one I had in San Francisco—at least I like to believe they would understand completely if they'd ever had such an experience. Of course ALL lives matter, but isn't it taken for granted that white lives matter? Black people have been so devalued that it is necessary to inform society that Black lives do indeed matter.

Society is an amazing tapestry of different cultures. Each and every one of these different cultures makes us who we are as a whole. Without any one of these differences, we simply would not be who we are. Life wouldn't be as bright and beautiful as it is. Any time someone, or an entire race, is undervalued or devalued, we as a society are truly depriving ourselves of a wealth of experiences and the opportunity to learn about and even embrace an entirely different way of looking at life. Taking the time to learn about and understand varying viewpoints adds to the depth and richness of life. When we decide we are better than anyone else, we come from a place of judgment that can only make each of us less than we can and should be. When we decide that an entire group of people is "wrong", or engages in criminal behavior, or should not be allowed to achieve their fullest potential, we degrade society as a whole.

Years ago, I served on a "back to work" panel established by a city in California. The panel was designed to help people get off welfare and back to work and included several small business owners, as well as a member of the police department, fire department and school district. During one break, panelists engaged in a conversation about the make-up of the audience members. The audience comprised people who had signed up for the free event. These were people who were really trying to get their lives back on track and did not "have" to attend. What struck me was how evenly divided the audience was as far as race. The audience seemed to be so evenly-mixed it appeared that someone had hand-selected the attendees, although we were assured this was not the case.

The reason I was so very surprised is because I had been a part of another similar panel convened by a different organization, and that audience was overwhelmingly white. I later discovered that the audience had been hand-selected – more white people had been chosen to attend. The lesson I learned from these two very different audiences was that even when organizations talk about helping people to get off welfare and back to work, the people they're often really referring to are white people. Why? My experience with the "open to everyone" event proved there are just as many minorities who want to get their lives back together as there are white people. Doesn't this reinforce the notion that the Black Lives Matter movement is necessary?

One of the most fascinating social experiments I've seen was on the *Oprah* show in 1992. You've probably heard of it. Diversity expert Jane Elliot was the guest and used an experiment she'd created in 1968 to demonstrate how racism not only still runs rampant in this country, but white people realize it is still happening and by their inaction are allowing it to continue. Elliot's experiment separated people waiting in line for the *Oprah* show not by skin color but by eye color: the end result being the brown-eyed people were given preferential treatment and the blue-eyed people were made to feel inferior. By the end of this experiment it was revealed that not only was this experiment about racism, the "majority" realized they were discriminating against the "minority" and certainly would not want to switch places with them. I've watched this experiment many times and it always brings home the same truth: racism is alive and well in our society and we need to be intentional about changing that.

If "Black Lives Matter" offends you, perhaps it's time to look inside yourself and see where you might need to do your own "inner-work." If you don't understand why the Black Lives Matter movement is necessary, it's time to reach out to a Black person and ask them to educate you; then really listen and take what they say to heart. Black Lives Matter is NOT anti-white; it's PRO-human and it's way past time that we all realize this.

Kellie Fitzgerald has arrived at this particular point in her life by taking the scenic route, often filled with pratfalls and new beginnings. After a life spent experiencing trials by fire while simultaneously navigating choppy waters, she is passionate about helping others navigate their own paths and become the

Mary Canty Merrill, Ph.D.

very best version of themselves they can be. Having been told early in adulthood that as an employee she would make an excellent entrepreneur, Kellie, has started, grown and/or run several small businesses. Currently, she is a publisher, Internet radio host and life coach in southeastern Arizona and, as usual, lives with a rather large menagerie of animals and way more gardens and other projects than any truly sane person would attempt to handle. Kellie can be reached at: fitzgeraldtoo@yahoo.com.

Confronting White Privilege

By MarySue Foster

Everything I have in life, as far as I can tell, is a result of my white privilege. By some standards, I don't have much. But I have a reliable roof over my head, and a family who will bail me out if I need them to. I live in a "safe" neighborhood, even though it is far below the standards I grew used to as a young adult. I have two advanced college degrees, one financed via a student loan for which the only requirement was that I could fog a mirror. (And it's a loan I will probably never be able to pay back but, because of white privilege, otherwise known as "connections" or "resources," I figured out how to apply for and get an Income Based Repayment plan. In my case, my monthly payment is zero. And that is perfectly legal. My balance has inflated from about $24,000 to $43,000 but that's another story.)

For the longest time, I resisted seeing or denied having seen my privilege. I thought "privilege" meant having a silver spoon, enjoying a lot of money and vacations and fancy cars: all things that have never been within my reach. About 20 years ago, already an old lady, after more than one long career working and volunteering for various causes including social justice and civil rights, I participated in a powerful workshop that my non-profit employer paid for me to attend.

Our entire staff of two dozen assembled in the basement of some nearby church and worked our way through two day's worth of training delivered by the Crossroads organization out of Chicago. About half our staff was Black and they were really more than generous that day. In retrospect, I can see that their generosity and love for us white folk was really extraordinary.

We started by taping up butcher paper around three sides of the room, floor to ceiling. We were to build a timeline of the history of humans. The leader put a mark about every 1000 years and we went to work. The depth and breadth of knowledge that was *not* mine was simply breathtaking. At one point, I sat in a corner and just watched the others work. They knew so much and their history was so rich and my paltry western history (what I could remember) just shrunk away. Even thinking about it today, I am exhausted and embarrassed and humbled at my arrogance and ignorance and privilege (now I knew the word).

When we said we were done, we started as a group and worked our way around the room, filling in the events we had missed, explaining how they were all connected to the whole, highlighting names in history that I was mostly blissfully unaware of. We spent hours talking about the impact of red-lining, the Jim Crow years, inequitable college admissions, white flight, loan practices and food deserts (although I don't think the term was in use then), and the portrayal of Black lives in the media—thinly disguised discrimination still happening in Dallas and other big cities, let alone the overt racism in small towns. My eyes were opened.

That weekend marked a turning point for me. I was also in the midst of a two-year-long program from Landmark Worldwide, training community leaders. One of the instructors frequently said, "Use what you've got in the service of your gift." What the heck was my gift? It didn't seem to be anything dramatic. My name would probably never appear in some *Time* magazine year-end issue of outstanding community leaders. I don't think I'll even make it to some Top Fifty local list. All of which is probably a good thing—I'll be spending the rest of my life taking a back seat, following the lead of my Black friends and allies I haven't met yet. I'm good at getting groups of people together to wrestle with ideas and action, to take on projects bigger than they ever thought, to reach out to the disenfranchised and include those on the fringes. I'm good at enrolling white people in those endeavors – and that's where I see the work is to be done.

Sometimes, I consider what we could be doing as humans if we truly utilized the talents of everyone we have. We could be finished with the work that we have to do by Wednesday noon and then play together the rest of the week! Imagine if all people were able to capitalize on their talents and use their intelligence and good spirits to build an inclusive community.

I don't have anything to say that's not a cliché. I don't have anything new to offer in this entire arena. What I bring to the table is an indomitable spirit, nurtured by years of white privilege, in service to Black Lives Matter. I'm willing to be embarrassed and prepared to be offended, to make mistakes, to humbly accept coaching and direction. I'm willing to give my money and my good name to causes that promote the well-being of people of color, and all of us, so that we can live in a world that works for everyone, a world where every voice is heard. We have nothing to lose and a whole world to gain. And we don't have much time.

MarySue Foster has more than 30 years' experience in community development. Her work has ranged from teaching, training and consulting, to serving as an

Mary Canty Merrill, Ph.D.

executive with diverse groups. Since 1981, she has participated in Landmark Worldwide, as a student and a leader. She loves language and inquiry and human development. She earned an MA in Religious Leadership for Social Change in 2010 from Starr King School for the Ministry in Berkeley, CA. She lives near her multi-cultural family of origin, volunteers widely, and plays seriously as a mixed media artist. In 2016, she is bringing a series of national speakers/workshop leaders to Dallas. MarySue can be reached at: marysue@earthlink.net.

Let's Never Return to "The Good Old Days"

By Susan Foster

A friend of mine, who I will call Marie, was a brilliant executive and worked with me in a well-known government Agency. She was the only black female executive in the Agency, and one of a very few black executives. Besides being a brilliant manager, she had a law degree as well as a masters' degree. As the first female (white) woman executive in my particular job, I admired how Marie negotiated the world of primarily white male scientists and engineers with professionalism, directness and humor.

One day we had an off-site team-building meeting, and at the table behind us were four white male managers. This was the social hour just before leaving, and they were having a grand time discussing how great it was in the "good old days." They talked about how in the "good old days" they didn't have to ask anyone who they hired or how they did things. They reminisced about the time when there were no "quotas." When they could ask their buddies for a job without worrying about competition. When they could assume that they would get promoted because they were there.

Very quietly and kindly, Marie got up to leave, walked over to their table, leaned down and said "It wasn't the good old days for everyone." And walked away. You could have heard a pin drop at that table.

It was one of those defining moments for me—one where you suddenly see clearly what "the good old days" meant to progress. It had never occurred to those managers that they were talking about white—mostly male—privilege.

They had grown up, career-wise, assuming if they did a good job, they would get promoted into a management position and keep rising – there was no reason to consider that they would suffer discrimination of any kind. Nor would they have to worry about people insisting they explain when they wanted to hire people who looked just like them, when others (read that black people) were just as qualified, or even more so. It would never occur to them that there were people outside this privileged group who could even become qualified to compete. They were in a specific enough occupation that most general engineers would never have the qualifications, if there wasn't some grooming and mentoring along the way in lower positions.

If you are black and in this Agency, you would never assume if you worked hard, you would get promoted, because you would have seen no evidence that might lead you to believe that. Except for my friend, Marie, you rarely saw executives who were not white.

Do you hear people talk about the "good old days?" Perhaps because of this experience, I've noticed this saying being used a lot lately, and it's usually coming from white people. This is what the "good old days" were to the managers who were at that table:

"I liked it when I could hire my white buddies and no one said anything. I didn't have to explain why I didn't hire someone at least as qualified."

"I liked it when I could work with who I wanted to and feel comfortable. I did not have to adapt to someone from a different race, gender or culture."

"I liked it when I could depend on getting promoted without my boss having to explain why that black candidate, who was more qualified and educated than me, didn't get the job."

"I liked it when the majority in the room was white like me. We had more in common, and I didn't have to watch what I said."

According to a recent poll released by Pubic Religion Research Institute (PRRI), 43 percent of Americans think discrimination is just as big a problem for white people. Half (50%) of white Americans agree that discrimination against whites is as big a problem today as discrimination against Blacks and other minorities. Not surprisingly, the poll found 61 percent of the respondents as identifying with the Tea Party. Some of the comments stated that there were more laws protecting Blacks and other ethnicities than whites. *Really?* Why do they believe these laws are needed if everything had been fair during the past? Further, the U.S. Census Bureau projects that whites will become a minority by 2050, which is also fueling fears that whiteness is no longer the norm.

I say, thank God and finally.

Now when people talk about "the good old days" I question them why it was a better time when racism was normal, acceptable, and insidious:

Was it better in the days when the country was torn apart because a whole race of people didn't have basic rights?

When human beings had to enter different doors, or use different facilities, because of the color of their skin?

When an educated, Black woman I worked with had to file a class action suit just to get a decent job, even though her college education made her more qualified than most of the people competing with her?

When racism was rampart in television programs, and there were no heroes except for white people?

When 42 percent of Black people were in domestic-type jobs, such as cooks, maids, yard workers, and busboys?

When the talents of a whole race weren't being encouraged, mentored, and tapped?

When "separate, but equal" wasn't equal in the least?

As an executive coach, I work with another government organization that also has specialized positions, and I see a cadre of every race and religion—men and women—that make it stronger. I remind them often that their diversity is their greatest strength.

This diversity matters to our economy and businesses. It matters that we grow Black leaders. There is now a plethora of research that shows diverse companies are stronger, healthier, and more profitable than non-diverse companies. The bottom line always speaks the loudest, and it has spoken.

How can we expect to have that kind of diversity and strength if our young people don't believe they have the ability, capability, and possibility of getting the right positions that lead to the top? How can young, black professionals see the possibilities without observing others like themselves who have accomplished great things?

We are all a part of this fabric called society. The fabric consists of richly woven colors and textures, with people of all different races, religions, and cultures. Only with this richness can we have a strong and beautiful fabric called humanity. When we tear or mar that fabric by not valuing even one of these colors, the fabric is weaker and less beautiful.

Black lives are such an important part of that fabric. They are mothers, fathers, doctors, lawyers, stockbrokers, engineers, entrepreneurs, business owners, ministers, artists, athletes, executives, and educators. When we discount those contributions, we degrade the fabric and ourselves. We make it weaker.

Those times when these contributions were discounted or not available to everyone may have been the "Good Old Days" for those who were privileged, but it wasn't the "Good Old Days" for everyone.

It was a time we should all strive not to return to. We *can* do better, and be much stronger for having done so.

Susan Foster is a Master Coach and author who believes everyone can become a great leader. She's the author of the best-selling book, "It's Not Rocket Science: Leading, Inspiring and Motivating Your Team to be Their Best" *and works with executives and managers in building strong organizations that value diversity. She can be reached at: www.susancfoster.com.*

Mary Canty Merrill, Ph.D.

Why I Teach My White Child That Black Lives Matter

By Shaay Gallagher-Starr

As a white mother to a white appearing daughter, why would I go out of my way to teach her that Black lives matter? Well, to begin with the obvious, because Black people have inherent value and worth, and I have many people of color in my life that I love deeply. By any measure of equality you care to name—housing, education, health, infant mortality, incarceration, hiring—the impact of racism on Black lives is clearly seen.

But why do I advocate for discussing such heavy topics as racism and bias with white children? Because racial bias begins in infancy and develops across childhood. White babies show preferences for white faces by 3 months, (Bar-Haim, 2006), white 4-year-olds display innate racial bias, (Best, 1975), and by age 10, white children have developed what is called an "empathy gap" for non-white people, (Dore, 2014).

That empathy gap, formed between 7-10 years of age, is responsible for the findings of a recent study showing that white pediatricians give less pain medication to Black patients, (Sabin, 2012). Another study revealed that white physicians touch Black patients less often, and don't engage as fully with them or their families in hospital settings. Faced with the needs of Black patients, white physicians are less likely to approach the bedside, and more likely to hold a chart in front of them or cross their arms, signaling more distance, (Elliot, 2016). These studies have profound implications for medical care and overall health in communities of color.

As white people, collectively, our decreased sense of empathy for people of color makes discriminatory practices in education, housing, lending and finance, law enforcement, and every other sphere in which we exercise power that much easier. An empathy gap also makes it difficult—if not possible—to form deep friendships between people of different races. I want my child to have friendships built on trust and mutual respect, to be able to share bonds of shared joys and pains with other people throughout her life. And I don't want her ability to create friendships to be impaired by her race.

The good news is that, though racial bias is a part of our evolutionary inheritance, it isn't that difficult to unlearn. The even better news is that unlearning racial bias creates opportunities for joy for our children and for us as white parents. And the best news is that it allows us to join in the effort to reduce the impact of white supremacy on people of color.

Before undertaking to correct our children's racial bias, we must become aware of our own. Reading books by authors of color, taking the implicit bias tests designed by Harvard University (https://implicit.harvard.edu), listening attentively to the people of color in our communities, and examining one's own beliefs are good places to start.

The next step is to open our doors and our hearts. Share books that feature Black characters with your kids. Foster friendships between your child and children of color by seeking out play dates and park get-togethers. Show your own appreciation for Black people in your life, and for aspects of Black cultures that you enjoy. Talk about Black history with your kids—there's so much more to the story of African Americans than slavery. If you feel lost about where to start, there are wonderful resources available online and at your local library.

As your children get older, share the words of Black people as they talk about their experience of racism. Please notice that I am not saying, "Talk about racism with your kids." As white parents, we haven't experienced racism. Let people of color speak from their own experience and put your children in a place to hear them. Talk with your kids about their reactions to what they hear or read. Questions such as, "How do you think that made her feel?" promote empathy. Remember that this tough subject matter is something we discuss by choice, and that it is a choice parents of Black children do not have. For Black children, understanding how racism and white supremacy work is a necessary survival skill.

Be aware of how race is discussed—or not discussed—in your child's educational setting. My daughter came home distressed because the 3rd grade unit on Civil Rights was "talking about racism as though it's over." After some discussion, she decided she wanted to write a letter to her teacher and principal about how racism is still impacting the lives of Black people. So we read articles on three recent examples of racism and I helped her create an outline for her letter. Her teacher shared her letter with the class, which prompted a classroom discussion about current racism in which the students were fully engaged. There were lots of questions about the water situation in Flint, Michigan and why it was affecting Black children disproportionately. The empathy gap was decreased in that classroom that day.

And if your children are older than 10? All is not lost. While it is easier to develop fewer racial biases than it is to unlearn them, unlearning is possible throughout our lives. We can—and should—be undertaking anti-bias work on ourselves, for all the same reasons. We should do our own anti-bias work in order to have deep friendships across races, to build greater trust with communities of color, and to have greater integrity around racism in all the work we do, in every sphere.

The rewards of challenging one's own biases are profound. Being able to listen attentively to another person's experience, without the barriers of bias, opens us to other people. Authors and poets reach us more deeply. Friendships ripen into the type of relationship that can sustain us across the years. We feel the joy of connection ever more deeply as we engage with care to not cause pain to the people we love. We can begin to act with certainty in opposing white supremacy and racism, knowing that what we gain collectively will be more than what any of us lose individually by dismantling racist systems.

Shaay is a mother through adoption and a speaker about gender bias and non-binary gender identities. She conducts workshops for educators about ways to combat gender bias in the classroom. She can be reached via her website at: http://www.rainbowworld.altervista.org.

Mary Canty Merrill, Ph.D.

#BLM Supporters Must Recalibrate So the Movement Remains Relevant

By Joella Glaudé

> *"It was the best of times, it was the worst of times, it was the age of wisdom, it was the age of foolishness, it was the epoch of belief, it was the epoch of incredulity, it was the season of Light, it was the season of Darkness, it was the spring of hope, it was the winter of despair, we had everything before us, we had nothing before us, we were all going direct to heaven, we were all going direct the other way - in short, the period was so far like the present period, that some of its noisiest authorities insisted on its being received, for good or for evil, in the superlative degree of comparison only."*
> – Charles Dickens, *A Tale of Two Cities*

It seems as though we're living through strange Dickensian times, doesn't it? I often experience a sense of cognitive dissonance reading material or watching breaking news whenever race is highlighted within a given article or segment. This is exacerbated whenever the Black Lives Matter hashtag (#BLM) is employed. Whether watching television coverage, scrolling through my Facebook timeline, or scanning my Instagram or Twitter feeds, the torrent is unyielding. Why does every reasonable call for justice to uplift the fallen get met with a barrage of hateful invective? Can we not acknowledge the toll taken on our collective psyche as such tragic events play out repeatedly? If we shift our focus from managing what really matters to assessing the messengers instead, we cede ground and share culpabililty in diversionary distractions. It doesn't take a genius to realize that much of the extremism one encounters must be filtered.

What are the forces that are driving so much negativity within our public discourse, especially around race relations and social justice concerns? Frustrated by public apathy and the systemic disparities that exonerate law enforcement officers as the minority civilian body counts rise, three Black women activists created the Black Lives Matter movement. The #BLM hashtag resonated with the public. Soon, citizens of all races and disparate groups across America began using it to organize local protest efforts. Citizen journalists uploaded violent incidents captured on cell phones; many went viral. Thought pieces centered on the #BLM phenomenon entered into the ether. Practically overnight, a serious grassroots movement was spawned.

Unsurprisingly, this reimagining of a revolution was not well received in certain quarters. At the outset, many affiliated with police unions and elected officials were combative toward those associated with the emerging movement. Civil rights leaders and traditional clergy were also skeptical of groups gathering under the auspices of the Black Lives Matter vanguard. Political operatives aligned with conservative and right wing media amplified this narrative. Backlash ensued and increased.

Further, #BLM's non-hierarchical, decentralized leadership structure didn't eradicate inevitable infighting. As contradictory narratives surfaced on social media, the movement's credibility was undermined. Combined with infinitesimal progress toward goals against harsh critiques, many speculate whether social media which allowed #BLM to thrive at its genesis, now threatens its momentum. What happens now as its message is morphed and maligned?

This is a critical moment for the Black Lives Matter movement, especially since it is set against the backdrop of the upcoming presidential election campaign season. Candidates are vying for votes. Activists have disrupted rallies to pose key questions as to whether or not social justice concerns feature prominently in the political parties' platforms. These are critical positions to stake out. Clearly, the feedback hasn't been all that impressive. Therefore, as of this writing, Black Lives Matter has not aligned with any political party, nor endorsed any candidate. Savvy.

On Election Day, Americans will elect new leadership to address future concerns. But, currently, the leader of the free world, President Barack Hussein Obama, Commander-In-Chief of The United States of America's armed forces is a Black man. He wields authority to dispatch resources of our world's most elite intelligence agencies and fearsome military. Yet, nary a week goes by without sad news of minority civilians violated by white law enforcement officers. There isn't a corollary of tragic death of whites apprehended by law enforcement. Frank discussions of these outcomes for people of color rarely elicit sympathy or outrage across racial lines.

Further, the slanted media coverage of these incidents favor police, despite activists' outcries or citizen journalists' evidence of brutality. Rarely are law enforcement officers held accountable for misdeeds against those they are sworn to serve and protect. Even so, the public remains highly polarized. We must contend with the changing face of power and authority in America. We must honestly assess the myriad factors that contribute to the failures of our system in order to reform it. These changes start with dialogue, but they do not end there. I credit #BLM with heightening public awareness and forcing many more people to engage their colleagues, families and friends.

We are all navigating as best we can in a complex world. As a parent, I have to help my children foster an understanding of why our world functions in the manner in which it does. It is not new ground; it's all the things Ta-Nehisi Coates covers in his latest book, *Between the World and Me*. It's of little consolation to me that many are similarly engaged in awkward conversations. It would be wishful thinking to presume that someday we'll have satisfactory answers to every question. Perhaps, that is precisely the point.

Failure to arrive at simplistic, neat answers to complicated, messy dilemmas should not inspire any of us to stop probing or searching. It should push us to continue this vital, meaningful work. Unless and until more Americans engage social justice issues consistently and candidly, we will not achieve a more just society. Civic responsibility involves more than laying the burdens of reforming society at our leaders' feet. The serious nature of contemporary social justice issues demands strong, able leadership as well as honed, synergistic followership. To remain relevant, the immediate challenge for #BLM is to recalibrate its model and refine its message to attract greater participation.

Allow me to close with a quote from the brilliant luminary Albert Einstein: *Striving for social justice is the most valuable thing to do in life*. I salute the visionary activists and everyday citizens whose tireless, collective efforts undergird the Black Lives Matter movement.

Mary Canty Merrill, Ph.D.

Joella Glaudé is a poet, art lover and non-profit fundraising executive. Across the span of two decades, she has served leading institutions in key fields: arts and culture, community development, social services and the healthcare sector. Hailing from Brooklyn, New York, Joella Glaudé is an esteemed soulsister of many, loving mother of three, and beloved babe of one. She can be reached at: jaye.glaude@gmail.com.

Why Do Black Lives Matter?

By Sandi Gordon

I picture a room of white women. We take turns around the circle introducing ourselves, similar to Alcoholics Anonymous®. Except that it goes like this: *"My name is Sandi Gordon, and I'm a racist."*

Those words are hard to write, and even harder to speak. My brain screams, "I'm a nice person! I don't engage in hate crimes! I value all lives! I have very dear Black friends!" All true statements. But... a deeper truth is that I have accepted racial injustice in our country. It is so entwined in our thoughts, beliefs, and actions that we as whites are all too often blind to it.

I had not recognized the systemic injustice and dehumanization of Black Lives until the Black Lives Matter movement started sharing stories... so many stories... on social media. I began to awaken, and passed on what I was hearing. But token posts and likes and shares on Facebook do not a warrior make. A warrior deeply examines what white privilege means and acknowledges that it exists.

Initially, I resented the term "white privilege." I have faced many significant challenges throughout my life, including gender bias. Of course I knew that men had the advantage in corporate America. But didn't everyone have the same opportunities? To be personally accountable for initiative, drive, taking action, doing the work? Didn't all lives matter? So as a researcher I started to study. And frankly, I was horrified to see the depths of blindness in most people – people like me. Beginning with the essay, *White Privilege: Unpacking the Invisible Knapsack* by Peggy McIntosh, I started the journey towards education and understanding.

A warrior searches out and fights against the stereotypes, the disparaging language, the blind assumptions, the "not like me" attitudes, the pervasive "slavery ended a long time ago and I had nothing to do with that history" beliefs. But until we remove our blindfolds to recognize the privilege that we enjoy is DIRECTLY RELATED TO THE COLOR OF OUR SKIN, we can't fight or be an effective ally.

And this fight is righteous, people. Because oppression is right here, right now. And reading *Black Like Me* (Griffin, 1961) is not enough for a white person to understand oppression. Nor will empathy bring about a daily lived experience of what it's really like to be Black in America.

Check out these statistics:

- A 2015 study by Britain's *Guardian* newspaper found that U.S. Blacks were killed by police at a rate roughly 2.5 times higher than whites.

- Studies show the presence of implicit (unconscious) bias playing a role in health care disparities.

- Almost every mainstream media outlet presents Blacks as dead beat, low life, low budget, criminal, uneducated, unemployed, oversexed, irresponsible, and more importantly, deserving of their environments.

"Films such as *Boyz in the Hood* and *Menace II Society* have become multi-million dollar success stories with criminal portrayals of young Blacks. These portrayals, over time, have fostered false beliefs in white America regarding the way we perceive and view Blacks. What the media refuse to acknowledge is that the vast majority of Blacks are employed, attend school, and are not involved in gangs or other criminal activities. It is now quite common for young African-American males to be stopped and questioned by cops for any misfits" (Balkaran, 1999). This quote is from 1999. Here we are seventeen years later, and I cannot see progress.

These statistics and experiences are our failures. They show our failure as a society and our failure as a country and our failure as a government and our failure as businesses and our failure as churches and our failure as schools and our failure as neighbors and our failures as friends and fellow human beings.

Yes, all lives matter, blue lives matter, lives MATTER. And from the cloudy lens of my privileged life, I see that Black Lives must be treated with truth and dignity and respect and equity from media, law enforcement, health care providers, landlords, employers, retail stores, and most of all, us. Each one of us. Because **Black Lives Matter.**

Sandi Gordon is a Senior Leadership Consultant and Executive Coach who helps individuals and organizations use strategic interventions to potentially double their own productivity, profitability, and engagement. She can be reached at: sandigordon@me.com.

Mary Canty Merrill, Ph.D.

We Hold These Truths to be Self-Evident

By Kjerstin Gould

Starting with the Declaration of Independence, our Founding Fathers drafted the documents that would become our country's touchstones, asserting Equality among men and a pledge of Life and Liberty.

I was raised to believe that the United States was the greatest nation on earth, founded on principles that promised the same opportunities to a person of humble beginnings as to one born to wealth and privilege.

I recall learning about the genocide of indigenous tribes; women being denied basic rights; and chattel slavery—but euphemisms were used and facts were glossed over. These pivotal chapters were treated as mere footnotes in the story of our country's greatness. Our Founding Fathers and every generation since has simultaneously committed atrocities against our own while declaring that ours is a nation of equality.

Growing up in a white family, not wealthy but with the advantages of college educated parents and world travel, I recognized that the story of American exceptionalism didn't quite add up. I was troubled by these outrageous lies, but white privilege permitted me the luxury of being only *somewhat troubled*.

I cannot imagine how it feels to be a Black American – to be raised on stories of our heroic Founding Fathers, some of whom *owned Black people*. I cannot imagine how it feels to be a Black American—to be taught that every citizen is equal, while our history relentlessly demonstrates otherwise. What toll does it take listening to the lie every day, while living the ugly truth?

Our government has never exemplified the ideals of Equality, Life and Liberty.

> *"We have come over a way that with tears has been watered,*
> *We have come, treading our path through*
> *the blood of the slaughtered."*
> – James Weldon Johnson

The entire history of Black people in the U.S. is an affront to those noble promises of equality, liberty, and life. Ever since African people were ripped away from their homes, Black lives have been treated as expendable. Black history travels through the unimaginable horrors of chattel slavery; white wealth was built on that free labor. Two hundred and fifty years of slavery were followed by a century of continued violence against Black people during Jim Crow. Next came sixty years of "separate but equal" laws; unbridled racist practices persisted for decades after those laws were struck down. More than four hundred years of compounding wealth has left Black American families impoverished and powerless compared to White families.

Black lives today are still treated as expendable. Poverty-stricken neighborhoods and school districts have become conduits into the criminal justice system. Every Black child born is at far greater risk of living in poverty, of being incarcerated, and of dying young. Within our racist criminal justice system, police act as judge, jury, and executioner of Black men, women, boys, and girls.

> *"We are not fighting for integration, nor are we fighting for separation. We are fighting for recognition as human beings.... In fact, we are actually fighting for rights that are even greater than civil rights and that is human rights."*
> –Malcolm X

In 2005, Hurricane Katrina devastated the Gulf Coast in one of our country's worst natural disasters. But the utter failure of emergency response and the abandonment of its victims was government neglect bordering on genocide. Media showed us the stranded victims of ravaged New Orleans: tens of thousands of Black Americans, many low-income, marooned in a city 80 percent flooded. Those who remained had no means of escape; victims navigated waters infested with human waste and human bodies, hunkered down on rooftops, waited day after day without food or water, electricity, or medical supplies. Three days after the hurricane when conditions were dire, a group of Black victims tried to cross a bridge from New Orleans into the predominantly White city of Gretna. Armed police barred them from crossing to safety. The mayor's justification for this betrayal was his assertion that some of them might be criminals.

Katrina was by no means an isolated tragedy. Today in Flint, Michigan primarily Black residents have been poisoned by an indifferent government. Similar atrocities of negligence against poor, Black American communities are rampant around the country.

People have long fought for the ideals set forth in the Declaration of Independence. Every day that we continue to withhold Equality, Life and Liberty from our Black citizens we malign those ideals. To claim a great nation, we are compelled to make the lie a reality.

Woven throughout even the most devastating chapters in Black American history are stories of unimaginable courage, resilience, and an indomitable spirit.

> *"Bringing the gifts that my ancestors gave, I am*
> *the dream and the hope of the slave.*
> *I rise. I rise. I rise."*
> – Maya Angelou

In recent decades, courageous Black American activists have risked their lives to demand equality, life, and liberty. Activists of other races have joined them in that fight. Their lives are our source of pride and inspiration.

> *"Freedom is never voluntarily given by the oppressor;*
> *it must be demanded by the oppressed."*
> – Martin Luther King, Jr.

As I continue to learn, I realize that the Black American Story is tremendous and humbling. Everyday heroes walk among us, have always walked among us. We find our inspiration from those who came before us, and we gain our strength from those around us.

> *"Change will not come if we wait for some other*
> *person or some other time. We are the ones we've been*
> *waiting for. We are the change that we seek."*
> – President Barack Obama

So we call out even subtle racism from our family, friends, and coworkers. We challenge the comforts of white privilege and learn to recognize the ways it has benefited us. We educate ourselves about the complex systems designed to deny equality for Black Americans. We listen to Black voices. We read the news with a discerning eye, looking for racial bias. We find opportunities to amplify Black voices. We become politically active.

> "We hold these truths to be self-evident, that all men are created equal, that they are endowed by their Creator with certain unalienable Rights, that among these are Life, Liberty and the pursuit of Happiness. –That to secure these rights, Governments are instituted among Men, deriving their just powers from the consent of the governed, **–That whenever any Form of Government becomes destructive of these ends, it is the Right of the People to alter or to abolish it, and to institute new Government,** laying its foundation on such principles and organizing its powers in such form, as to them shall seem most likely to effect their Safety and Happiness."
> – The Declaration of Independence

> "The cost of liberty is less than the price of repression."
> – W.E.B. Du Bois

It will take enormous effort to rebuild our country based on Equality, where Black Americans have the same rights to Life and Liberty as White Americans. Without doing so, those noble words are a lie. In the fight for Equality, *any* effort is worth it; and *every* effort is necessary. It starts with Black lives mattering as much as White lives. It starts with Black Lives Mattering, Too.

Kjerstin Gould lives on the Pacific Coast with her four-legged friends and near her adult son and extended family. Raised as a white liberal feminist, it is only in recent years that she has truly woken to the systemic racial injustices in the U.S. She spends much of her free time listening to the voices of People of Color, relearning history, and adjusting her perspective of current events. She writes two blogs: www.TheRangerChronicles.com is an exploration of life with PTSD; and www.LifeSimplyIs.com chronicles her ongoing journey of social justice and feminist advocacy. Kjerstin can be reached at: https://twitter.com/LifeSimplyLife *or* https://www.facebook.com/LifeSimplyIs/

Mary Canty Merrill, Ph.D.

Why Black Lives Have Always Mattered to Me – And the Result

By Susan Oldberg Hinton

BEGINNINGS. Picture a little white, suburban-U.S. toddler—like anyone, trying to grow up in a confusing world. This girl, at a 1950's pool party, seeing the *most beautiful Black girls... a-sparkle in sunlit droplets.* Watch them now, still playing in my memory amid a sea of white children... on the far side of a strange boundary.

Inside, feel an early, painful confusion igniting a passion for Justice. I felt invisible... and *so* yearned to be friends, too! No one was there to dispel that boundary, but I remembered the desire. Surely, this early encounter underpinned my embracing the BLM movement, from which I've gained welcome focus with Black leadership for my justice efforts.

ADULT LEARNING. Through participating in Anti-Racism workshops, I've learned so much about the how's and why's of the completely artificial boundaries created by Systemic Racism. In our church's workshops, a small-group segment explores "Some Privileges of Racial Power." Each person first, individually, reviews a number of statements about everyday US life activities such as, "I can arrange to be with people of my race most of the time." Then each of us counts how many statements are true for us. When all have finished our count, we are asked to stand up at our tables. Participants with fewer than 20 true statements are asked to sit down; more sit with fewer than 15; more sit with fewer than five... three... one. This offers an opportunity and structure to see and acknowledge one's own daily, unearned privilege—or its absence.

As we stand or sit to embody our tallies, we notice who has a full set of privileges, and who does not. At the end, those still standing are invariably the lightest-complected people in attendance, looking down to meet the eyes of table-mates of a darker hue. Very often there is one white male left standing in a very quiet room. All then discuss how we felt as we were reviewing the statements individually; how we felt when we looked around to see who was standing and who was not—and the implications of having these different amounts of Privilege. For me, one result of participating in these workshops has been a persistent calling from my heart, to use 'my' White Privilege (until it is gone).

Every human being is a unique person, created expecting fairness and thinking about Justice. I've found that the more choices I make to use White Privilege as I follow Black leadership to dismantle the system—the fewer privileges I can check off as true in my everyday life, when I repeat the training. I find myself increasingly glad to have less Privilege as I celebrate more of it for others too long "sitting" while others "stood."

THE RESULT. The more I *know* 'my' White Privilege—and *use it for Justice—the less Privilege I can wield.* Specifically, at present, for many of the training exercise's statements **(the boldface in the below),** I can describe where that privilege went—and the 'upsides' I love growing into *(italics below).*

- **I can** *no longer* **arrange to be with people of my race most of the time**, in my eventual-retirement neighborhood; there, I have become identified as a "N-lover," and find certain folks not letting me into their lives the minute they get that memo. *(Upside: more cultural openings.)*

- **I can be pretty sure of getting housing in an area I can afford and in which I would like to live,** *BUT:*

- **I can** *no longer* **be pretty sure that my neighbors will be neutral or pleasant to me,** because my views are known, communicated with signage. *(Upside: more Black friends.)*

- **When told about "civilization," I am** *no longer* **shown that my race made it what it is,** because I have educated myself to see between the lines of any text purporting to show white/European "credit." *(Upside: I know and can teach many of the facts about global and US injustices done in the name of white 'civilization'.)*

- **Whether I use credit cards or cash, I can** *no longer* **count on my skin color not to affect the perception of my financial reliability.** This is because I have shopped in the company of Black people– especially Black men. Once this is noted, I am grilled for ID and denied certain store privileges, whether I am with a white person or a Black person. *(Upside: lots of practice in interrupting "micro-aggressions".)*

- **I can** *no longer* **arrange to protect my [visiting] children most of the time from people who might not like them,** because my nieces and nephews are likely to hear "N-lover" flung from passing neighbors. *(Upside: opportunities to teach about Systemic Racism.)*

- **I can** *no longer* **swear, dress in old clothes, or not answer letters without people attributing these choices to my race's bad morals, poverty, or illiteracy–** since it is now assumed that I must be "poor white trash" for associating with Black people socially. *(Upside: I can cultivate humility and give up victimhood.)*

- **I can** *no longer* **speak in public without putting my race on trial.** "What can you expect from a white-trash N-lover." *(Upside: teaching moments when I see that face.)*

- **I can** *no longer* **do well without being called a credit to my race.** ("Not bad for a white-trash N-lover.") *(Upside: teaching moments when I smell that thought.)*

- **I can** *no longer* **remain oblivious to the language or customs of people of the global majority (POC) without penalty,** because more and more whites know the truth, and hold each other accountable for speaking it. *(Upside: living in the real world.)*

- **I can** *no longer* **criticize the US government and talk about fearing its policies and behavior without being seen as a potential terrorist,** because BLM is part of my public face. *(Upside: sharing the real world.)*

- **I can** *no longer* **go home from meetings feeling that I belong— rather than isolated, out-of-place, outnumbered, unheard, or feared,** because now I go where there is fear from every side. *(Upside: seeing change from the inside and confronting those toddler feelings from the pool.)*

- **I can** *no longer* **be sure that if I need legal or medical help, my race will not work against me.** Amazing and different, how many white attorneys would not return my call last winter. *(Upside: Black attorneys know the system so much better!)*

CONCLUSIONS. This 'loss' of Privilege doesn't mean that I'm not 'white' anymore; *physically* I am as white (and racist-conditioned) as ever. But I *can* become more multi-culturally curious. I *can* be comfortable engaging beyond 'whiteness,' by ever moving towards discomfort. I *can* deliberately learn (and dismantle) the roles my culture of origin played and still plays in systemic, racist injustice. The system still cuts me White Slack when I step into a new environment, *until they know me there.* So—staying focused depends on being known as my authentic self.

"Why Black Lives Matter" is because "Black Lives Matter" makes sense logically, as all the above "upsides" evidence.

THE FUTURE. My personal change is a tiny hill of beans relative to the big picture. But *collectively*—this massive coalition-swelling, with so much of it now finally coming from the demographic that's had the disproportionate amount of power?—*that's Power that will work!*

As I look forward to living full-time in the diverse community chosen for retirement, I also look forward to seeing more of that Privilege disappear. I long for a society I hope to see in my lifetime—a happily and peacefully diverse society, where no one wears invisible knapsacks full of invisible power tools, no one has to carry a reserve stock of items to replenish others', and no one's culture is forced to adopt unnatural limitations.

Susan Oldberg Hinton is a blunt-spoken, smart, semi-retired clergy wife working towards full retirement for two, with a lifelong ally and justice orientation, who enjoys learning, music, and people—preferably together and with dogs. A white, raised-poor, self-educated woman leading where necessary, and following where possible, Susan can be reached at: motormice@hotmail.com.

Mary Canty Merrill, Ph.D.

Shifting the Paradigm

By Erin Hooton

"We knew we could not be free in the same paradigm that had oppressed us. If the construct is the same, then we are going to remain in the same situation. We had to talk about revolutionary change." – Elaine Brown

How do you talk about why Black lives matter? Why is it necessary to keep asking why *Black lives matter*? How is it that we still have such a gaping void in our human community that we have not grounded an answer?

Because the paradigm never changed.

Mainstream society has continued to enforce the belief that the value of life is sourced from a comfortable and measureable contribution to others. It declares that, in actuality, there is no baseline of human value, unless you are white. We never stopped telling Black people that what they can *produce* defines their worth, and the *personal comfort* of the white mass determines the validity of their experience. In other words, whether or not white society *believes* Black people have value, based on their *perception*. Throughout history and into the present, the 'limits' on the value of Black people have continually been defined by the limits of white perception. Whites have territorialized Black value to begin and end in sports, entertainment and criminality—a continued commoditization of life for white consumption and disregard—and convinced one another of the validity of our imperceptions.

I do not believe that Black lives need to be justified by accomplishment or contribution, by visibility or notoriety, by what they can provide, or what we can consume from them, in order to *have value*. Black lives matter because they are *lives*, and because they are *Black lives*. And Black people have fought extremely hard to solidify this fact, against ever-present white dehumanization and control; against jails, institutions and death. At the very least, when considering the value of individual lives, we should look at a person as a center for creativity, for self-actualization, forms of communication, expressers of the exterior experience through an interior filter. From the mass kidnapping and enslavement of Black people for colonial development (Drescher, 1999), to the conflation of skin color as biological information on human character (Long, 2003), to the creation of laws that oppressively regulate Black life outside or into prisons, to terminology, eugenics, medical experiments (Alexander, 2010), police brutality and murder (Krieger, Chen, Waterman, Kiang, & Feldman (2015), we have refused to understand and pronounce that **Black Lives Matter.**

Racism is the most deadly moral and social defect of this country. Though disguised in various modifications to systems, institutions and day-today personal interactions, racism (and other isms) has continued to deform the way that we function as a nation divided, because racism was never eliminated. Greed, power, ego, denial, insulation from truth, and fear; all these ever-pervasive defects of white society have been somewhat dampened, but not cured. From the national media, to politics, education, financial institutions, laws and prisons, the narrative (and actions) still being reinforced are that Black people don't matter *as much as*.

The deceptive nature of inherited racism and racial bias has continued to camouflage the *necessity* for responding to whether

Black lives matter with a resounding **YES**. We have seen concessions in laws and social mores, certain types of racism receding from public exhibition, but the roots of hate and oppression have never been excised. We've not been able to build a new foundation so that no one group of people can be held up or held down by others because of their color or national origin. White people have failed to hold one another accountable in the way in which we must, believing our national moral development is complete.

We have forgotten that, at the cost of their freedom, dignity and lives, in unfathomable numbers, Black lives have been the source of inspiration and propulsion for some of the biggest leaps in our moral development as human beings, and its radiating global effect (Earl, 2013). In spite of racism's best efforts, every leap in human rights in this country, every national conversation about equality, and evolution of thought is predicated on great loss and cruelty and savagery against Black people, and subsequently by the leadership *of Black people,* towards a future that holds the value of every human life as inalienable, deserving of freedom and the right to thrive.

We are at the place again, where the paradigm of white supremacy is pointed out and so desperately trying to stay alive. It is imperative that we change the paradigm, by again following Black leaders, so that there is no need to ask, because Black lives *do matter.*

Black lives matter when we stand up to and against racism, in conversation, in politics, for strangers, in families.

Black lives matter when we recognize that white children, the potential oppressors, are absorbing and emulating the narrative that we are perpetuating, and we show them how to honor and love differences.

Black lives matter when we stop allowing the characterization of a group of people to be created by media headlines.

Black lives matter when we value positive change over personal comfort.

Black lives matter when we actively listen to the experience of others, regardless of whether we can identify with it.

Black lives matter when we stop feeding the prison-industrial complex.

Black lives matter when we stop killing unarmed Black people.

Black lives matter when white people step down from the podium, and step beside our compatriots of color in solidarity.

Black lives matter when we tear down standards, laws, institutions and ideas that uphold white supremacy.

Black lives matter when we stop requiring people of color to be superhuman, in order to be human.

Black lives matter when we stop derailing national conversation about inequality with whiteness.

Black lives matter when we turn ideals into actionable evolution.

Mary Canty Merrill, Ph.D.

Erin is a 30-year-old artist and writer living in Mexico. While she doesn't have any special qualifications, she is a human being who cares deeply about the human experience, and the human condition. She grew up in both the U.S. and Mexico, and has seen and experienced many wonderful and horrifying facets of human character, including within herself. She's been on a journey in adulthood to expand her awareness in order to be of maximum service to her fellow humans. Erin can be reached at: erin.hooton@gmail.com.

Why Black Lives Matter

By Steven Jarose

When I was growing up in the 1950's, the Fourth of July meant picnics, parades and fireworks. It was a time to show our patriotic pride in America and the people who made us a great nation. This view was shaped by my family, my teachers, my faith tradition and the media. It was entirely white.

The veterans and firemen and scouts and musicians who marched in the parades were white. The people who lined the sidewalks waving the flag were white. The history I learned in school was a white history, as were the stories of valor of men who made us 'great.' My view of being 'all-American' was a white football player and a blonde, blue-eyed cheerleader. Every role model I had in my formative years was white. I was steeped in whiteness and did not know it. No one told me I was white. I knew it without having consciousness.

The story I was told about America went like this: The United States was a land of liberty and opportunity for all. Our vast migration from East to West was a testament to our initiative, our intelligence and desire to make a better life for those who came after us. Anyone who worked hard and applied themselves had access to the American Dream. Success and prosperity were open to all because we were all equal.

How does such a whitewashed view of self and country get challenged by reality? Not easily. If my family and I were Black and had the very same experiences, challenges, struggles and financial difficulties I had growing up white, my life view would be very different. I would know what it means NOT to be white, not to have my history validated or the contributions of my people honorably included. It would mean being stonewalled and severely restricted in my access to education, career, financing, and where I'd be allowed to take up residence. It would mean having to work twice as hard and left to wonder why I am so invisible to so many.

I did not know that the story I grew up with didn't apply to everyone. It was a story for white America. Manifest Destiny was meant for those whose skin color was like mine. While I was being told the playing field was equal, I was also being shown that my group was morally, intellectually and physically superior to others. The messages were subtle as well as blatant. They were everywhere. And I was blind to them.

I was shocked to be awakened to such a reality. Being born white had given me a head start on others? You must be crazy! I denied it. I became defensive. I took my anger out on the messenger. I isolated myself even further in the comfort of segregated living.

It took time to own that I carried privilege as white and as male. I realized that I could not claim pride in those identities until I healed from the injustice of being told or shown that I was less than or more than any other human being. Gradually, my reasons for keeping silent or avoiding conversations on race no longer comforted me. Fears of being politically incorrect, of thinking it was not my issue, or that I might offend someone, or be called out on my racism gave way to a desire to learn how to redirect my privilege in ways that could benefit everyone and lead to greater equity.

If every day for the rest of my life I noticed one more thing about the personal and systemic impact of racism in the U.S., I would still be woefully ignorant about the racism people of color encounter every day in multiple ways. That said, I can not afford to let ignorance prevail. I have two eyes and two ears to see and hear in new ways. Accessing my senses forces me to un-numb; get the wax out of my ears and the sleep out of my eyes so I can better understand what's going on. It means that I notice who is in the room and who is not; where we meet and the places we don't; where I shop and where I don't; which bus routes have shelters and which do not; whose voices get heard and whose voices are shut out.

It also requires that I use my thinking and my voice to speak up. It is too easy to disengage these days; stay within my comfort zone or 'go elsewhere' physically and mentally. But I could take initiative and start the conversation. I could share an idea, thought or article with someone and ask their opinion. I could wonder aloud why it took so long to recognize Ebola as a world health crisis, and why we Americans were not concerned until the reality set in because it was at our doorstep. The same could be said for the Zika virus, since both were first identified on continents inhabited by people of the global majority.

I admire what Paul Tillich said: *"The first duty of love is to listen."* Really listen. I'm just too quick to pass judgment because of my (white) urgency to inform, educate and correct those I see as other. What kind of learning is that? What kind of listening is that?

I've noticed how my tone, posture, relaxed presence and willingness to be informed can make a huge difference. It is an extraordinary gift of generosity when we appreciate or acknowledge another person's point of view. "I take your point" or "You've expanded my way of seeing this issue. Thank you." And we get to share our thinking, too, or the conversation remains a monologue rather than the dialogue we are striving for. We can add "My experience offers another perspective that I'd like to share" or "I'd like to build upon the example you gave."

The time to engage and act is now. If we wait until the stars are aligned or we have the perfect opener or response, we will lose the opportunity to cross the conscious and unconscious distances keeping us from one another.

I'm learning that not speaking up is a form of violence. And when I do speak, there can be violence in my choice of words, especially if they are designed to cut off conversation, intimidate another, or carry unintended consequences. If I didn't intend to hurt another person by what was said, it in no way diminishes its impact. When I say racism is not my issue I am committing an act of violence; towards myself and towards the person I am engaging, regardless of color. In fact, I am colluding with the institutions and structures that keep racism so deeply entrenched.

I recently read an article describing the critical need to care for the natural environment. I was moved by the language: strong, visceral and emotive. Words like destruction, degradation, suffering, exploitation, damage, dumping ground, genocide, theft, marginalization and exclusion. We treat the earth as a commodity to be exploited. We treat one another in much the same way when we avoid confronting the toxic environments of racism and economic disparity we live with every day. What if those same strong powerful words were used to describe the history of racism in the U.S. and how vividly it flourishes today in myriad ways?

In fact, such words have and continue to be written and spoken through the pens and voices of Black Americans across the country.

Race matters. Black lives matter. Being treated 'less than' matters. Are we awake? Are we listening?

Steven Jarose is the Director of the Rochester, New York Chapter of the National Coalition Building Institute, a nonprofit leadership development organization dedicated to eliminating racism and all forms of oppression wherever they occur. Engagement, rather than blame, shame, or guilt, is the key to understanding. He is an educator by training, an interfaith minister, LGBTQ advocate, and active in community-wide initiatives promoting equity and justice for all. He can be reached at: sjarose@ldagvi.org or sjarose@frontiernet.net.

Mary Canty Merrill, Ph.D.

Being Black Does Not Mean Being Less Than

By Christie Kendzior

It saddens me that some white people place a value judgment on skin color, which manifests both consciously and subconsciously, but which ultimately boils down to the belief that white is synonymous with good and black is synonymous with bad. It's not only an irrational way of thinking, but it's dangerous as well, because it can have deadly, real-life consequences.

It's a message that has been drilled into the minds of people via many avenues, such as family structures, school systems, the way communities are organized, and media portrayals. Sometimes it's not even explicit, and said people might not even know that they've been harboring such feelings, but they will surface when certain situations arise. For example, some people will always take the side of the police when yet, another unarmed Black person is gunned down, or they will assume that every Black person who is arrested is guilty. Whatever happened to "innocent until proven guilty?"

I grew up in a small town where this type of thinking reigned supreme. Yet, I never bought into the white-is-better rhetoric. I'm thankful that my family didn't exude racism, even though I was surrounded by it in many other ways. It has been said that racism is taught, and that is true. However, just because it hasn't been specifically taught to you, does not mean that you're not susceptible to it. I am susceptible to it. We all are. I was horrified and embarrassed to learn that I hold a moderate automatic preference for white people, after taking Harvard University's Project Implicit test. This test is designed to identify an individual's unconscious racial biases; and unfortunately, I ended up having quite a few.

Taking this test and engaging in other cultural awareness efforts make me realize that I have a lot of work to do. And I'm thinking: if someone like me has these biases, then what about all of the other white people out there?

We live in a society where Black children are sent to crumbling, failing schools. A society in which many Black communities are poor and devoid of affordable, nutritious food and where good paying jobs are non-existent. A society where Black men, particularly young Black men, are being killed by police at alarming rates. A society where the college graduation rate is significantly lower for Black students than it is for their white peers. A society where the incarceration rate disproportionately affects those with dark skin. A society where the scales of justice tilt in favor of white people.

The Black Lives Matter movement arose because of these aforementioned atrocities, but especially after the killing of Trayvon Martin, an unarmed teen walking along in his neighborhood minding his business and gunned down by a suspicious self-appointed neighborhood watchman—who was not convicted. The Black Lives Matter website states that they are "working for the validity of Black life." And I think that says it all. It's obvious that some segments of our society do not value Black lives. The message that being Black is somehow 'lesser than' seems to permeate certain neighborhoods and towns. Fortunately, though, there are a lot of us who reject these prejudicial messages, and who wholeheartedly believe that Black lives do matter.

I can clearly see that our society isn't fair and is leveled against Blacks and other people of color. Blacks have been subjected to atrocities for hundreds of years within our system of white supremacy and white privilege, beginning with the days of slavery.

Mary Canty Merrill, Ph.D.

In order to do my part, I try to actively listen to people of color as much as possible to better understand what they have been through. Having not walked in their shoes, I can never fully empathize with Blacks and other people of color. Nonetheless, I'm committed to advocating in every way that I can. This includes: writing and calling legislators, protesting, speaking up whenever I hear racist talk, and talking to other white people about their own privilege and white fragility.

Black lives matter because we're all in this together. Life can be cruel, unforgiving, and painful, yet it can also be beautiful, special, and loving; and there is no reason why someone should have a harder life merely because of their skin pigmentation. Equality is the goal, and I will always work toward it in some capacity. Onward!

Christie Kendzior has a Masters in Social Work and her focus has been on educating and empowering underprivileged children, and teaching them how to overcome barriers and obstacles. She is married with four children, and is currently a stay-at-home mom. Social justice matters mean the world to her, and she is also interested in politics and global issues. Christie can be reached at: Christie.pavlock@gmail.com.

What Black Lives Matter Means to Me

By Susan M. Kuhn

Black Lives Matter originated in the Black community as a campaign against police violence against Black people. The movement began with the #BlackLivesMatter hashtag after the acquittal of George Zimmerman in the shooting death of Trayvon Martin in Sanford, Florida. It became nationally recognized during protests following the police killings of Michael Brown in Ferguson, Missouri and Eric Garner in Staten Island, New York. Since that time, the movement has protested against numerous other murders of Black people at the hands of law enforcement officers.

There are three reasons why Black Lives Matter is important as a concept and as a movement. First, because the idea that Black people are "lesser" than is baked into American law and American history. I hadn't thought about this history much recently, until Ferguson, and until the anger of many Black friends and colleagues set me to reflection. I thought, I read, I discussed and I realized something: The America I, as a white person, thought I knew, isn't the same America my Black friends and colleagues experience. I recognized how my white skin affords me a very different life experience. Perhaps my biggest wake-up call was realizing that our racial history was far worse than that of South Africa, which was of course horrid. I was ignorant and didn't know it.

A quick look back lends clarity to this other thread of our history. Many founding fathers of this country were slaveholders. The 1787 constitutional convention that established the Federal government counted Blacks as 3/5 of a person. Blacks were forbidden to learn to read, bought and sold as property in slave markets, deprived of family ties, raped without recourse, and subject to labor without compensation. Even lynching was not considered murder. The Dred Scott decision declared that no one of African ancestry could be anything but a slave, even if they lived in a state where slavery was illegal. If that isn't a message that Black lives don't matter, I don't know what is. 'Saying All Lives Matter' is not only lazy, but extremely ignorant. The official policies of this country have supported, and in many areas of our society continue to support the notion that Black lives don't matter.

Second, Black Lives Matter means that Black lives and Black culture IS American culture. One recent Sunday, driving to my church, I sat at the light as a Black congregation adjourned. I watched the well-dressed couples, and children leave the service. I thought: every one of you is descended from slaves who were beaten, raped, treated worse than some animals and deprived of freedom. Yet, look at you: elegant, independent, and believing in God. Each of you has climbed a mountain that no one ever required me to climb. Each person seemed nothing short of a miracle to me.

When starting college, I had an opportunity to move from what former singer and composer Rick James called "the rough ghetto" of Buffalo, New York to the more cosmopolitan Washington, DC area. Buffalo was harsh. Everyone around me thought Blacks were inferior. My father had a vocabulary of cuss-words for Black people that made me lose all respect for him. In a new city, slowly, Black culture became a part of my life. Charles Drew made transfusions possible, and "The Real McCoy" refers to a Black inventor. We have a Black president, sports stars and oh, do we have some awesome Black music. But I am talking about the more subtle goodness, the values and nuances of culture that make up America. So much of it comes from African Americans. Black Lives Matter greatly in the nation we have become.

Third, Black Lives Matter is a necessary movement and a necessary corrective. It speaks to the history of systemic abuse that is part and parcel of American history. It points to the remnants of those abuses and demands that we root them out. Shooting a Black man in the back is not a legitimate exercise of police authority. Killing a Black mentally ill woman in her cell with a taser, with no mental health professional present, as happened to Natasha McKenna in Fairfax, Virginia, is not competent handling of a Sherriff's department. Failing to see the teachable moment when a student wears a "Confederate Lives Matter" shirt to a school that excuses itself simply because it's in Virginia—the capital of the Confederacy—underscores a pervasive weakness and ineptitude.

We have not yet come to grips with the fact that the white mass murders across the U.S. have racist backgrounds. We have had a very difficult time taking down the flag of the vanquished Confederacy which fought to preserve slavery. Most disturbing of all is that it took the Charleston, South Carolina massacre of nine innocent Black parishioners attending Bible study to accomplish that.

At my church, we work towards racial reconciliation. There is not much reconciliation in these aforementioned examples. As recent visitors from the Episcopal Diocese of South Africa said at a conference I attended, "When we peel back one layer of racial issues, there is another layer waiting to reveal itself." I have been thinking about these white male mass murders, as well as the "garden variety" racism that permeated by upbringing. What are these shooter's back stories? What would it have taken to change their hearts and minds? At this juncture, we are no closer to knowing this now than we ever have been. There is a painful blindness, a willful immaturity among many whites. Even among those who care, there is a lack of skill in terms of moving from private empathy into true and public reconciliation. I count myself in this group, although I am open to listening and learning to help promote racial justice and equality for all.

It is a long-term process, this coming to terms with racism and systemic injustice and inequality in America. There is a lot to learn, and a lot to be done. We are still wallowing in the denial stage, and Black Lives Matter is our country's urgent wake-up call.

Susan M. Kuhn is a Washington, DC-based writer, digital strategist, fundraiser and social activist. She has extensive experience in the national philanthropic, nonprofit and technology sectors. Her blog, Un(do) Poverty, will soon become a book. She can be reached at: susankuhndc@gmail.com and on LinkedIn as Susan M. Kuhn.

Not for Your Convenience, Nor for Your Service

By Nicole Lattery

The more things change, the more they remain the same. Being Black is hard, criminal even. It always has been. At least that's how it seems. And while some pundits argue that America is Post-Racial, virtually all Black people deal with some type of racism each and every day. A comedian coined the acronym DWB meaning "Driving While Black," putting a name on the trend of Black men being targeted in traffic stops. Racial profiling is quite prevalent in the 21st century. Unfortunately, there is no evidence that white supremacy and its ugly child racism ever died.

When slavery was abolished, we were set free but not deemed equal. And with each attempt to advance the cause of Blacks in this country, the system was set up to keep us under foot. Today, with the establishment of the Black Lives Matter movement we continue to struggle for inclusion and fair treatment. How ridiculous is this? Here we are proclaiming that *Black Lives Matter*, then someone in the penny section hollers "All Lives Matter!" Yet, I am not aware of a time when whites had to defend the validity of their existence.

Europeans came to this country claiming that they discovered America, despite the fact that indigenous people were already living here. Historical records reveal how Native Americans were mistreated, intentionally given diseases, and slaughtered by the white man at will. These atrocities speak volumes about how far white people will go to retain a sense of superiority.

I am from Jamaica. The island was originally inhabited by the Arawak and Taino peoples. Yet, Christopher Columbus claimed to have discovered my native country. I am angered by the sense of entitlement that whites have about virtually everything feed their egos shrouded in what I call, "a superiority complex."

We have been led to believe that white is better. That white is good, and Black is bad. That is until white women decided they wanted Black lips and thus began the lip injection phenomenon. Black buttocks also became quite appealing, so now there are butt injections as well. I will not go any further on the point of black appropriation, but wanted to provide a few examples of the sheer hypocrisy perpetuated white people. It seems that Black Lives Matter only when it's convenient for whites to appropriate our culture.

Here we are in 21st century America having this conversation about the validity of Black lives. I have heard the argument "free but not equal." And still our 'freedom' comes with certain caveats. For example, our freedom to vote is accompanied by the machinery that exists to suppress those votes. Freedom of speech allows racists to spew their venom against Blacks without retribution, but when Blacks exercise free speech, we are met with unrelenting anger, criticism, and threats. A case in point is Beyonce's *Formation* movement which has many white people up in arms, accusing her of being anti-police. Yet, there is a significant difference between "anti-police" and "anti-police brutality."

Dr. Martin Luther King, Jr. was assassinated because he spoke out against the oppression of Blacks. Our right to bear arms was not welcome when the Black Panther Party took up guns to protect themselves and their community against police brutality. Unfortunately, many white people skew the Black Panther story, omitting crucial humanitarian efforts of the movement, such as providing meals and health care programs that were sorely lacking in the Black community.

There is the argument that they kill us out of fear. Not the lame "fear for our lives" crap, but a fear that Blacks are a force to be reckoned with, so must be contained and constrained lest we take over the world. The last time I checked, we didn't want to take over the world, we simply wanted equality... to not face oppression at every turn. We want the same access to economic basics such as a quality education, housing, health care, safe drinking water and safe neighborhoods. We want to not be targeted and shot as if a bull's eye has been painted on our backs.

Black lives matter. I have a son who I must raise under a lot of pressure: pressure to not speak a certain way; pressure to not wear his pants sagging; pressure to not go to certain places, lest he is considered a "thug." The pressure is on, simply because he has one strike against him—his Blackness. Until we convince people that Black lives matter, too, I will always fear one day getting that dreadful phone call. Even worse is that I have very little hope that justice would prevail.

Black lives matter. It seems the central argument is how much we matter. Let me explain. Black communities receive less funding for schools; it's hard to source quality foods. What you will find is a plethora of junk food. Here in Florida, as in most areas of the country, there are lower income communities where even supermarkets are lacking. The basics of life are limited, if not altogether withheld. Meanwhile, research indicates that funding is liberally provided for building prison complexes. The lead poisoning of the residents of Flint, Michigan through the water supply is yet another example of the widespread disrespect and maltreatment of Blacks in the U.S. The system is rigged us: less funding for education, health care, housing, and quality food sources, but more than sufficient funding for prisons.

Mary Canty Merrill, Ph.D.

This troubling trend prompts me to ask a number of questions of white people. Am I to understand that you think I don't matter? You seem to be of the opinion that you are somehow superior to me and that your life is worth more than mine. Are you saying that because you kidnapped and brought my ancestors from Africa to America in chains to tend to your crops, plow your land, and nurse your babies, so you still own me and my right to life? Am I worth more if I provide cheap labor for landscaping, nursing and housekeeping? Does my value decrease if I ask for more pay or stand up for my rights to the same benefits and perks that you enjoy? With all the money that we made you from our blood, sweat and tears, you still perceive us as property? And even though slavery is abolished you still perceive us as inferior? Well, I've got news for you. We are worth more than the money you paid when you bought and sold our ancestors into slavery. We are more valuable than the plowing of your land and the picking of your cotton. And although you took our wives and daughters for your pleasure and forced them to carry your seed, we are more valuable than you will ever know or accept. So whether you acknowledge it or not... Black lives matter – we always have and we always will!

Nicole Lattery was born in Kingston, Jamaica and has worked with youth to empower them to be their best at all times. She has advocated for equality on all levels. She lives in Florida with her husband and four-year-old son, and is concerned about the racial inequalities that persist in our society. Nicole is eager to help shift the narrative and the dynamics of race that will impact the life of her young son, and can be reached at: nyqui2002@yahoo.com.

When Others Suffer, I Suffer

By Matthew Lecki

I vow not to harm, but to cherish all life.
– The First Buddhist Precept

More than a decade ago, I took the Buddhist Precepts and was given the Buddhist name Sudo by my Dharma teacher. In doing so, I vowed to live my life guided by basic Buddhist morality. These guidelines include undertaking not to harm, not to steal, not to lie, and avoiding other behaviors that cause suffering for me and for others. It's that "for me and for others" concept that is so very important when attempting to live by the precepts. Buddhist philosophy frequently reminds us of the interconnectedness of all life. There really is no difference between "self" and "other." We are all one, just as individual waves on the ocean are not really different from the ocean. If others are suffering, I suffer. If others are not free, I am not free. If others cannot breathe, I cannot breathe.

The preciousness of all life is a widely held principle, but it's not enough to say it and move on. Upholding this precept requires some introspection. It demands looking at the details. It requires accountability or it is just an empty promise which harms me and all living beings. It demands the acknowledgement of the suffering of others. It takes a deep and honest look at my role in that suffering and how the possible alleviation of that suffering might take place.

As a white man, I have benefited enormously from the suffering of people of color. My nation was founded on colonialism that stole land and resources from indigenous people and committed genocide on an unfathomable scale. My nation captured and enslaved millions of Black Africans and grew its economy on this brutal, inhumane, and immoral practice. My nation fought a war to preserve the institution of slavery and only begrudgingly abolished it. My nation then committed de facto slavery, violence and lynching, segregation, and discrimination on Black people for another one hundred years before it saw fit to pass the Civil Rights Act of 1964. Since the passing of this law, Black people continue to be marginalized and oppressed and White people like me continue to benefit from systems and institutions that discriminate, oppress, and harm Black people. Despite anti-discrimination laws, the Black community is harmed by disparities in education, employment, home ownership, medical care, and law enforcement and justice. As a white person who has participated in and benefited from these systems, I will spend my life unraveling my twisted karma. The absolute very least thing I can do is to remember the First Precept and acknowledge when Black friends and family are suffering.

When others suffer, I suffer.

Among the most shockingly unfair and brutal aspects of racism experienced by Black people is the widespread discrimination and violence from the systems that should be protecting them and ensuring justice. For example, Black people are disproportionately arrested on drug charges by more than 25 percent, despite the fact that drug use by Black people and white people are approximately the same. Police stop Black people at a rate four times higher than that of white people. When stopped, Black people are frisked 85 percent of the time, whereas white people are frisked only 8 percent of the time. In a recent year, Black people were stopped by police over 600,000 times and contraband was found less than 2 percent of the time. When charged, Black men are incarcerated at more than six times the rate of White men and serve longer sentences for the exact same crimes.

When others are not free, I am not free.

John Crawford, an unarmed Black man in Beavercreek, Ohio, was killed in a Walmart store in an "open carry" state for holding a replica air rifle that he picked up from a shelf in the very store he was killed in. Michael Brown, an unarmed Black teenager, was gunned down by a police officer in Ferguson, Missouri. Tamir Rice, a twelve-year-old Black teen, was killed by police while playing in a park in Cleveland, Ohio. Sandra Bland, a Black woman, was pulled over by police for a turn signal violation and was arrested, physically brutalized, and died in her jail cell in Waller County, Texas. An unarmed Black man, Eric Garner, was killed by police with an illegal chokehold for selling cigarettes in Staten Island, New York. He died of asphyxiation after repeating "I can't breathe" 11 times—*11 times*!

When others cannot breathe, I cannot breathe.

Black Lives Matter. I say this because all life is precious and one way that I can uphold this value is by noticing when others are suffering.

Black Lives Matter. I say this because Black children, women and men are suffering.

Black Lives Matter. I say this because I choose to acknowledge their suffering and push back against racist systems and my nation's shameful history that continuously show they do not.

Mary Canty Merrill, Ph.D.

Black Lives Matter. I say this to acknowledge my own complicity and privilege and take a very, very small step toward redressing this terrible imbalance.

Black Lives Matter. I say this as a reminder to speak the truth, confront racism, and show up for my Black friends and family.

Black Lives Matter. I say this as a mantra and a prayer for an end to the suffering of Black people.

Black Lives Matter. I say this because I love my wife and want her and every Black person to live in a world where having Black skin doesn't mean risk, fear, and suffering.

As I sit on my cushion and prepare myself to meditate, I take a breath for Eric Garner, who cannot breathe, and for every Black person who has suffered and is suffering.

Black Lives Matter. I vow to remember that for "all lives are precious" to ever be realized, Black Lives Matter NOW.

Matthew (Sudo) is a white guy living in Ann Arbor, Michigan. He is a practicing Buddhist, full-time student, and IT manager. He can be reached at: <u>mcl@districtx.net</u>.

Little Activists Need Information, Too

By Teresa C. Lewis

See Dick Run. See Jane Protest. See Sally's eyes water from tear gas. Children must be prepared for activism with appropriate tools, language and understanding so they can nurture lasting change when they become the leaders of tomorrow. At only 2½ years of age, the Black Lives Matter movement is just a year and a half from its own infancy. As Black Lives Matter toddles toward its childhood with all of its growth stages and growing pains, parents and others who live and strive for social justice can embrace and share conversations about activism with children just as they would their primary colors, numbers, games, feelings and manners. This type of sharing is a ripe opportunity to prepare the hearts and minds of children who will become the youth that inherit a maturing iteration of the Black Lives Matter movement 20 years from now.

Well over 20 years ago, I was a mini-Afro-wearing, baby Panther kid with raised fist. Part of my reality was that all of the caring adults seemed much too busy with revolution to educate and coach the children who were on the periphery. As a young girl during the civil rights movement, I was woefully unprepared for the hazy, scary, unknowing that was the movement seen through my lens of childhood. Late nights. Long rallies. Strangers shouting. Meetings. Microphones. Fear Noir. I might have benefitted greatly from a children's primer on what it meant to "liberate" the local public swimming pool or on how to use milk as an antidote for tear gas in the eyes, and perhaps, what emergency hiding space to retreat to if the "revolution" spilled over into our front room.

No such primer existed for us then. However, primers will emerge as adults tap into their own snaggle-toothed, elementary memories of wanting to make a difference and not knowing how to matter. Conjuring up the nostalgia of our grade school "I Have a Dream" essays could help adults who are involved in transformative work to stay attuned to how activism may affect children. Fresh ideas can be explored and safely dissected with youngsters using low and high tech multimedia options. A child's natural naiveté and optimism is a good place to begin non-threatening conversations that start with a simple question; *"I wonder how that felt to have that happen...?"* The ideas that flow from simple questions can be woven into transparent, teachable moments guided by a caring adult. The Internet and other advancements allow extended reach for adults who wish to ensure that children are not considered superfluous to the movement.

Political activist Angela Davis confirmed that she and her sister were activists from a very young age. Angela Davis said in an interview: *"I remember that strange sounds would be heard outside, and my father would go up to the bedroom and get his gun out of the drawer, and go outside and check to see whether the Ku Klux Klan had planted a bomb in the bushes. That was a part of our daily lives"* (van Gelder, 2016).

Decades after, I lay wide-eyed in the dark, hands folded in a type of self-assuring hug, while my militant parents made militant bumps in the militant night, a heartening voice has emerged. Author Kenneth Braswell has written a book to address his children's questions about protesting. His book *Daddy, There's a Noise Outside* could spark conversation and provoke questions that require adults to meet children at their level of understanding. He asserts that children have long been participants in activism and protest.

He wondered, "... in those cases where we have used children to protest a particular issue, whether or not adults take the time to actually explain to their children what [they're doing] and why they're doing it" (Edwards, 2016).

In retrospect, I know I did not understand why I was marching and chanting as a fourth grader. I should have. The children of revolution need guidance to sort out real and perceived fears. Children are too well advanced for the old school, "See Spot Run", primers of yesteryear. They are inquisitive and resilient. They need practice on how to prepare for times of controversy as well as lulls of peace. They need words to express the ways that they matter to the movement. Adult activists must invest early in opportunities to be transparent and inclusive with the children. The primer we write that empowers children with relevant information today will inform and aid youth in articulating the manifesto of tomorrow: Black lives matter!

Teresa Lewis is a Social Light, Social Media expert and Lifestyle blogger who encourages people to be more SELF-ish in order to serve others. She can be reached at: lewisteresac@gmail.com.

Mary Canty Merrill, Ph.D.

Black Lives Matter... Of Course They Do!

By Candace Lilyquist

Recently, while completing a training session to address racism, a white woman says to an African American male participant, *"I just wish people could know that men like you exist. It would change everything."* There are many people who do not know that men like JES exist. JES is the man any woman would want her son to become. He even understands others so well that he has the ability to navigate an unpleasant situation in which a young white woman, sitting from a place of privilege and superiority, chooses to express herself without pausing to consider the impact of her words or how they make him feel in a group setting.

Let's flip the script on that last scene. What if *all* people had as good a life experience as this lil' white girl? Wouldn't that be grand? What if people of color could be certain that they will experience the exact same privileges as she does?

Racism is a collective distraction. And many white people fail to consider how much they lose as a result of institutionalized racism. Thus, the statement 'All Lives Matter' is merely more noise in an already distracting system. 'All Lives Matter' is a phrase chanted by people who refuse to acknowledge and confront the daily slights and abuses that are imposed on people of color.

The Black Lives Matter movement emerged in response to police brutality (i.e., the killing systematic killing of Black men, women and children). Today, contemporary civil rights movement has morphed in many directions, with many collaborative leaders. In fact, the Black Lives Matter structure closely resembles that of a starfish. When one limb drops off, the remaining limbs continue to operate, spawning new growth to replace the missing limb No entity will be able to cut off the head of this movement and disband its followers, because leaders are present everywhere. Because the Black Lives Matter movement has no single figure head, it has the flexibility to branch out anywhere it chooses. Black Lives Matter isn't comprised solely of Black and brown people, but engages a multitude of racially diverse individuals who care about the issues that people of color are currently facing and are willing to spread the message that Black Lives matter – today and every day!

The majority of people in the United States live in population dense areas. According to the 2010 U.S. Census, eighty-one percent of U.S. residents live in suburban or urban environments, and is common to see people from all racial and ethnic backgrounds represented in these environments. However, as we venture into less populated areas, the communities are less racially diverse. In fact, no racial or ethnic diversity exists in some areas. For example, in Western states an individual can drive for miles and miles before approaching land owned or managed by a person of color.

National news networks are sharing the stories of Black Lives Matter protests to people who live in population sparse areas who have little to no capacity to understand why these protests are occurring. The mayor, the sheriff, business owners, and government employees are the only people they know, and the vast majority of those people are homogenous. The concept that people of color suffer disparate treatment by police, the justice system, the educational system, political systems, and other institutions is beyond the comprehension of many people living in sparsely populated areas. This is because their life experiences provide little, if any, opportunities for social interactions that might inform their knowledge and understanding of racial injustice and inequality.

How does one explain to a white man, who has been driven home by the local police on numerous occasions when intoxicated, that a person of color might not make it home after a police encounter in most major cities? How does one explain to an ill-informed white person that a police encounter gone awry involving a Black person could very well result in an automatic death sentence?

When white people lack connectedness to the realities of people of color whenever they interact with the justice system, they (whites) cannot grasp the concept of social injustice and inequity that is dictated by skin color. It makes no sense to them. Consequently, all they see is a particular group of people demanding to be treated more 'special' than they already are.

Many white people go about their day-to-day lives with little interruption. They have not experienced the pain and agony of losing a child to a gun, knife, or drug battle in the streets. They have not experienced drinking water filled with lead that create health issues for them and stunt the growth and development of their children. They have not experienced having "the talk" with their sons in an attempt to save them from deadly police encounters. They have not experienced living in unsafe neighborhoods where a walk down the street can result in a gang-related death. They have not experienced attending schools in which the building, because of unsafe structural conditions, mold and other hazards, should be condemned. They have not experienced having a merchant follow them around a store suspecting they might steal merchandise. They have not experienced being relegated to eating unhealthy foods because there is no neighborhood grocer to offer healthy fare. They have not experienced being considered an affirmative action hire simply to meet some government quota. They have not experienced be discriminated against because of the color of their skin. They have not experienced being related or connected to someone whose life was cut short, whose future was destroyed, or whose dreams were crushed because of institutionalized racism and systematic injustice

So how do we shake people out of their unconsciousness? How do we wake them from their deep slumber? How do we challenge them to move beyond the status quo, instead of accepting it and going on with their lives? Demonstrations that shut down traffic will garner attention. So will angry protests. So will having difficult conversations with people inside and outside of our families and communities to educate them about the ultimate destruction that apathy exacts on *all* communities, not just communities of color.

Racism is a very real problem in 21st century America, and Black Lives Matter's efforts have emphasized disruption of "life as usual" in communities to raise consciousness surrounding the racial disparities that continue to negatively impact the lives of people of color. These advocates are asking all people to look beyond their immediate day-to-day activities – their commute to the workplace, within their faith community, and at the mall – to acknowledge what is happening three blocks, ten streets, or half a city away to the lives of Black and brown people. None of us is whole until we are all whole. None of us is free until we are all free.

Mary Canty Merrill, Ph.D.

Candace L. Lilyquist is a Minnesota native transplanted to the Washington, D.C. Metro Area. Her life's work is focused on saving the public education system in the United States while transforming it to include kinesthetic and tactile learning styles, with a constructivist approach. She believes public schools are formed in community and reflect community. She also recognizes that adults must get along and connect in order to build the schools our children, students, families and communities need. Her views were formed from living the first eighteen years of her life in a city with a sign that reads population 154 (today). Candace can be reached at: candalily@gmail.com.

Mamma

By Emma Kate Lomax

"Mamma?"

"Yes, Lucy Kate?"

"Why are brown men bad?"

Astounded I took a sharp deep intake of breath as I peered at her in my rearview mirror. We were travelling down Interstate 95 and I felt disappointed that yet again here was the sad image of another Black man at the side of the road deep in conversation with a uniformed police officer.

As he started to gesticulate with emotion, I recall wanting to turn around and free him, or yell, *"Just stay calm and breathe deeply."* The view of the men got smaller and smaller and here was my innocent six-year-old daughter waiting for an answer to her question.

"Mamma? Why are brown men bad?"

As I looked at her face, I knew this was a pivotal moment as a parent and it was the most important question my daughter had presented me with thus far. Even if I had a lifetime could I ever do her question justice? Having to formulate an answer in a split second I recognized that rather than skillful handling, this required an authentic heart.

"Brown men aren't bad sweetheart. What made you ask that?"

"Well every time we pass the police, they are arresting brown men."

In the UK our politically correct terminology is Black, Asian, Mexican, Muslim, and Syrian. And as the refugee migrant situation escalates the use of terminology becomes even more confusing and controversial. But to use the word brown is definitely not okay, but that is another conversation.

She was right. On this short journey alone, this was the third time a man she perceived as brown was on the side of the road with another man she identified as a police officer.

So, was my initial response to the BIG question appropriate or a complete abdication of my responsibilities as a parent?

"You know how some police wear uniforms and others don't? Well, how do you know that the conversations you have just seen aren't between two work friends discussing where to go for their lunch or what job they are going to next?"

My mind was focused on teaching my daughter that people of any color can be anything they choose to be, even undercover policemen. But as the response came out of my mouth I realized it was a lame attempt to answer her question.

So I wondered, 'Where did I learn my lessons that Black lives matter, which I could share with my daughter?'

At nine years of age, I sat vacantly staring out of the window across the barren desert. I was daydreaming, completely in my own world, away from the babbling youngsters jumping across the school bus seats firing taunts. The mayhem escalated and half strewn sandwiches were hurled like missiles. As the bus driver turned around to admonish the children, the whole pack of white American and Eurocentric children revolted. In a moment their warring stopped and with a shared allegiance they turned on kind, patient, gentle Hafeez. I remember a half eaten sandwich slapping his taqiyah skullcap and a young boy not yet 10, sneaking up the aisle of the bus to empty his packet of half eaten Crumples Chips all over Hafeez's headwear. The feeling of my blood boiling, my utter outrage at the injustice and the malicious nature of the attack has stayed vividly with me for over 35 years.

I recall Hafeez anchoring the brakes. As the bus stopped abruptly on the desert road, Hafeez turned to us children and uttered words in Urdu. The children responded with silent gestures, mockery and titters that this man could not even tell them off in English. He left the bus, fell to his knees at the side of the road and started to cry. He had been subjected to the most humiliating attack by a bunch of over-privileged expat children. Children who had already been taught to hate people because of the color of their skin. As I rose to my feet, shouting that people were idiots, I too was mocked. I left the bus, dropped to the sandy floor and hugged Hafeez. That one act of kindness attracted the most horrendous names and I can recall a small part of me regretting my actions although I knew what I had done was right.

Following the bus' abrupt stop, a few children who were rampaging the aisles did fall over. There was nothing more than bumps and bruises; the greatest initial injury was some bruised egos. However by the time of the parental debrief the following day, those bruised egos had managed to spin a yarn worthy of an Aesop's Fable.

My memory of the parents' debrief is vivid. A young Texan Mamma hollering that her precious brat could have been seriously injured or even killed as Hafeez 'recklessly' brought the school bus to a complete standstill. This Mamma wanted Hafeez sued for negligence. *"That will teach him to take care of my family, if he has no money to send to his family in Pakistan this month".*

As a white woman, my awareness of my fragility is a gift. I have lived amongst siloed segregated cultures and communities. On a superficial level, I've tried to understand it but I will continue to always be safe, and be able to rest in my privilege. But speaking out is the essence of who I am. I want to help chip away at a system that is broken and is hurting the world.

I want to mother a white daughter without a white perspective, but I know that's not humanly possible. All I can do is raise a child that nurtures and develops her relationships based on trust and mutual respect, not on skin color and ethnicity. I want to raise a daughter that is as passionate as her Mamma about inspiring change.

Eight months have passed since that day on the highway, and it is seven weeks until her seventh birthday. It's time for her to begin to learn that on the streets of America, Black people are gunned down because they can't, and more importantly wouldn't, want to change the color of their skin. The police do not attack white people and, as she experienced during her five weeks in North Carolina, Black people are not arrested every day on the side of the road because they are naughty. Black people are arrested every day on the side of the road in North Carolina because of the color of their skin. All brown men are not bad. Most brown men are good sons that their Mammas are very proud of just like I am proud of you.

As a Mamma, I want my daughter to come to the table. I want her to learn about the personal struggles of others that first brought me to the table. So this weekend, we will settle down to watch Roots and together begin the journey of Kunta Kinte. I will be fully prepared for the difficult questions that will most certainly arise. With some sadness, I will reflect on the little change since 1980, when as a nine-year-old girl my heart first reached out to Kunta. And hope that during her lifetime Lucy Kate knows deep in her own authentic heart that Black Lives Matter, Too and she can quietly reflect on real transformational change.

Emma Kate is British and attended American schools in Dhahran, Saudi Arabia and Islamabad and Karachi, Pakistan while her father worked in the oil fields for Haliburton, an American multinational where former Vice President Dick Cheney presided as CEO after his tenure in the White House. These experiences shaped her mindset and as a white English woman, she is committed to influencing lasting social change as an independent social worker, criminal justice consultant and author. Emma Kate can be reached at: emmakatelomax@googlemail.com.

Mary Canty Merrill, Ph.D.

Smacked in My White Face

By Autumn Lubin

"Privileged? Oh, hell, no. I grew up doing without many tangible things that "privileged" people have. I lived in subsidized housing, ate dinners paid for with food stamps, was eligible for a governmental summer work program that taught teenagers work skills, and went to college on grants and loans. I grew up with a mother who had mental health and alcoholism issues that overshadowed hope. There was no solid ground in my childhood. There was nothing privileged about my earliest years."

Yes I did. I said that.

Another day. I'm having dinner with several of my colleagues, in an out-of-town restaurant and the conversation turned to parenting. "I'm getting ready to have 'the talk' with my son," one woman said. There were murmurs and nods of support. I tried to not show my shock. Her son was 6. What would cause her to talk to a kindergartner about sex?

Yep, I thought that.

The conversation continued. It was animated. Frustration that bordered on anger tinged the words. It became clear that they weren't talking about the birds and bees. I finally interrupted because I have learned in my aging that asking a question, even if it sounds stupid, is better than being stupid. "What is the 'talk'"?

I said it out loud.

The table grew quiet. I watched many thoughts flash across faces. In the end, the genuine affection we have for one another won the day. Without a sigh or any indication of weariness of teaching yet another white person, the woman who started the conversation answered my question. 'The talk' is one that Black American parents have with their children, particularly their male children. It is designed to teach their children how to respond to authority in our world in a way that will allow them to come home safely each day.

I had no words.

This was a conversation I had never even considered having with my son. I taught him to be respectful – not to keep him alive but to prevent sending another brat out into the universe. I had met my friend's adorable, extremely polite and funny little guy. Pieces of my heart silently and permanently shattered at that table in some unforgotten restaurant. I instantly sank into my friend's heart and felt the heavy everyday terror that resided there. There is no greater loss than that of a child. To have to consider this as a real possibility each time your young child leaves your protected sight is shattering. Every day.

I quit talking. Started listening closer.

My vocabulary grew. *White privilege. White fragility. The color blind myth.* The powerful juxtaposition of never giving thought to my whiteness and the blackness of my friends that required near constant attention. I have the luxury of being considered a mom, a wife, a business owner, a neighbor. The adjective describing my skin tone or race was never enjoined with my identity. In our world, my friends and colleagues will nearly always be identified as black before anything else. The more I learned, the more I came to know the raw nakedness of my ignorance. Humility wrapped me in its sheer cape.

I shook in my incredulity that I had made it to middle age not knowing this.

I walked my days in a watchful silence, recalibrating all I thought I knew. I had worked in racially mixed communities for a long time. My friends span the color continuum and the globe. I have an open mind, a caring heart and I've sought out knowledge about all people. I'm thoughtful about my word choices and respect the cultural norms of other ethnicities. I truly thought I had a good idea of what it meant to be something other than white in our racially charged world.

I knew nothing.

All I had learned, all I had experienced, all I could discern, was from a place of whiteness. My judgments, my perspectives, my way of helping, all came from walking in a world where my own skin tone was never a thought. Until I removed the protective gear of my whiteness, I remained part of the problem even while sincerely believing I was working towards the solution. I had to really get it, all the way to my soul, that walking black in a white world was nothing I could experience and therefore, never fully comprehend.

I was sat down on my humble white ass.

I began to understand that just standing with black people wasn't enough. Shaking my head at the racist atrocities that occur in black and brown and every color but white communities wasn't nearly enough. Changing my profile picture on Facebook to this week's dead child wasn't nearly enough. Signing petitions wasn't nearly enough. Empathizing with the broken hearts of moms, dads, sisters and brothers, even whole communities, wasn't nearly enough. While I didn't personally perpetuate any hate acts, if I sat back quietly, I was a co-conspirator.

Still sitting, trying to absorb the enormity of it all, I breathed.

A Black colleague told me that racism wasn't a black person's problem to solve. Only white people could fix it. It took me quite some time, thinking, reading, researching and listening for her words to resonate. I believe there is a continuum of understanding racism and I was in the beginning phases. I believed initially that I was further along than I was because I was missing an essential piece: vocabulary. I thought I knew what a lot of words meant. I was wrong. I didn't know the sub-categories of racism. I am certain I used racism, bigotry and prejudice interchangeably, not understanding the nuances of each. The whole concept of white privilege was not in my deck of words. The list is long. The work is hard.

I began to learn how much I didn't know.

Humility is quite a teacher. All true learning starts with the essential declaration of I don't know, but I want to understand. Once I accepted my vast lack of knowing, once I created the void, understanding crept in. Claiming knowledge I didn't have, was a do not enter sign to real knowing. I had to sit down, open my arms, my head and my heart and be receptive to all that entered. The blinding flashes of the obvious that brought clarity, the words that made me chafe and especially that which created discomfort. All of this is a needed companion to my white privilege. I can't give up my privilege but I can own it and marry it to genuine understanding, authentic conversations and a willingness to keep talking about it until it resonates with every soul I can reach. I will agree to stand in the messiness these conversations create and maintain your dignity and mine. I will make a sacred vow to keep learning. I will no longer stay silent.

White people, we need to talk.

Autumn is a middle aged white woman who realized how much she didn't know about all the implications and manifestations of racism, and is now working diligently to get herself as well-informed as she originally thought she was. She manages her own business, Yellow Wood Pathways and is a national trainer and online educational facilitator. She writes and produces national training curricula and writes her own blog. She is also writing a memoir entitled, "Lies My Father Taught Me and Other Stories of Love" as well as writing a Christmas story with her teenage granddaughter. She hopes to marry her ability to teach and write to connect with other people who are also on a racism learning curve and seeking to change this world so future generations won't have to explain why Black lives matter. She and her husband, Chris live their lives by a creed of hospitality and a sign by their front door reads, "The Lubin House. Where everyone is family." Autumn can be reached at: amlubin@gmail.com; www.yellowwoodpathways.com; or www.enterwithagentleheart.wordpress.com.

A Sleeping Giant Has Awakened

By Natalie Manuel

"I CAN'T BREATHE." These were Eric Garner's final words before he died, while being restrained in a chokehold by police officers on July 17, 2014. His words perfectly frame the African-American experience in the United States. Being Black in this country is absolutely suffocating. There are some days when it leaves you feeling breathless.

African-Americans are dying in epic proportions in the US, and much like the other officers on the scene of Mr. Garner's death, many fellow Americans are standing idly by watching it happen. However, while much of America sleeps on the injustices that continue to plague communities of color, a sleeping giant has awakened. People of all races and from all walks of life have had enough! Many have taken to the streets to declare: BLACK LIVES MATTER.

In August of 2014, reports of police brutality began to dominate the news. I remember being on Facebook, when the story of a fatally shot, unarmed teen made its way across my news feed. His name was Michael Brown, Jr., and his body had been riddled with bullets. My first reaction was, *"Wow. Not even a dog is treated this way."* I was angry, but sadly, I wasn't surprised, because Black men in America have been brutalized by police officers long before the days of Rodney King.

As the investigation into Mike Brown's death continued, I recall watching on CNN, as protesters gathered in the streets of Ferguson, Missouri. My emotions were all over the place on that fateful evening. I was extremely grateful for the young people who bravely took a stand in the name of justice. While I was angry that it took something so tragic to bring attention to an issue that has been problematic for so long, I felt a sense of empowerment because our voices were finally being heard – thanks to the people of Ferguson.

Being perfectly honest, the killing of the unarmed teen Michael Brown, Jr. single-handedly changed my view of humanity for the worse. On the one hand, the protesters made me proud. I never knew I could care so much for a group of people that I didn't know. I fell in love with their tenacity. I love the fact that they refused to "go home," as so many had been calling for them to do. The Ferguson protesters represented all the things I wish I had the courage to do myself. On the other hand, I felt like we had suddenly stepped into a time machine to revisit an ugly past.

At a time when African-Americans were simply seeking justice and equality, along came racism and bigotry, slithering their way to center stage, in all of their hatefulness. As I scrolled through the comment section of an article posted online the day after the first protest in Ferguson, I remember reading the vilest, most cruel things that literally brought me to tears. When I tell you it felt like I had walked into the middle of a Klan meeting, I am not exaggerating. There were people referring to Blacks as the n-word, savages, apes, gorillas, monkeys, criminals, thugs, and a host of other racially charged slurs and expressions. Some individuals even thought it would be cute to create and post memes of the deceased teen, as he lay bleeding out into the street. As if all colorful language and insensitive memes weren't wounding enough, everywhere there was the "Black Lives Matter" hashtag, a resounding "All Lives Matter" hashtag followed. The fact that bigots, even to this day, attempt to derail the conversation, and try to turn this space in history into a debate over a hashtag, is overwhelmingly vexing.

Fighting racism, while simultaneously fighting for the right to live is completely exhausting. There are days when I am so weary and worn, that I have to be intentional about seeking the good in life. Nevertheless, the fight must continue.

One of the more difficult tasks of this modern-day Civil Rights movement has been the attempt to explain to individuals that Black Lives Matter does not aim to exclude. Instead, this movement includes anyone who recognizes the existing racial disparities against minorities here in the US. It's not about tearing down White lives, or any other lives for that matter. It's about holding law enforcement accountable for the years of abuse against communities of color. If the people who are chanting that All Lives Matter is truly concerned about all lives, then there should be no reason to take issue with the Black Lives Matter movement.

Black people are the ones being hunted down and slaughtered like animals. Therefore, we are the ones who have a responsibility to be vocal on this issue. Until the status quo truly reflects liberty and justice for all citizens, then the continued amplification of Black voices is a must. Black people are Americans too, and we deserve to have the same rights as our fellow Americans.

Eric Garner got it right. Some days it gets hard to breathe. Not only are Black people fighting for equality, we are fighting for our very existence. This is not about a hashtag, nor is Black Lives Matter merely a slogan. It is a pronouncement. We have raised our voices to let the world know that we are tired. We're tired of being overlooked. We're tired of having our experiences dismissed. And we're tired of being shouted over by the likes of people from "All Lives Matter." No longer will we allow ourselves to be pushed around by the barbaric system of White Supremacy. Black lives matter. They always have, and they always will. Black people know it, now we just need the rest of society to get on board. If you are not for Black liberation, then step aside because the rest of us have work to do.

Natalie is a 39-year-old single woman who has been advocating for social justice and equality for many years. She was born and raised in Texas, and now resides in Mississippi. She's a full-time nanny to her two beautiful nieces. She can be reached at: Pinknailpolish76@yahoo.com.

Hoodie

By Jennifer Watley Maxell

February 12, 2012

Today we wore our hoodies to church to bring attention to the senseless death of Trayvon Martin. As I dressed my children in their hoodies, the irony was not lost. I thought about Trayvon's mother and the number of times she must have done the very same thing, never imagining that one day her son would be the one to die. I am sure she never imagined that she would be on the national news demanding justice. I am sure she never thought that she would have to find a way to clear her son's name. As I pull my son Max's hoodie over his head and explain the significance of our efforts, I pray that I will never have to feel the pain that Trayvon's mother and so many others have felt. As I look into his little 6-year-old face, I witness his furrowed brow denoting the slipping away of a piece of his innocence.

Having grown up in a predominantly white suburban community for most of my life, I know what it's like to be a target. To be followed around the pharmacy and offered too much help in an effort to be kept in view. I know what it's like to have guidance counselors tell me not waste my parent's money going out of state; a state school is good enough for me. I know what it's like to be told that I'm pretty for a Black girl and that if I were white, I would probably be prom queen and I know what it's like to want to believe that my children will never experience those same things. I have grown up in "post-racial" America or at least that's what the politicians and media outlets want me to believe. In this version of America the racial dividing lines are so faint that many try to deny their existence. The political pundits, politicians and powers that be try to assert that discrimination is a figment of our imaginations and that the reason for the violence, low testing scores and lack of adequate housing in Black communities, lies within those communities.

Since racism and discrimination no longer exist, these power brokers want us to believe that the playing field has been leveled and opportunity is available for all. While I agree that people should pull themselves up by their bootstraps and work to make their dreams a reality, I also believe that in a country like ours, everyone should receive bootstraps as their birthright. I was sickened and appalled by Newt Gingrich's comments about President Obama's remarks that Trayvon Martin would look like his son if he had one. Mr. Gingrich's comments only demonstrated how out of touch and insensitive he really is. There was no need for the President to infuse the issue with race, because the countless Black people that have been profiled recognized it when they saw it. This time though, it's not just us, there are countless white people, Asians and Latinos who recognize it also and donning their hoodies in protest.

While I don't consider my family to be disinherited, I am feeling the pressure and lamenting the reality that my children, especially my son, will too. Deep in my heart, I always knew they would, but I wanted to believe it would be different for them. Trayvon Martin's death and the fight for justice following it represent a renewed loss of innocence. For so many of us, we thought the days of picket signs and marches had passed but as we raise our hoodies we remember the words of our forefathers that "injustice anywhere is a threat to justice everywhere" and "power concedes nothing without demand".

This was a reflection that I wrote four years ago while in seminary for a Theology of Howard Thurman class. Howard Thurman was an African American mystic, author, theologian and civil rights leader who was known for his many writings including his book *Jesus and the Disinherited* wherein he draws on the personhood of Jesus as a poor disinherited Jew to assert a Christology that puts Jesus on the side of those on the margins of our society. I wrote this reflection not knowing that Eric Garner, Tamir Rice, Sandra Bland and so many others would follow Trayvon Martin. I wrote it not knowing that #Blacklivesmatter and #Sayhername would become a part of our lexicon. I wrote it not knowing that the paradoxical pendulum of hatred and violence would continue to swing further and further back to the Charleston Nine, a sitting U.S. senator calling a sitting U.S. President a liar on national television, and the comparison of The Black Panther Party to the Klu Klux Klan as a reaction to a Super bowl halftime show. I wrote it as a mother trying to figure out how to prepare my son...my 6-year-old son... to live as boldly and freely as any other child, knowing that the assertion of his freedom could cost him his life.

Howard Thurman believed that Jesus' radical love ethic, an unconditional love of God, and the God within all of humanity allows the disinherited to resist oppression but at the same time do no harm. This radical ideal of love allows people to endure and resist oppression by maintaining the sanctity of personhood within the soul. My son is 9 years old now and he isn't innocent anymore. He is still sweet and respectful but he's also a little angry, a little on edge. While he laughs and enjoys the normal joys of boyhood, he isn't quite as carefree as his peers. He is still a boy and yet I as his mother struggle with raising him in a way that is safe and maintains the sanctity of personhood within his soul. *Black Lives Matter* because my son matters and he deserves to grow up worried about sports, his grades, girls, or weather he'll ever complete his baseball card collection. My son does not deserve to grow up worried about whether or not he will see 12 years old, and if he does, whether he will be someone's target. As his mother, I don't deserve to worry about the sanctity of personhood within his soul. Even though we donned our hoodies four years ago for Trayvon, we don them today for all the Trayvon's we hope our children never become.

Rev. Jennifer Watley Maxell is a writer, educator, church co-founder (The Breakthrough Fellowship in Smyrna, GA), life coach, motivational speaker and preacher. Jennifer received her Bachelor of Arts degree in Philosophy from Howard University, and her Master of Divinity degree from Emory's Candler School of Theology with Certificates in Black Church Studies and Religious Education, and was ordained an Itinerate Deacon in the AME church. Jennifer currently resides in Smyrna, GA with her husband, Charles and their three children, Madison, Charles III and Skylar. She can be reached at: jennmax@msn.com.

White Child on a Bus

By Auburn McCanta

"Does this wash off?" I asked the man in the bus seated next to me, leaning into him, rubbing his arm with my small fingers. I was four. Living in an all-white neighborhood, I'd never seen a person with a skin tone different from mine. Wonder and curiosity swelled inside my body. This was a teachable moment, and my mother (a staunch Eisenhower Republican) was seated two rows behind me and unable to hear my question to the man—the first Black person I'd ever seen.

"No, this doesn't wash away," the man said, smiling, soft, generous to a small child. "In fact, lots of people look like me. Some people are born with skin like yours, some people are like me, and lots are somewhere between," he said. I nodded gravely at the significance of this new knowledge. I made a note about the shape of his ears, and then offered a list of the books I liked. I was a curious and chatty child—no subject was left unexplored. As we bumped along rainy Portland streets, I grew to love that man with his dark skin, his broad smile. I cheered that he too loved my favorite book, *Br'er Rabbit*. I think he liked me.

I knew I liked him.

The man on the bus was my first diversity instructor. There have been many since. There was my high school biology teacher, Leon Jordan, who was selected as a top-four finalist for America's teacher of the year. He threw chalk at me if I didn't have the right answer. There was Mary Carter who flagrantly cheated off me during an important college mid-term exam. She then turned herself into my dearest friend and, together, we helped every one of our classmates not only pass that class, but excel to graduate with high-honors. None thought of our skin color. We were each simply students working to help others become a little better the following day.

I'm now at the cusp of my 71st birthday. I was two years old when Jackie Robinson became the first Black baseball player on a major league team. I was nine when the Supreme Court decided on Brown v. Board of Education, frustrating the notion that school segregation was a noble and lofty idea. I was ten when Emmitt Till, a fourteen-year old boy, was brutally murdered for allegedly whistling at a white woman. And only ten when Rosa Parks was arrested and jailed for not giving up her bus seat to a white man. I was twelve when I watched the quiet, dignified resistance of the "Little Rock Nine" students who simply wanted to go to school. On the news, I learned of sit-ins and freedom rides and church bombings, as well as the horrific Mississippi burning.

I've watched moon shots on television. I've danced to Elvis. I've grieved the deaths of Martin Luther King, Jr., President John F. Kennedy, Bobby Kennedy, and so many others who have yearned to make us a more inclusive nation. I listened to Martin Luther King, Jr. and heard his "I Have a Dream" speech, gasping with tears and hope. I voted for President Barack Obama. Twice.

I cried for the historical beauty of America's first African American President, while still weeping for our country's obsolete and offensive ideas that continue to encourage a system of chronic and intractable racism.

I've watched us dismiss one another and include only those we think are "our" people. Although I see our young people embracing the benefit of loving one another precisely *because* of our perceived racial and cultural differences, so many still carry on with the horror and sadness that skin color is the proper, albeit illogical, factor in determining who is advantaged and who is left out. Who is jailed and who is celebrated. Who gets poisoned water and who benefits from its sale.

I'm disturbed that we still live with the notion that skin color is what gives advantage to some, while dismissing the humanity of others. We continue to separate ourselves with a color fissure that insists on jailing Black boys at an alarmingly high rate, while white boys are given hardly a lecture for the same thing. When a self-appointed "neighborhood watchman" was unbelievably acquitted after he had profiled, followed, and shot to death a young Black teenager, a collective spark ignited and the Black Lives Matter movement flamed into being. The white response was, "Well, all lives matter, don't they?" Yes. But, the institutional racism that has chronicled the Black experience is something that no white person (including me) can truly understand or incorporate into their family history. Since the first white person set foot on this country's shore, people of color have been denied safety, self-respect, economic and educational opportunity, decent housing, healthcare, and many of the hidden advantages that white people easily enjoy. As a white woman, I'm ashamed. Black lives *do* matter—equally and without equivocation or exception.

For me, diversity is a journey that started on a rainy bus day with nowhere to sit but next to a man who looked like the drawing of Uncle Remus from a favorite story. I was enchanted by the magic of his shining skin, his deep and smiling bass voice. But the striking thing—the thing that most impressed my small years was the wrinkled disapproval on my mother's face, the firm yank on my narrow arm, as I was trying to wave good-bye to the man whose skin baffled me only long enough to know that it didn't wash off. Without an overt word, I learned that a friendly gesture was forbidden when it came to people other than *our* kind. I was a white child on a bus, yet it was a kind Black man who whispered me forward into embracing and finding the truth in knowing that his life mattered—no matter what my mother's face told me. My marching days are over, but I can still stomp my feet and write my truth. I can still be a voice for positive forward movement, and I can still vote for those candidates who truly understand that—Black Lives Matter!

Auburn McCanta is an award-winning fiction writer and poet. With a background in homeless advocacy and environmental law, McCanta served as Founder and CEO of the Homeless Advocates and Service Providers Association. She served as an Ambassador to the National Alzheimer's Association, and was a primary member of the Arizona Alzheimer's Task Force. Her advocacy is fierce and uncompromising. She can be reached at: amccanta@gmail.com.

I Am Not A Racist… Am I?

By Don Miller

I understand "white fragility" and now understand I have it. Because of my "white privilege" I did not even know I had it. I know other people who refuse to recognize their "white privilege" or that white privilege actually exists. I guess they, like me, have an excuse although not a good one. You see for sixty-five years I have been white and have no desire to change who I am. I just want to change the way I think about certain issues such as race. I do not apologize for the fact I am white or that I view the world through white eyes. I just want to learn and understand…and be a better person because of it. For the first twenty-three years of my life I swam in a culture awash with "whiteness." Schools, textbooks and what little media there was, were all presented from a white viewpoint. In most cases I "feel" little has changed. Back then, in the fog of my youth, African-Americans were on the fringe of my peripheral vision or in some distant city, seen only through the screen of my black and white television. It would be impossible for me to view the world any other way. But…I do have a brain and a desire to change the way that I look at the world.

I grew up in an area and in a family neither racist nor prejudiced… overtly. Now I realize there were covert lessons to be learned and I learned them well…even though I didn't realize it at the time. When I went off to an all-white college the lessons became more overt. The fight song was officially "Hail to the Redskins," racist in its own way, but we played "Dixie," much more. I hate to admit that the de facto anthem of the Confederacy still causes chills to run up my arm. I CAN admit it because it is my "Southern white privilege" to do so. My first collegiate history course was taught by a disciple of the "Lost Cause" history of the Civil War although I would not realize this fact until I heard him speak at a "Sons of Confederate Veterans" meeting...the only one I ever attended. I decided, on my own, that despite their claims to the contrary, they were, in fact, racist...as am I. It was the only class I took under Dr. "White Supremacist" and I was fortunate to have a "damn Yankee" husband and wife team for most of my American History courses. They did not believe in the "Lost Cause." As I have been too slow to realize, I don't either.

The first time I came into contact with large groups of non-white races was in the teaching setting...students, players and teaching peers. I studied all of my new black friends and students...and Asian or Hispanics. I also studied my white friends and I had an impossible time reconciling what I was hearing about groups of people with the people I knew. The group "stereotypes" did not fit with the individuals I had gotten to know. The stereotypes could not be correct. For me this was an epiphany, not caused by a lightning strike on the Damascus Road, but rather a realization that occurred over time. Much like Job, I attempted to avoid being called to a cause and admit to having been a "closet non-racist" racist for too many years. I also admit to continuing to think of the "stereotypes" when I looked at groups of people I don't really know. I believe many of us, of all races, continue to express this view and can't seem to admit to the creation of a "system" which, in itself, is racist.

We sit back in our "Ivory Towers" declaring how non-racist we are and wring our hands over what is happening in cities like Chicago. We rail about how the "liberals" or "thugs" have destroyed the city and make jokes about turning the presidential "rallies" into "job fairs" to keep the protestors away. We are blinded by our own "whiteness" and refuse to admit that those of us at the top of the racial strata have caused the problems not only in Chicago but in cities throughout the country, despite the money we believe has been thrown at the problem.

After the "Great Migration" of Southern blacks to Northern and Western industrial centers to escape Southern Jim Crow, "we non-Southerners" defended our "birthright" with violence, intimidation and legal maneuvering that included mortgage discrimination and restrictive covenants in order to restrict where people of color could live, work and chase the "American Dream." Later, in the Seventies, cities underwent what was called "White Flight" as whites with means fled to the "burbs" and a better life "away from those people." So why didn't the people of color just leave the decaying inner cities for better opportunities? I am reminded of a Chris Rock standup routine bringing attention to starvation in Sub-Saharan Africa: "Why don't you just take them to the food?" I posed that question to a group of ninth graders in a geography class and was not surprised to find their answers to be quite mature. "Lack of resources to move, unfamiliarity with the new area, not wanting to leave families behind, fear of the unknown, civil and religious wars, and people did not want to accept them." I would say most of those statements are true about Oakland, Atlanta, Baltimore, or any of the other areas "we white folk" proclaim to be bastions of free loading and democratic liberalism, along with the thought "Why should they have to leave." More to the point "These people" are right where "the system" wants them and "these people" are angry about it...something we racist can't see or understand.

I have been fortunate to make contact, through social media, with many former students. Some are very conservative, others very liberal and they represent a broad spectrum of races and religions. I read some of their post and am shocked and appalled at their thinking. Recently I made contact with Dr. Mary Ann Canty Merrill. I remember her as a pretty little black girl with a big smile who sat very quietly in a ninth grade class many years ago. She went by the name Mary Canty back then. Today she is a beautiful and capable woman who is anything but quiet. Among her titles, which includes psychologist, teacher, life strategist, author and humanitarian, are the descriptors warrior and provocateur. I would add activist. She is ACTIVELY involved in a WAR over the way people view and think about race. The term provocateur is defined as someone who provokes and she has certainly provoked me into thinking differently about my past life and what I want to do with the years I have left. She has also provoked me to re-edit a dozen or so "essays" I had written about "Heritage and Hate" as it relates my home state and the Confederate flag issue. Oh well, it's just time.

Mary is not a "thug" looking for a "handout" as many of "these" people are being "wrongfully" portrayed. She is actually a "white bigots" worst nightmare. A successful, intelligent black woman who is not going to sit quietly on her hands. That sure goes against the stereotype presented by "certain" people. All of my friends of color go against the stereotype I see advertised by "certain" people. My friends and acquaintances are educated, black home owners, with families, who go to work every day and pay their taxes...just like me. Despite their successes and their hard work to realize them, they too are pissed off at the "system" that I believe "we white folk" have created and maintained for the past one hundred and fifty years. I cannot imagine how people who have spent decades without resources are feeling.

This former student has certainly become the teacher and the new student has become a rapt and uncomfortable learner. After being allowed to join Mary's website "Voices for Equality," I have found myself shocked, appalled and quite uncomfortable with the anger I found. I also find myself being "educated" as to why there is anger. Like Saul on the Damascus Roads, the scales have fallen from my eyes but the landscape, bathed in bright sunlight, causes me to squint and cock my head to the side in wonder. "How did we get ourselves in this hot mess?" My conclusion is that the "system" has always been a hot mess, now suddenly uncovered and stinky. Because of my comfortable "white privilege" I had been able to ignore it.

I say these things because I am still learning, still evolving as a person, an "old dog" attempting to learn new tricks...something I wish the rest of my generation might emulate instead of sitting back and being comfortable looking through their "white eyes." I have been told repeatedly that people are flocking to a certain presidential candidate because they are unhappy. Shouldn't we also recognize that the unhappiness spans all races and our history? Shouldn't we ask the question "Why?" There is an answer somewhere if you are willing to allow yourself the opportunity to find it. You might start by asking a black friend...or making a black friend.

I salute you Dr. Merrill. I'm writing this piece during Women's History Month and want to acknowledge that you are carrying forward the same traditions of women who have passed before you. Thank you for carrying on with the standard.

From your racist student.

Don Miller is a retired history and science teacher and coach of forty-two years. He has a Master's Degree in Administration and Supervision from Clemson

Mary Canty Merrill, Ph.D.

University and a Master's plus Thirty in Science Education courtesy of almost every college in the state of South Carolina. He was named state coach of the year twice in baseball and once in soccer. Drawing heavily from his rural upbringing and career, Don hopes to continue writing while operating his "organic" hobby farm with his wife Linda Gail, also a retired teacher and coach. He can be reached at: cigarman501@gmail.com.

Dear White People: It's Not Always About Us

By Jared Lucas Nathanson

Fellow white people... **Black Lives Matter.**

Does this statement seem hostile or confusing to you? No pressure or judgment, I'm only asking how you first feel when you hear it, because we should be honest and we should take a moment not to say what we feel people want to hear. We should analyze what we feel when we first hear or read the statement "Black Lives Matter."

Do you feel that the phrase is needlessly exclusive? Does it make you feel left out or less important? It's okay to admit that. It's understandable that you feel that way. We white folks often feel that when we hear voices of struggle demanding parity. We often feel uncomfortable or left out, but the question is, "what are we left out of?"

We are left out of the need to demand our relevance, because we are relevant. We are secure. We are left out of the inability to be recognized for our importance in our communities and places of employment. We are left out of the need to demand safety, the need to convince authorities that we are not a threat. We are left out of the terror of worrying that our children will be treated without compassion, with actions rationalized and protected by imagined or concocted fears and poorly formed bias, again and again hardwired into systemic action, so that every interaction is a potential risk with catastrophe.

We are left out of pain, fear and the struggle to...matter. Because we matter. White lives most assuredly matter. White lives most unequivocally matter. White lives are treasured, protected, loved, respected, defended, nurtured, redeemed, considered, valued, avenged, mourned, remembered, canonized and considered meaningful.

The statement "Black Lives Matter" does not need a caveat about us. Our society hums with the significance of white lives. There is no question about how much white lives matter, and still it makes us feel weird, because the statement is one that does not include us. As I've already indicated, we are very accustomed to the conversation always being about us.

We don't need to exclaim that "All Lives Matter." This statement, while a nice idea of general equality, allows us to water down our focus and dilute the demand to matter for those that need to demand that they do. Those that are oppressed and hurting need the focus. It's simply good triage.

The question isn't *"Do all lives matter?"* The question is *"Which lives matter?"*

Right now, in this country, looking for pure equality between Black and white Americans, what is the discrepancy? What is the difference between two people up on the same drug charges, what are the possibilities of indictment, conviction, length of sentence, even arrest in the first place? What is the difference between two people up for the same job, what are the possibilities of hiring, salary, promotion, firing? What is the difference between those two people's chances of accumulating wealth, property, education, general health, or lifespan? What is the difference between those two people's chances when encountering police?

These questions have clear answers. Scientifically irrefutable evidence that comparably, Black Lives Do Not actually Matter as much. Blacks are, when all other conditions are exactly the same, more likely to be arrested, indicted, convicted, sentenced longer, not hired, paid less salary, not promoted, more often fired, poor, renting, homeless, under-educated, less healthy, live a shorter lifespan, suspected, feared, threatened, harassed, beaten and murdered.

In fact, feeling excluded is an actual sign of our privilege, as much as not getting to take medicine is the privilege of those who are not sick.

We feel uncomfortable and excluded from needing to demand our basic rights, because comparably, we have them. So much so, that we lack the empathy to understand the horror Black lives go through every day and we embrace the ridiculous concept that we are upset for being excluded from having to fight for our right to matter.

Be careful what you wish for. We could not take it. Not a week or a day of it. The strength that comes from centuries surviving oppression holds weight that would push down on our unburdened shoulders with deep and heavy reality. We would scream and shout and go mad with the pressure to need to look at everyone we pass on the street, in stores, at work and interact with in our daily lives and project onto them that *"I am not a threat." "I am a competent person." "I am where I belong." "I am capable." "I will not steal from you." "I am valuable." "My life matters."*

We would do better to affirm the question "Do Black Lives Matter?" with the answer **"Yes Black Lives Do Matter!"** We would be better off to accept that sometimes, if we truly care about equality and parity, it is not about us.

Black Lives Matter is triage. We need to stop distracting the discussion and actions of activism by asking "Why were we left out?" The answer is "because we are damn lucky!" It's not always about us.

Jared Lucas Nathanson is the lead singer of the Boston-based band, The HeartSleeves and an activist involved in anti-racism and anti-oppression politics. He can be reached at: jared.nathanson@gmail.com.

Coffee Makes You Black

By Linda Neff

Front of the line
Class line
VIP line
Coffee line
County line
Redistricting line
Cross the line
Worry line
Voter ID line
Lead pipe line
Back of the line
Shackled line
End of the line
Line-up

Lines. They surround us. They define us. Lines drawn by the powerful to create spaces to sort and delineate society into any number of categories: rich, young, privileged, poor, educated, disadvantaged, suburban, ghetto, uptown, downtown, race, gender, political bias.

Lines with the power to box and trap us within our own lived experiences. Lines of entrapment designed to keep the privileged safe and the disadvantaged at risk. Lines seemingly etched in place since the dawn of slavery in this country.

While etchings can fade with time, this is not the case in Milwaukee, Wisconsin, one of America's most segregated cities. Milwaukee also claims one of the highest incarceration rates of Black males in the country. The demarcation between rich and poor, Black and white is all too visible.

Nearly half of my lived experience as a white female has been in Milwaukee. It wasn't until the last seven years working for the country's largest reproductive health care provider that I began to find the edges of my entrapment and slowly venture beyond.

In earlier years, I had briefly caught a glimpse of the edge of my lived experience as a freshman at Purdue University in 1979 when a cross was burned on the front lawn of a Black fraternity—of which I did nothing about, other than go to class. That experience of not standing up and allowing myself to remain trapped within my own female identity of privilege served as an important precursor to more actively engaging in social justice.

The story I want to share though is about the power of finding the edges of our own lived experiences. The story of physically moving beyond those lines to seek knowledge and understanding allowing each of us to become the change we want for the world—especially for one of the most important movements of our times—Black Lives Matter.

This is a story about a Saturday in July. Specifically Saturday, July 13, 2013. On that particular Saturday, I hurried to finish my chores and errands to attend the debut of Kwabena Antoine Nixon's first book, *Eye Write What Eye See*. Kwabena is best known for his advocacy work among African-American youth and as a powerful spoken word artist.

Kwabena's book signing was only a few miles from my home. Sadly, I needed to plug the address into GPS. You see, my destination, Coffee Makes You Black, was beyond the not-so-imaginary line segregating Milwaukee. Despite its closeness, its location was a distant land for me.

During my short drive, I listened to radio reports detailing the Trayvon Martin case as the jury deliberated behind closed doors. The media speculated on what the jury may or may not be discussing as I crossed the line between predominately white and predominately Black. My thoughts, however, were focused on the violent end of Trayvon's life and the risks associated with being young and Black in our country.

With Trayvon and his family on my heart, I walked into the coffee shop. I sat down and listened to Kwabena share his story of growing up a young Black male on Chicago's west side... his father murdered when he was 11, his mother strung out on drugs leaving him in the care of his grandmother, aunts, uncles and cousins. He talked about the constant fear of being in the wrong place at the wrong time. Waking each morning knowing this was the day he could be killed... the continual sadness of another friend or family member being gunned down.

In contrast to his untenable circumstances, Kwabena was surrounded by the grace of his family, friends, teachers and his beloved grandmother who sacrificed significantly so her family and Kwabena were always first. Together their voices supported his big dream: to become a poet and a writer. He spoke of how important his grandmother's voice was in shaping his path and her examples for walking it boldly.

Despite his path riddled with danger, danger from which he will never entirely be free, Kwabena achieved his dream. He is a published author, poet and activist using his words and his voice for the greater good of Black lives while bringing awareness to the lived Black experience.

That day, the day the world would hear the jury's decision regarding Trayvon Martin's death, Kwabena's words and story were validated and cheered by children, peers and elders. As an invited attendee, I too wanted to cheer Kwabena shouting my own words of encouragement as he spoke. I wanted to place my arms in the air like others were with palms facing upward as an outward sign of support. As the only white person in the coffee shop, I recognized our separate and distinct lived-in Black and white lines. It was not my place, nor my right to co-opt this rarified tradition of exuberant support.

While the energy, love and excitement filling the coffee shop that Saturday were palpable, I walked out feeling despondent. Throughout the telling of Kwabena's story, I struggled to comprehend the life he and so many others in the room had experienced under the same sky I call America and Kwabena writes about as AmeriKKKa. A country where the rules are different if your skin isn't white. A country where being young and Black is an unforgiving and unsafe place. A place where running out for Skittles is a death sentence.

Coffee Makes You Black. Despite the coffee shop's name, coffee will never make me Black. I will never know what it is to be Black in our country. And I will never know what it is to be a Black mother and raise a Black child in this country.

What I do know is I want to strive for peace and understanding to help bridge these dividing lines that exist in communities across our country. To do this is to believe and have faith in an America where people of color are no longer trapped within the lines of economic slavery. Where social justice moves with fluidity throughout the Black lived experience.

While coffee won't make me Black, it is the medium in which we can all begin to cross society's drawn lines in our own efforts to build peace, understanding and equity for Black lives – one cup of coffee and one brother and sister at a time.

Linda believes in the power of individual and collective voices to share uniquely, compelling stories to positively shape our lives, our communities and our world. In 2013 she created the **Selfies for A Cause Project** *which has been profiling a different non-profit each day since its inception. She is also a contributing author to the* Women on Fire Volume 2 *in which she shares her story of finding her voice later in life. You can learn more about Linda on her blog at* www.voicesofpearls.com *or contact her at:* lrneff@gmail.com.

Mary Canty Merrill, Ph.D.

Living in a Dystopian World

By Leslie G. Nelson

That's how we stay young these days: murder and suicide.
—Eugène Ionesco, *Man with Bags*

Most of us love dystopian stories. Whether we are looking down the arrow shaft with Katniss, fighting with Tris, or looking over our shoulder for Big Brother, our fascination with dystopian novels is unmasked. Concepts from dystopian novels like "Big Brother" and "the red pill" have become part of our everyday vocabulary. And why not? It's fun to be scared and know at the end that you can turn off the movie or put down the book and return to your normal life.

I remember the first dystopian novel I ever read; it was George Orwell's *1984*. Ironically, I read it in 1984. Even though it's been just over 30 years I still remember vividly the chill of Big Brother watching my every move. My deepest fears are realized at the ending. Since then, I've reveled along with everyone else in *Brave New World*, *The Hunger Games*, *The Giver*, *Divergent* and many others.

But what if we were truly living in a dystopian world? Dystopia is defined as an imaginary place or state where everything is unpleasant or bad. It is said to be totalitarian or environmentally caused, but all the dystopian novels I've read were totalitarian in nature. Considering this I thought about Stalin, General Mao, and of course, Hitler. As Americans, we are fascinated with the Holocaust as much as dystopian fiction (if the number of books and movies about this time period is any indication). We shudder at the horror of it, but can't look away. What must it have been like to live in fear of your own government? To know that one wrong word,

Why Black Lives Matter (Too)

one listening ear and you could find yourself hauled away by the Nazi's. A universal question plagues us, why did the German people allow this to happen? Why didn't they stop it? Surely we would do something if that happened today. Or would we?

Contemplating all of this, a disturbing thought hit me. Is that what it feels like to be Black? To feel as if you are living in a real life version of a dystopian novel? The thought was chilling, but I couldn't shake it.

I'm white, and one of my sons is currently living in Ghana. I smiled at the thought that he could meet a young woman there. What beautiful children they would have. And then it hit me: a tiny glimpse of the fear that comes with raising a Black child (and suddenly White Privilege took on a whole new meaning).

Like the people in the districts of *The Hunger Games*, Black parents fear for their children's safety daily. All parents have fears about their children, of course, but as a white mom, when I gave my children 'the talk', it's about the birds and bees. When Black parents give their children 'the talk' it's about how to respond when a police officer stops you. In an article, *"What black Parents Tell Their Sons About Police"* Jazmine Hughes explains, "Being a black parent, especially of a black boy, comes with the added onus of having to protect your child from a country that is out to get him—a country that kills someone that looks like him every 28 hours, a country that will likely imprison him by his mid-thirties if he doesn't get his high school diploma, a country that is more than twice as likely to suspend him from school than a white classmate."

That is what it means to live in a dystopian world. And their fears are not ungrounded. Some of their 'tributes' have been Emmett Till,

Trayvon Martin, and Tamir Rice. The trouble doesn't stop with the police. Black children are in danger in schools as well. According to nationwide data by the U.S. Department of Civil Rights Office, "In the most extreme case, more than half of all 4th graders retained—56 percent—were black, according to the data, which account for about 85 percent of the nation's public school population. In 3rd grade, 49 percent of those held back were." While education is important for everyone, the stakes are particularly high for Black men. For example, according to the Brookings Institution, there is an approximate 70 percent chance that a Black man without a high school diploma will be imprisoned by the time he reaches his mid-thirties.

The worrying doesn't stop when a Black son is grown up. A recent sociological study has proven that even those Black men who do not do time in prison will have a harder time finding employment than a white man with a prison record.

Like Jewish people and other "outcasts" in Hitler's Germany, Blacks must be ever watchful. Things that white people do without thinking can lead to devastating—even fatal—consequences for African Americans. For example, I grew up among rednecks and guns were common. Many boys received shotguns for their twelfth birthday. People carried them in the window of their pick-ups. But it's different when you're Black. Tamir Rice was twelve when he went to the park with a toy gun that a friend had given him. Police drove up and shot him within seconds of arriving on the scene. John Crawford III was walking through Walmart, talking on his cell phone when he picked up a pellet gun that was out of its package, lying on a shelf. Crawford then walked around the store, carrying the gun idly while still talking on his phone until police arrived and shot him. He later died at the hospital. The officers were not indicted in either case.

It's not just carrying a gun that can endanger a Black man. Akai Gurley died simply because he was in the wrong place at the wrong time. He and his girlfriend walked into the stairwell of his apartment building and Gurley was shot by a jumpy new police officer. The officer was indicated in this case.

If your child has a mental illness, the stakes get even higher. Tanesha Anderson suffered from schizophrenia, and her family called the police to get assistance in getting her to the hospital for an evaluation. Tanesha resisted the police officers and died on the sidewalk before her brother's eyes. Unfortunately, this family's tragedy is not an anomaly.

If a Black child falls ill, they are also at a disadvantage. ABC News recently reported on a study revealing racial bias in medical care. This was not the first study to discover such findings.

For those who are willing to seek it, the truth is far scarier than fiction. To be Black is to live in a dystopian world. The only question that remains is what we are we going to do about it? Will we ignore the pain of others just as the people in *The Hunger Games Capitol*? Generations from now, will people look back on this era and wonder why we didn't do something to stop the cruelty and injustice?

What are we *actively* doing to let Black people know that their lives DO matter to us?

Mary Canty Merrill, Ph.D.

Leslie Nelson lives near Seattle, Washington with her husband, five children and one crazy dog. She loves writing and reading and is awe-inspired by Toni Morrison. Leslie is the author of Touching His Robe: Reaching Past the Shame and Anger of Abuse. *She can be reached at: lesliesillusions@gmail.com.*

Black Lives Matter, and There's Nothing Debatable About It

By Kevin Odom

Why do Black lives matter? The short and simple answer is this: Because live all other lives, Black lives matter, too. The unfortunate thing is the manner in which Blacks have been and continue to be treated in this country which has forced the establishment of the Black Lives Matter movement and the resounding phrase "Black Lives Matter."

It is very sad that saying "Black lives matter" is so threatening and discomforting to white people. It's the truth, so shouldn't make any white person feel threatened at all. It is an outcry from the Black community that their lives are consistently and disproportionately being threatened and snuffed out merely because of the color of their skin.

Black lives have been devalued since the first African slaves arrived on the shores of America. They have a documented history of being kidnapped, stripped of their families and culture, sold into slavery to the highest bidder, tortured, whipped, raped, lynched, and even today, profiled, harassed and murdered at the hands of police who have taken an oath to protect and serve. This insane behavior *must* stop, because Black people are human beings and their lives *do* matter.

Despite popular belief, the Black Lives Matter movement is not anti-white or anti-police. It is anti-white supremacy and anti-police brutality. The Black Lives Matter movement is not saying that other lives don't matter. It's saying that Black lives matter, too. In fact, the movement would have never been created if Black lives *really* mattered at all in America.

When we examine the recent police killings of unarmed Black men, the underlying assumption that police were created to serve and protect the community is all but erased when we consider that although Black men make up only 6 percent of the U.S. population, they account for 40 percent of the unarmed men shot to death by police in 2015. This is beyond reprehensible!

We white people have and continue to collectively disregard and devalue Black lives. We often ignore the racism and injustices that are leveled against them. We want to live comfortable in our own white privilege and turn a blind eye to the disenfranchisement and maltreatment of Black people. But don't you understand that our silence is complicity?

Another issue looming large is the appropriation of Black culture. White people will claim to feel threatened by and superior to Blacks, yet we don't think twice about stealing and proudly embracing elements of Black culture, as if it's our own: innovations, art, music, dance, language, style, food, and many other aspects of Black culture. Why can't we honor Black culture through homage rather than shamelessly steal? Why can't we love Black people as much as we love Black culture?

It is not the responsibility of Black people to inform or educate us. It is incumbent us white people to challenge our outdated values, beliefs, assumptions and perceptions of Blacks. Black lives are not only valuable, but they have made significant contributions to American society. In fact, this country was built on the backs of Blacks and the very soil is infused with their blood, sweat and tears.

Why Black Lives Matter (Too)

While we may not want to remember the tragic history of Blacks in this country, we can never forget it.

Let us examine our values, beliefs, attitudes, assumptions and behaviors as we drop the white guilt, white tears, and feelings of superiority.

Let us stop claiming to be colorblind as we acknowledge, appreciate and embrace racial diversity in all of its forms and richness.

Let us open our hearts and minds to the stories, pain and plight of Black Americans as we eradicate injustices that are perpetrated daily.

Let us live and let live as we demonstrate love and compassion for our sisters and brothers as human beings, regardless of race, creed or color.

Let us use our white privilege to challenge racism, prejudice, discrimination, police brutality and every other injustice leveled against Blacks in America...

Let us overcome our smugness and boldly proclaim that Black lives matter, too!

Kevin Odom is a free-spirit from the mountains of East Tennessee. He believes in every human's right to "be and let be." He sees everyone's color, because he is not color-blind. He also values the differences in the color of humanity and celebrates those differences. He is proud to have been afforded this opportunity to share his thoughts on why Black lives matter, too. Kevin can be reached at: thekevinodom@gmail.com.

Mary Canty Merrill, Ph.D.

Taming the Beast of White Privilege

By Kendra Penland

I am white. I'm not sanctioned to speak for all whites, but I will. If so many can ask the one person of color you know to represent the "Black community" at every board or department meeting in your community, I guess I can stand in for my lily white brethren just this once.

My entire life's perspective, regardless of how accepting and inclusive my upbringing, is based on the generational tradition of indoctrinating children into, and perpetuating in adults, a cultivated and socialized racism. We are all subject to it. This is why otherwise "reasonable" people tense at the sight of a group of young Black men walking down a street. This is why a young Black child receives the "most athletic" award at a kindergarten awards ceremony, when all other awards are academically focused or character-based. This is why non-Anglican names are punch lines for subtly racist jokes and barriers to employment or advancement. This is why a Black 12-year-old child, playing in a park, is now dead instead of enjoying life with his family.

I have spent most of my life being told that where, how and to whom we are born is all secondary to what we do with our lives. It was a precious gift given to me by my parents. It is also wrong, a patent falsehood, at least in terms of the greater context of the world in which we live. To have the capacity and the requisite context to entertain such luxurious thinking is afforded only to those enjoying white privilege, and often with an added dash of economic comfort.

To hear that, and not question it…to believe you have the world at your feet, there for the very taking (funny, because that's just what whites have done since time immemorial: taken) and you can be anything you like if you are willing to work for it, is most certainly a truth, especially if you know the right people. But mostly, because you have a hope and a future story as a result of a cultivated white manifest destiny. What a *privilege*.

For centuries, there has been a dedicated effort by whites to elevate white members of society via efforts that vary from suggestion, to coercion, to physical torment. In order to elevate one group, another one, in this case people of color, must necessarily be diminished. See how rational this all sounds? So, you oppress and/or enslave the very ones who provide the labor, literal blood, sweat, and tears, required for your elevation. So they will continue to have no choice but to comply, because you have the power and they have no choice.

The greater the temporal distance between white cultures who instituted this inherently racist system and the whites of today, the less responsible and more removed contemporary whites feel they must be from the onus. They didn't own slaves. They didn't segregate their stores. Why can't you just get over it, people of color?

Because, in the grand scheme of things, as whites have advanced, they have done so while many people of color struggle, or even be purposefully limited. And as society has "progressed," it has done so to the detriment and on the backs of people of color.

It has been proven that women of color have to work twice as hard as anyone else to attain the same level of accomplishment, thanks to a double whammy and healthy non-stop dose of misogyny and racism.

So many whites are adamant that there is no longer an issue with racism in this country, because they know, deep down, it means acknowledging disparities and examining themselves. In doing so, they fear, and they are right to do so, that they will discover some very uncomfortable truths about themselves and those they revere.

White fragility is a thing. Whites don't want to believe this, because it fractures their carefully constructed world of white supremacy. To believe that they are only superior because they have done so at the expense, and to the detriment, of an entire group of people is too much to bear. Or maybe that's too much credit. Maybe it's just about fear of being "less than."

Acknowledging that fear requires a logical and fair-minded intellect to consider the fairness, or lack thereof, in this arrangement. It would then follow that restoring balance requires relinquishing privilege. A life without privilege—what does that look like? Feel like? How does that change one's life? How does that change one's value—in the eyes of self and others? Why would one ever want to know if they didn't have to?

All life has value. Yes, in the grand scheme of things, all lives matter. Except that argument hasn't existed until whites felt threatened by a changing tide, by a movement and a growing lack of acceptance of "how things are." For hundreds—thousands—of years, people of color have been used and abused by people in power, institutions, and systems of government, as if they were commodities. And not only have they not derived any benefit from this abuse, they have been systematically marginalized and intentionally prevented from accessing information, public facilities, private businesses, basic rights, educational and career opportunities, being able to love, being able to live in peace as a family without fear of being separated for the profit of a master...people of color have been denied human and civil rights in the this country in ways that no white person—even those in poverty—have been. And it's all because of the color of their skin.

Black lives matter uniquely because white lives have always been drawn to, and ultimately absorb, usurp, steal, and appropriate the value from Black lands, music, fashion, food, art, the very images of people of color, benefit—even profit—from them. Yet, the same white culture that finds Black culture a business opportunity, a fad, an object of desire, will marginalize, condemn and criticize people of color for daring to claim—or reclaim—what was theirs to begin with. It is about damn time that Black lives not only mattered, but also received preferential—at least equal—treatment.

White privilege is an insatiable beast, with a cruel and contradictory need to devour the lands, the cultures, the lives, and even the very souls and spirits of the people of color from which it derives its strength and sustenance. Always taking, slashing and burning as it goes, until it has used up all there is to be had, then moving on to the next quarry.

This is our beast, white people. We must domesticate it, train it, or kill it. This is our charge alone, white people. It is not the responsibility of people of color to guide us or to tell us how we must rectify the situation. We know how. We just don't want to believe and accept our complicity in it. However, until we accept our role in creating this monster and make peace with our culpability, it will never die. This beast is a creature of white society's creation, and

Mary Canty Merrill, Ph.D.

it is our birthright and responsibility to dismantle it by intentional, daily practice while sitting in the discomfort of knowing that we have a bloody, horrific pedigree. It requires forgiving ourselves. It requires getting past the white tears and living daily as allies and accomplices for social justice and equality.

Kendra Penland is a proud mother, the Executive Director of an industry trade organization, and a committed rabble-rouser with a lifelong commitment to benevolent Machiavellianism. She likes bourbon, singing jazz, and asking questions. She can be reached at: <u>kendrapenland@yahoo.com</u>.

We Have to Say Black Lives Matter... Because in America, They Don't

By Michelle Rashid

If Black lives *really* mattered, we wouldn't need to say it. If they *really* mattered, we wouldn't have developed this concept or this rallying cry. We need something to align with and to provide clarity and truth about racism and what we can do to eradicate it and support the struggles. We need clarity about what the problem is – how wide spread it is.

Black lives matter is the right phrase and the right movement, because Black lives really don't matter in this country... although they should. How can anyone argue that All Lives Matter when there is pervasive racism in our society? White lives matter. Wealthy lives matter. Blue lives matter. These groups do not need a rallying cry, because they are not being oppressed and dehumanized.

Black men, women and children are murdered and mistreated by our society and the majority of people don't seem to care. Are we in denial? Do we not care? Do we not feel connected to Black people as fellow human beings? Is it fear? Is it apathy? Is it a sense of not knowing what to do or what to say? When death doesn't open our eyes, what will?

Racism is so pervasive and deeply ingrained in our culture that it actually seems normal and people don't even see the problem. The denial is almost as staggering as the problem. Racism and prejudice are subconscious in all of us. *"We can change the world but some of us are not tryin'"* is a lyric by Tru ID, a Seattle-based band. So let's change the world or at least try. How?

Mary Canty Merrill, Ph.D.

As white people, we must examine the alarming statistics that highlight the injustices that are occurring all around us. We must work to raise our awareness and increase our cultural competence and sensitivity. We must work harder and use our privilege to bring issues of racial injustice and inequality to the forefront, talk about them, and take purposeful action to eradicate them.

W. E. B. Du Bois said that at the heart of all prejudice lies ignorance and fear. To address ignorance, we must raise awareness and tell the truthful stories that need to be told about America's shameful history of racism and oppression. We must face the glaring statistics and engage in difficult conversations. We must stand beside the victims of racism and oppression to acknowledge their experiences and understand their feelings. We must support the struggle and hold one another accountable to promote racial justice and equality. We must exercise our voting power and actively participate in changing our decision makers when their policies fail to represent the equal rights of every human being in this country, regardless of race, creed or color.

Fear is a huge issue because it is connected to power. People in power fear losing it but they only need to share it. To address fear, we must first acknowledge ignorance and do our part to educate others. Only through awareness and education can we begin the process of understanding and eventually healing. We must rally around movements like Black Lives Matter. We must take deliberate and consistent action to speak out and stand up for injustices whenever we see them. We must intentionally fight the systemic and blatant disregard for an entire race of people.

Former United Nations Secretary General, Kofi Annan said *"Ignorance and prejudice are the handmaidens of propaganda. Our* mission, therefore, is to confront ignorance with knowledge, bigotry with tolerance, and isolation with the outstretched hand of generosity. Racism can, will, and must be defeated."* We must create the spaces to confront racism and then actively listen to the stories and experiences that are shared. We must take responsibility for the individual role that we each must play in overcoming racism and oppression for a better humanity.

Stop sitting on the sidelines or merely rendering lip service. Get actively involved. Do something constructive—anything—starting today. It's going to be a messy journey, and it's going to be hard. But the time to act is NOW… because Black lives matter, too!

Michelle is the Director of Culture and Organizational Development in her own firm. In both her professional and personal life she is deeply driven to support fairness and equality and fight against injustices. She is committed to being open and continually increasing her awareness by taking responsibility for more than just her own life. She believes in a collective effort to serve the community in which she lives. Michelle can be reached at: mrashid@virtuoso.com.

Mary Canty Merrill, Ph.D.

Thoughts of a Recovering Racist

By Rhonda Lee Richoux

Why do I care about my brothers and sisters whose skin breathes Africa and whose pain breathes America? This isn't Disneyland, this is reality. Dog eat dog. Every man for himself. Pull yourself up by your bootstraps and you can be anything you want to be. We have a BLACK PRESIDENT so everything is hunky-dory. GET OVER IT! Yeah. That's what the white man says.

The white man: killer, kidnapper, rapist, enslaver, the white man does his thing. The white man will be king. The white man makes us sing "God Bless America", but his America is not my America. My America hasn't been born yet. My America rejects the "separate but equal" compromise of the modern day racist. My America rejects the disparity in justice along racial lines that dominates our system. My America rejects the police state that exists to administer its racist two-second street trials by which police become judge, jury and executioner in the time it takes to identify Black skin and draw a gun. My America rejects white history as the only history, rejects white feelings as the only valid feelings. My America rejects white privilege, even as I benefit from it. My America has yet to be born.

I've written three drafts of an essay about why Black lives matter to me. I threw all of them out. They were very nice, very thoughtful, and very interesting. But they were disingenuous. It felt wrong to tell the quaint story of how I found my way through the passive racism practiced by my family and peers in New Orleans. The realization as a teenager that I was a racist, and the realization that it would take a lifetime to repair my mind, heart and soul, overwhelmed me at one time. It doesn't overwhelm me anymore, but it makes me angry that I was indoctrinated by good people that I trusted for truth. New Orleans, for the most part, was not like the rest of the South. We didn't attend KKK rallies, but the "otherness" assigned to Black people by the non-Black residents was no less shameful. Separate but equal. Yeah, I remember. I remember the white and Black water fountains. I remember the separate lunch counter at Woolworth's. I remember being the darkest person at my school, and feeling out of place because of it, but understanding that I was allowed because I wasn't Black.

Having been raised in New Orleans in a diverse neighborhood, racism wasn't taught in word, but in deed. I learned by observation. I learned that we don't call Black people "Nigger", but we don't invite them to dinner, either. I learned I could have a Black boy for a friend, but I couldn't date him. Filipinos, who had faced discrimination themselves, wanted to distance themselves from those on the bottom of the heap, always trying to be good citizens, to have the approval of the white ruling class, to stay at least one layer above the bottom of the social heap. I learned that being brown didn't mean I was "white enough" in every situation, just that I was white enough to go to school with white kids. I learned that white people were afraid when Black people started speaking up and demanding their rights, because they were sure "they" wanted to take over the country. I also learned that my family talked equality but walked a different walk, and I had to face the fact that my brown skin didn't shield me from receiving the indoctrination of racism. I am 63 years old, and I am a racist in recovery.

So why do I think Black lives matter? Because they do! Latino and Filipino migrant workers were abused and mistreated in the farmlands out west and in the fish canneries of Alaska. Native Americans are subjected to blatant racism in states with large

Native populations. I know I was mistaken for a "dirty Injun" in Arizona. I went through one month of degradation and got just a tiny taste of what it means to be a part of the "other."

But ANYWHERE IN AMERICA, Black people are still at the tail end of the social order that is dominated by white, male superiority. I am a racist in recovery, and I must face my complicity in the shameful behavior of the society in which I participated if I am ever to find healing and serenity. That's why it's so important for me to say, loudly and clearly and with absolute purpose, **"BLACK LIVES MATTER!"** In a time when I hear white people scream "We want to take our country back", I want to tell them their country is dead, so they can have it. Their America was built on the blood of the red man and on the back of the black man. It's not my America. My America is yet to be born, but the labor pains grow stronger every time I hear someone say, **"BLACK LIVES MATTER"**.

Rhonda Lee Richoux is a retired paraeducator, freelance writer and native of New Orleans. She is currently researching her Filipino family history for a book she hopes to publish in 2017. She lives in Picayune, Mississippi, where she paints, writes and engages in social activism. She can be reached at: <u>rhondarainbow@aol.com</u>.

A Love Letter to Black America from Her Native Sister

By Bee Schrull

When asked the question *"Why do black lives matter to you?"* so many reasons flood my mind. I consider all the advancements in technology that have benefited our society, contributed by the brilliant minds of Black inventors.

Without Alexander Mils, a Black man, would the elevator have been invented?

Without Richard Spikes, a Black man, would the automatic gear shift have been invented?

Without Lee Barrage, a Black man, would the type writing machine have been invented?

Without Frederick McKinley Jones, a Black man, would the refrigerated truck have been invented?

Sarah Breedlove, a Black woman entrepreneur, was the first female self-made millionaire in America after she started her own line of hair and beauty products for Black women. Her company, the Madame C.J. Walker Manufacturing Company, is considered the most widely known and most successful African American-owned business of the twentieth century.

Marie Van Brittan Brown and Albert Brown were the husband and wife team who invented the home security system.

Granville Woods, A black man, invented the Multiplex Telegraph to send messages between train stations and moving trains. His invention ensured safer public transportation for cities across the United States.

Most importantly to most of us, Frederick Jones, a Black man, invented the air conditioner and Alice Parker, a Black woman, invented the heating furnace. Without access to homes with heating and cooling, lives are in danger during hot summer days and cold winter nights.

These are just a few examples of Black inventors who have truly blessed our society with their genius.

I celebrate these inventors and their intentions. Then, I consider what could have been.

Trayvon Martin wanted to fly or repair airplanes when he grew up. He was never given that chance. Trayvon could have piloted Air Force One.

Tamir Rice could have discovered the cure for cancer, or invented new green technology that changed the way we harvest energy and helped us reverse the effects of climate change.

Sandra Bland could have passed legislation that changed the nation's use of police for the better or become a legendary Black filmmaker, author or professor.

Throughout America's history, the minds of Black Americans have given birth to countless inventions. For every Black life devalued, we rob ourselves of one possible solution to great problems. We rob ourselves of one possible cure to a dangerous disease. We rob ourselves of one possible advancement in science. We rob ourselves of the possible solution to global poverty. We rob ourselves of the love and caring one human life is capable of producing—the kind of love and caring that got me through the hardest times in my life.

As a child, my life was very dark. I was abused at home in every way imaginable. The only time I ever felt happy and safe is when I was at school or at a real friend's house. As a young girl with very few safe places, my safest places were in the homes of my Black friends. Black mothers played mom to me. Black fathers stepped in as dad when mine was absent. Black shoulders felt my tears. Black arms surrounded me with love during the times when I needed it the most.

Kimberly was my very first best friend who tried, and failed, to teach me how to double Dutch. She failed not in being a teacher but in choosing a student. I laugh because my coordination in second grade was lacking at best, and she didn't make me feel insecure about it. We laughed together when I tripped or yanked the rope out of her and Amy's hands.

In fifth grade at the very beginning awkward stages of puberty, it was Vanessa who taught me to take what others said to try and hurt me and turn it into a joke to aggravate them. She showed me how to handle being picked on with grace and dignity.

Sixth, seventh and eighth grade, Brandy and I were inseparable. Singing "Motown Philly" by Boys II Men as her mother took us shopping. Watching TV together, doing homework together. Talking about the boys we liked together. She opened my eyes to what Black girls experience that I would never experience at such a young age. I remember one day she was sent home from school for wearing Bantu knots, something very, very popular among all of the female students at the time but has been worn by Black women and girls for thousands of years. Other girls in school were allowed to sport this hairstyle. She was sent home after she was told that her hairstyle was distracting and threatening to the other students. I asked her, and I still ask myself to this day, "How can a hairstyle be threatening?!?" I didn't understand then that it wasn't her hair. I came to understand as I got older that it was the color of her skin that threatened those around her. This was perhaps my first experience with misogynoir: the unique oppressive combination of sexism and racism that Black women and girls experience their whole lives. It turned me into a warrior at twelve years old.

Throughout my teenage years when I was trying to live my life with independence while at the same time needing guidance, my trusted friends surrounded me and didn't let me doubt myself. All the way into adulthood, making the right choices in life as well as the wrong ones and having the Black women I've grown to love by my side the entire time, having Black men who give me hope for the future of fatherhood constantly encouraging me, having Black women who showed me what it means to be a friend, a woman, and a fighter every day made a remarkable difference in my life. Without the love and support of Black men, women, boys and girls throughout my life, I would not be as capable as I am today of handling anything that life throws my way. Simply put, I am the woman that I am today because of Black lives... and those Black lives matter.

Every human life has value. Every human life carries with it the divine. Every human life must be protected. The justice system, the educational system, the healthcare system and every other system in this country is currently failing Black Americans in countless ways every day. Every single aspect of our society spells out the message to Black people that their lives don't matter. But Black lives DO matter. They matter immensely and they always have.

This country was founded on the blood of natives and it thrived because of the blood of Black people. This nation has come so far in its young existence BECAUSE of our sacrifices. America MUST show us some deference because of all that we have contributed to this society. America must do better by the Black community. America must bring centuries of racism and oppression to an end. America must send one message and one message alone to every single Black child in this country: "Your life matters. You can and will achieve great things. You are crucial. You are necessary. We need you, and more than ever we need what you have to offer this world. Rise. Rise and claim your place. Proudly wear your crowns because you are the future kings and queens of this nation. Rise."

Until our nation is filled with carefree, happy and hopeful Black children, our future will look very much the same as our present and our past.

Black Lives Matter.

Bee Schrull is a 35-year-old Native American woman. She hails from Tacoma, Washington and now lives in Cleveland, Ohio. Her entire life has focused on civil rights and matters of racial justice and equality. As an activist for Native Lives Matter, Black Lives Matter, and Not Your Mascots, she spends her time counseling others and fighting for the rights of all oppressed people. Bee can be reached at: beeschrull@twc.com.

Mary Canty Merrill, Ph.D.

What's Going On in America?

By Judy Shepard

For the past year and a half, the hashtag #BlackLivesMatter has been a rallying cry for a race of people who are sick and tired of being sick and tired. It's a call to action by a new breed of civil rights activists, revolutionaries, and visionaries. It's a means of gathering the people in the market place to stand together in unity to speak courageously and loudly about the frequently-occurring injustices in communities of color.

Black Lives Matter dares to pose this question to mainstream America: *"When will our lives be as valued and worthy of respect in a country that claims that "All Lives Matter", yet continues to see the color of my skin as a threat and a weapon that needs to be contained, restrained and destroyed?"* The movement dares to pose the question, *"Why are Black lives purposely, systematically, and deliberately snuffed out without thought, rhyme, or reason as society sits silently by, while another man, woman or child is gunned downed without provocation or cause, and then turn around and place the victim on trial while the accused is applauded for 'doing their job'?"* Black Lives Matter dares to pose the question, *"When will those, who defy the very laws that were meant to protect and serve all people, be held to the same standards as the people whose voices have been needlessly silenced?"*

How can anyone attempt to justify an individual being killed because their life is not valued and not feel any sense of compassion or empathy? Yet, will quickly flip the script when the victim happens to be white? Say their names: Trayvon Martin, Tamir Rice, Michael Brown, Sandra Bland, Eric Gardner, Freddie Gray,

Why Black Lives Matter (Too)

Amadou Diallo... these and countless other Black lives have been lost, without provocation. Every American should be outraged over these senseless murders and asking the question, *"What the heck is going on?"* It's sad to say that double standards continue to characterize the laws of this country. However, a groundswell of woke people is beginning to challenge this troubling and damaging status quo.

It boggles my mind how a slogan meant to convey that Black lives matter, too has been vilified by both the media and the general population as being racist and hate-filled. The Black Lives Matters slogan and those associated with it have been labeled anti-police, anti-white, and anti-establishment for simply speaking out and bringing to light the horrific murders occurring in communities of color. The Black Lives Matters movement may be many things, but racist is *not* one of them.

What needs to be clearly understood among the masses is this: In and of itself, the Black Lives Matter slogan is mere words. To add depth and meaning requires citizens to rise up and demand that America keeps her promise of justice and equality for *all*, not just some. It requires open and honest dialogue to acknowledge the reality of what is happening to people and communities of color. It requires courageous people who will take their heads out of the sand, devise strategies and implement actions to ignite change.

Like it or not, the Black Lives Matter movement is here to stay. Its roots are deeply entrenched in the history of this country. It was conceived through the blood, sweat, tears and struggles of our ancestors who came before us. It was born of the refusal to be treated as less than human. It was cradled in the arms of those who walked a long and tumultuous road to pave the way for a proud race of people. You may try to bury us, but we are seed. We have taken root and will blossom, bear fruit and inspire a whole new generation of warriors who are willing to stand up and speak out in the name of social justice and equality, because Black lives matter, too!

Judy Shepard is a Southeast Queens, NY native currently living in Floral Park, NY. She is a gifted singer-songwriter and is currently one third of the Joyriffic Band as a singer and arranger. Judy holds a B.S. degree in Management and is currently working on her M.S. Certification in Marriage/Family Counseling. This is her first published piece. She can be reached at: sugar1049@gmail.com.

Why Black Labeling Matters, Too!

By Dan Spencer

Let me state for the record that I am about as white as a homo sapien can be genetically. I recently submitted a DNA sample to an online site primarily to find my birth family, since I was given up for adoption at two days old. My ethnicity was also determined by this procedure. I was really hoping to have something interesting in me like Native American or African ancestry, but my hopes were dashed when the results became available.

Being white, some people who share my ethnicity feel that it's okay to make racist remarks about Black people around me. Obviously, these are people who don't know me very well. These very same individuals feel that racial epithets are okay to label Black people who are otherwise behaving badly in some manner. Under the same circumstances with white people, a nonracial, but unflattering term would be used instead. Let's not mince words. The only difference is their deep-seated hatred of Black people.

I met my birth mother for the first time in my life two months ago. She lives in North Carolina adjacent to the border with Virginia. Our first face-to-face meeting took place in the comfort of her living room. We sat side by side on her couch and chatted for four hours straight. We shared many personal anecdotes with each other. My maternal grandmother died around three years ago. She was in her early 90s at the time of her passing. During the last months of her life, she was cared for by a Black woman. My mother insisted on making that abundantly clear to me at the beginning of the story. Once an allegation of embezzlement of my grandmother's checking account was made by my mother, her caretaker suddenly became an N-word. Okay. I understand that the caretaker might have stolen money from my grandmother, but why is a racial slur necessary to describe the suspect? While I did not speak up as I probably should have due to the circumstances of our first meeting, I did give a look of disapproval that I think was lost on my mother.

My mother's husband took me back and forth to my mother's house from where I was staying during my trip. On the way back, he also thought that it was appropriate to describe another Black person with the N-word. Once again, the person in question was alleged to have done something wrong. I don't remember what that was now. Did it even matter that the accused was Black?

I have found over the decades that some white people are prone to emphasize that it's understood that when a Black person commits any form of misdeed that they definitely need others to know that the person in question is Black. In the vast majority of cases, the person's race is irrelevant. It's only pertinent, in my view, if the person has committed a racial hate crime against someone of another race. That very same relevancy works for all races.

So when is it necessary to identify someone's race apart from your local *gendarme* looking for the alleged perpetrator of a crime? Let's say that you're at a party with a large group of people of vastly one race. For example, it might be helpful in a sea of white people to point out someone of another race with whom the person that you're socializing with might want to meet and discuss the ethics of GMOs. It's no more racist than identifying a redheaded person in a throng of blondes. There's no problem factually stating that Obama was the first Black President, especially given the historic aspect, but his detractors will frequently articulate and frivolously cite his ethnicity when speaking out against him or his policies. Was

Obama the first President who created unpopular and controversial policies?

When you are describing a person of another race to another individual of your race, please remember this: If your story does not require that subject's race to be identified, just don't do it.

Dan Spencer is a free-thinking ethical vegan and father to three non-human children. He was given up for adoption at two days old and recently reunited with his birth family. Dan is in the process of preparing for the next exciting phase of his life. He can be reached at: 4dandroid@gmail.com.

Mary Canty Merrill, Ph.D.

How Did We Get Here, and What Will We Do About It?

By Valerie Stephens

The reason I committed to being a contributing author for this book project is because I am currently living in a country that does not value Black lives. It never truly has, at least not for the right reasons. America itself was built on the subjugation, exploitation and degradation of Black lives stolen from Africa. This is indisputable, and yet rarely discussed in detail.

The propaganda and lies promoting the falsehood of white superiority were immense and widespread and used as a form of justification for the atrocities of enslavement and worked to dehumanize Black lives in every way imaginable. These lies were rampant and in perpetrated in our media, newspapers, radio, movies and educational system. This propaganda still affects us and is in effect to this day. The trauma is stored in DNA, the lies instilled and enforced with terrorism and direct violence for hundreds of years. It lingers still, in the form of exclusion and coded character assassination.

My argument is this: As a society, we have yet to hold ourselves accountable for these atrocities. The falsehoods of white supremacy have been allowed to rot and trickle down through the centuries, affecting generations of people.

We can see this at work in the adamant denial of facts, especially by those of us who are white. Countless videos of Black men shot and killed by the police, hauled off to jail wrongfully, their civil rights violated and the majority of white society hardly blinks.

Cold, hard facts available online with a single click showing that Black Americans are incarcerated at higher rates, die earlier and are more likely to be subjected to environmental pollutants – none of which is actively addressed by those in power who just so happen to be predominantly white and male.

Many do not see what is before their very eyes. Some white people live in so great a bubble of privilege that they are blind to the realities of institutionalized racism. Others see it, but are overt racists who actively seek to devalue Black lives whenever possible.

Each day, more of us are waking up to the stark realities in this country. We see the crimes against humanity that have occurred and that are ongoing. We want to hold our country and ourselves accountable. We are ready and willing to flip the script, to say it loudly, to boldly affirm that BLACK LIVES MATTER, TOO!

That time is now.

Valerie Stephens is a white anti-racist living in Northern California, born to the movement after the death of Sandra Bland. Sandra awoke in Valerie a capacity to see institutionalized racism for what it really is and speak out against it. For this awakening, she will be forever grateful. Valerie can be reached at: Val576@gmail.com.

Mary Canty Merrill, Ph.D.

Vigilant At the Gate: Black Lives Matter, Too

By Susanne Sulby

Every human being born into this world deserves the same amount of love and adoration. Babies come to us as these beautiful little beings, tiny hands, warm skin, lips smiling with peals of laughter pouring out of their mouths. They come with the hope of the future. What is it that happens between that beautiful beginning and the onset of adulthood that turns our love into suspicion of the 'Other?" That turns white against Black and Black against white? I believe it is a quiet indoctrination that begins in our earliest years and is handed down through generations. This prejudice is often delivered in hushed whispers, indifference, and at times, blatant unapologetic disdain for Black people, culturally and systemically. It's insidious and sometimes difficult to see, when one is not the recipient of it.

In contemplating this subject, it hurts me to realize that many people still do not believe that there is a deep vein of systemic racism and personal bigotry in American culture. And then there's this recurring thought: If I, a white woman, feel uncomfortable with the pain of just *thinking* about this kind of racism, what must it be like for those who have to *live* it?

I believe I bring a unique perspective to this question. You see, I grew up in a prison. My father, a retired Marine, was the last live-in warden at the Bucks County prison in Doylestown, PA. I learned early on that once a prisoner was brought into the prison, my father held the responsibility for that person's safety. These responsibilities were taken seriously. Numerous safety measures were taken during the admittance to the prison. For example, prisoners were required to turn in belts and shoelaces to ensure

Why Black Lives Matter (Too)

they would not kill themselves or harm other inmates. One would expect the same standard of responsibility to be upheld by law enforcement officials. I do understand and deeply respect the job that law enforcement officials are tasked with. There are plenty of very dangerous individuals who can and do cause them harm. However, they are the ones in positions of power and must be held to a higher standard.

On my father's first day of work, one of the guards ran in to his office and explained they had a problem with a new inmate and they did not know what to do. When my father, a 6'5" retired Major in the Marine Corp heard this he jumped to his feet and accompanied them to the holding cell. Here he witnessed a newly processed inmate, a large Black man, running from one end of the cell to the other end of the cell and bashing his own head against the wall. Apparently the prospect of spending time in prison was too much for this man to accept, death by any means was his choice. This was a county jail with 130 inmates and the guards did not know what to do. My father needed to act or this man would surely die. He had the guards open the cell door, tackled the man and sat on him until medics arrived and could sedate him. He understood his responsibility to protect this man, even from himself. As I grew up I learned that in his tenure as a Warden he started the first work release programs, Education programs, counseling programs and Drug and Alcohol treatment programs in the country. He explained to me that he believed his job was to rehabilitate not punish. The punishment was already meted out in the loss of freedom.

It has been more than 50 years since that event took place. Currently, Black men are incarcerated at much higher rates than whites, making up only 13.2% of the U.S. population and 40% of those incarcerated. It would be easy to say that the Black community creates this, that we all have a choice to be criminals, and in many ways that's true. However, even if someone has committed a criminal act or is suspected of committing a criminal act, they are still human beings. They have rights. Additionally, I challenge the idea that this is solely a Black cultural problem. With lower high school graduation rates, unemployment rates for young Black men at nearly twice the rate of their white counterparts and an ongoing national cultural storyline that paints young Black men as dangerous "thugs," is it really true that young Black men are free to create their own destiny?

When I drive my car, I'm not going to be pulled over because I'm in the wrong neighborhood; when I go into a store I'm not going to be followed around because I'm white. When I apply for a job or an apartment or credit I am not going to be dismissed *because* of my skin color. Therefore it would be easy for me to believe it's not happening. Yet I know that it is.

We are one race, the human race. Human beings created the concept of race, as well as racism. Race is about the pigment in our skin, the same thing that determines eye color. It is absolutely ridiculous to believe one group of people is better/smarter/more deserving than another because of the color of their skin. I am paraphrasing Jane Elliott, the anti-racism activist, here. Her message is powerful and true.

Black lives matter because if my brother suffers, I suffer. We truly are all connected. The only way to not feel this is to remain disconnected from yourself, to live in such a way that you feel inferior and must project that onto others. Slavery, bigotry, and fear mongering are not new ideas. But they are very tired old ideas.

What *is* new is that we are in a time where vast groups of people from all different walks of life agree that equality is a good idea. Slavery ended a little more than 150 years ago, the Civil Rights movement took place just over 50 years ago and globally apartheid in South Africa ended in 1994! My point is this: we have made progress, and we should use that as leverage to keep moving forward. It is our responsibility to speak up and continue to call out violence and racism whenever it happens.

This is why the Black Lives Matter movement has caught on so rapidly. Many, many people are outraged by police violence. Many more are aware that we must insist on fair pay for hard work. This is, in my opinion, extremely important. If a parent must work two jobs simply to pay rent and put food on the table, there is little time left to invest in the development of the beautiful children in that family. We need to level the playing field in order to give Black families and youth a fair chance at building a future. We need to tell the truth about systemic racism. And we need to be vigilant at the gate of our own hearts so the cancer of racism can no longer grow.

Susanne Sulby is an author, actress, producer, coach and teacher. Her most recent project Sanctuary, *a play about the cycle of war, was recently produced off-Broadway to critical acclaim. In addition to* Why Black Lives Matter (Too), *Ms. Sulby's writing will be featured in the upcoming book* Essential Wisdom. *She lives on the East Coast with her beautiful family, and can be reached at:* susannesulby@gmail.com.

Mary Canty Merrill, Ph.D.

Black Mental Health Matters (Too)!

By Erin Conyers Tierney

Depression is a scourge that is ravaging the African American community. According to the Health and Human Services Office of Minority Health, African Americans are 20 percent more likely to experience serious mental health problems than the general population. Although anyone can develop a mental health problem, African Americans sometimes experience more severe forms of mental health conditions because of unmet needs and other barriers.

Depression can be prompted by a chemical imbalance, stress, and general despair. It can also be triggered by institutional racism and poverty. Studies have revealed that the painful effects of racism may trigger not only short-term sadness or anger among African Americans, but also deep bouts of depression, anxiety, and other serious mental health issues that tear at the very fabric of the Black community.

With racial tensions at an all-time high in America, Blacks are very likely to suffer battle fatigue as they combat persistent stereotypes, institutionalized racism, discrimination, microaggressions, a lack of empathy and other social ills that are imposed upon them daily. All of these factors can and do have a detrimental impact on mental health. Even perceived maltreatment has been associated with adverse psychological and physiological consequences.

Another disturbing trend is economic disparities. African Americans are disproportionately affected by poverty. People experiencing homelessness and exposure to violence are at a greater risk of developing mental health conditions. According to the 2012 U.S. Census Bureau American Community Survey, the poverty rate for all African Americans was 28.1 percent. This concentrated poverty extends out the door of a family's home and occupies the entire neighborhood. Consequently, many African Americans are forced to live in blighted communities where they cannot feel safe in their own neighborhoods, let alone their homes. A family's home is supposed to be a safe haven where they can take refuge from the ever-present hostilities of this world. Yet, for many Blacks, the lack of a domestic sanctuary can trigger and exacerbate depression and anxiety. Unfortunately, no amount of antidepressants, anti-anxiety drugs, or counseling can transform a home into a place of refuge.

Along with constant stress, anxiety, and violence, comes Post Traumatic Stress Disorder. While the rate of PTSD is the same for Blacks and whites, it is often misdiagnosed in Blacks and may be more difficult to assess because of their emotionally blunted presentation (avoidance and numbness).

Socioeconomic factors play a vital role in African Americans' ability to treat their depression. Many are subjected to tenuous, low paying, high stress jobs, making the ability to afford a co-pay or being able to take time off work, which might be unpaid, is an undue burden and a substantial barrier to a Black person wanting to seek treat for their depression. In fact, this only makes it worse, feeding a vicious cycle.

Despite these alarming statistics and because of racial stereotypes and stigmas surrounding mental illness, many African Americans continue to suffer in silence. They do not want to be perceived as weak or accused of "airing their dirty laundry" in public. Therefore, rather than seek medical treatment for mental health disorders, Blacks will generally turn to their faith and prayer. One study also revealed that African Americans who knew they suffered from depression preferred to "handle it" themselves, while a smaller percentage sought help only from family and close friends.

In addition to mental illness being a taboo topic in the Black community, mental health providers can be insensitive to the cultural experiences and needs of African Americans. It is important for mental health professionals to keep in mind the pressures and cultural differences of African American clients, as well as clients of other races. Establishing boundaries and knowing the proper limits is crucial when counseling patients of color. Most importantly, it is vital to provide communities of color quality mental health care services and properly diagnose the mental health problems that plague their communities.

While it is unwise not to seek treatment, it is even more disheartening to know that disproportionate barriers impede African Americans' access to mental health services. In order to encourage Black people to seek treatment for depression, mental health professionals must be ready, willing, able and available to serve lower income clients. Access to effective mental healthcare is paramount to promoting social justice and equality! Effectively diagnosing and treating depression and other mental illnesses among African Americans will provide immeasurable benefits not only to their Black community in particular, but to our society in general. Black mental health matters, too!

Erin Conyers Tierney is a graduate student at Liberty University and is studying to become a school counselor in order to help future generations of children. She is recently married to her husband, Kyle. Erin can be reached at: getkreative@aol.com.

Say Her Name: Blackness at the Margins and the Erasure of Women in the Movement

By Muthu (Jordan) Weerasinghe

On a warm night in May of 2015, a rally for Rekia Boyd was held by "Black Lives Matter NYC"; the turnout was less than a hundred to honor the 22-year-old, slain by an off-duty police officer. It was a less than modest turn out for a city that has seen thousands of mourners for the Black men who have been murdered.

In the era of Black Lives Matter, of civil rights, of abolition, Black women have always positioned themselves at the frontlines demanding justice for the state sanctioned violence committed with impunity on Black bodies. Yet, while we lead this charge as we always have, the narrative remains centered on cis-heterosexual Black men. While credit is begrudgingly bestowed upon few of the Black women in leadership, we are still struggling for an acknowledgement of our pain. The number of protesters present at the rallies of Black men versus those present at the rallies for Black women are proof of the lack of interest surrounding Black women. It is without question that the highest rates of unemployment, incarceration and support of the prison industrial complex are attributed to Black men, while they conversely have the lowest rates of high school and post secondary educational attainment. These malevolent facts sound the alarm: Black men are in distress. But so are Black women and girls.

Regardless of some progress made by and for the Black community, the gross disparities in income, homeownership, educational attainment and justice within the race is still best illustrated by troubled lives of Black men. If President Obama's initiative designed to address the unfavorable odds in the lives of young Black men (named "My Brother's Keeper) is any indication of what the general consensus is on Black lives in general, then Black women have once again been left behind. The minds of many still believe that addressing the pernicious circumstances of Black men by elevating them somehow uplifts the entire race, as a whole. The largest impediment in this equation is the conviction of social justice advocates that any discussion of Black women and girls in the larger context of Black issues is inherently divisive, a distraction from the real problem at hand. In addition to this, any strategy or initiative that could enhance the lives of Black women and girls are foiled by the lack of information surrounding them or the conditions that they may be subjected to.

The erasure of women is hardly a new development. Black women and girls have long been seen as what renowned feminist Michelle Wallace termed "Black superwoman." Impervious to the same struggles faced by Black men, Black women have always been expected to place their needs second to keeping the race as a collective on a forward trajectory. The professed heroines, the mothers, aunts, sisters and friends who both fight alongside their beloved fathers, sons and brothers, all while experiencing a very specific gender inequity within racism, are somehow still less deserving of consideration by virtue of their purported resilience and strength; we are somehow shielded.

While the contributors of this body of work seek to convince you of why Black lives matter, too, the conversation inevitably surrounds the same subjects of Blackness. I can assure you there is never a discussion of Blackness at the margins. It is never about the sisters, the queer sisters, the trans sisters, the non-gender conforming sisters.

Even as I write this, I struggle to name the very unique and persistent challenges Black women face in attempting to center our struggles of victimhood as well as being leaders in the liberation movement. My tumultuous emotions surrounding the low turnout for Rekia Boyd and other Black women are continuously dismissed. Yet my own personal struggles cannot hold a candle to the erasure and consistent suffocation my queer and trans sisters face. Perhaps the most strange in this second wave of the civil rights movement is that cities across America are being flooded by chants of Black Lives Matter without consideration of the fact that it was founded by three Black women, two of which identify as queer, yet the narrative is still only focused on Black, cis, hetero males as the only victims of state sanctioned violence, of institutional racism, of any Black burden that was ever endured.

So I urge you to take into consideration that the burden of combating oppression in the face of misogyny upon which the entire toxic patriarchal system is built is overwhelming, it is killing us. The purpose of building these movements is to free all those that labor in the chains of its oppression, but it cannot be done if the oppressive ideologies are actively perpetuated in activist spaces. Today and every day, let us say the name of every Black woman that has been forgotten, murdered, left behind, let us be our sister's keepers and never again leave them out of the discussion, because their lives matter, too.

Muthu (Jordan) Weerasinghe is a native of Washington, DC. She is a social justice activist and book worm hailing from very humble beginnings in the Diaspora. She aspires to return to Howard University to complete an M.D. She can be reached at: Jordan.s.weerasinghe@gmail.com.

Mary Canty Merrill, Ph.D.

Why Do Black Lives Matter At All?

By Crystal Combs White

On September 28, 2005, Former Department of Education Secretary William Bennett told a caller on his syndicated radio talk show that, "You could abort every Black baby in this country, and your crime rate would go down." As reprehensible as Bennett's comments may be to some, this "end justifying the means" social agenda has been embraced in institutions, law and ideology. In the ten years since those comments were made, America has reenacted a page out of Bennett's *Book of Virtues*, and put it into play in classrooms across America. There are four million Black children living in poverty and at least forty percent of those children are not ready to enter kindergarten.

Has America decided that we waste entirely too much time and money trying to prove that all children can learn, in particular Black children? Why should we bother at all to educate Black children that live below the poverty line if the facts tell us that these children will more than likely have learning disabilities and developmental delays?

"Conscientious" law makers have embraced the rationale in voting against "misappropriation of resources" to target a population that is unfit to learn. House Republicans proposed in the 2016 budget to eliminate 14.6 billion dollars in education by targeting Head Start, Title 1, and some special education programs. Schools in high poverty areas already receive less than 45 percent of state and local funding than other schools in the same district. For some Black children this means by fourth grade they will be two years behind grade level. If they are fortunate enough to even reach 12th grade they will be at least four years behind.

America is clearly incapable of addressing the achievement gap through public policy, teacher recruitment or legislation. We are striving for equality, not equity right? Teachers have enough to do without trying to figure out how unfair disadvantages and privileges impact students. Let's honor the American dream by keeping more money in the hands of tax-payers; after all, wouldn't it be a drastic measure for education financing to be overhauled to address these inequities? Without any data from sustained and adequate funding in any disadvantaged communities how can we make the case that Black children living below the poverty level matter?

Democracy is sustained with a commitment to equality. Institutionalized racism, like that existing in education is the greatest threat to a democracy. All children deserve a quality public education. When we close the gaps in equity and access we can address the democratic deficit. We say "Black Lives Matter" to remind everyone that "all of us matter. President Barack Obama said, "We are true to our creed when a little girl born into the bleakest poverty knows that she has the same chance to succeed as anybody else."

If we are to believe the persistent counterpoint to the Black Lives Matter movement that "All lives matter", we will need to start with how America treats its children. There is a contradictory nature to our democracy because America has shown no mercy on Black children. Black children have been used to dig the deep ditch of the racial divide that has grown during the eight years of Obama's presidency. That deep ditch of racial hatred is threatening to engulf all of us. Black children are drinking contaminated water, sitting in mold-infested over-crowded classrooms in schools without libraries, books or certified teachers and they are angry. Black children in America are being fed into the "grinding wheel of education" which no longer serves as the "great equalizer."

The core belief of American democracy is that access to education will ensure success. Instead, education has become a point where access and inequality collide. Data compiled by a 2012 Department of Civil Rights indicates a persistent pattern of racial disparities in discipline and academic achievement. Black children are being placed at risk of failure by the inequitable allocation of resources to education. We can't sustain a democracy by neglecting children. Education is a crucial starting point in addressing the challenges faced by racial disparities. A child realizes or loses their potential in education. The moral failure of inequitable opportunity is the heart of the Black Lives Matter movement. As a result, America can no longer avoid this conversation about race. Until these glaring disparities have been acknowledged and effectively addressed, we will continue to shout: Black Lives Matter!

Crystal Combs White is a Cleveland, Ohio native, wife, mother and grandmother. A graduate of Wayne State University, she has coordinated community and parent engagement for K-12 school communities since 1986. She also provides health and nutrition education for Michigan State University. Crystal can be reached at: cwhiteconsulting@yahoo.com.

Removing the Stain of Racism

By Rebecca Wiggins

It is a unique time in history. We are more connected to one another through technology than ever before, yet seemingly more isolated and divided at the same time. Social and news media have created a culture of constant information-sharing that often resorts to sound bites, shallow connection, and a lack of critical thinking. We are less involved in one another's lives, and struggle to keep pace in our high-stress society. It is easy to overlook or ignore injustice when it happens to someone else, which is why each of us must be even more intentional about how we live our lives, build community, and shape the future.

Growing up in a predominately white suburb afforded me the privilege of being oblivious to the reality of racism. It was not until I formed friendships with people of color that I learned the truth about what it's like to be a minority in this country, and the daily microaggressions they endure, like being followed in a store or overlooked for a job because of an ethnic-sounding name. At first, I felt ashamed of my ignorance and the lack of diversity in my life. However, once my eyes were opened to these experiences that were so different from my own, I could no longer keep wearing the blinders of privilege. I felt a responsibility to break the cycle and foster an appreciation for different cultures, perspectives and beliefs with my children.

The uncomfortable truth is that the roots of racism run deep within the structures and laws of our country, and are embedded in our psyche. *Whiteness* and *Race* were deliberately fabricated to discriminate and dehumanize groups of people for power and economic gain. Since colonization, our country has perpetuated white supremacy. This includes the Trail of Tears, the denial of the fundamental rights of citizenship and land ownership to people of color, and immigration policies that limited particular ethnic and religious groups from entering the country. It was not until the Immigration and Naturalization Act of 1965 that racial, ethnic, and religious diversity among Asian, Latin American, and African people in the United States began to increase.

Our country has worn the shameful stain of slavery and segregation for all but the past 50 years. While the Civil Rights movement led to laws for equal rights, no meaningful steps toward reparations or reconciliation were taken. It is unreasonable to assume that such atrocities, systemic oppression, and deeply held beliefs and biases can be wiped away in such a short span of time, particularly without substantive efforts for education, healing, and lasting equality. The concept of "colorblindness", or not seeing race, was intended to signal progress and inclusion. Instead, it created anger, ignorance, and division. As a result, discrimination continues unabated against many people of color, often on a subconscious level.

Even though we may oppose racism and bigotry, we are often unaware of how we benefit from a system created and dominated by white people. For example, white people accumulated and passed down generations of wealth before Black people were even able to start. According to Pew Research Center, the median household wealth disparity between whites and Blacks is the highest point of inequality since 1989 (13-to-1). A wage gap remains today where white women earn 79 percent compared to white men. However, the numbers are far worse for women of color. The American Association of University Women reports that African American women make 63 percent, and Hispanic women make just 54 percent.

Each child holds a key to our future, and should be given a fair chance for a better future that is not based on ethnicity, income, or zip code. Unfortunately, the average poor Black child lives in poverty 3 to 4 times that of the average poor white child. Further exacerbating the problems are underfunded school systems that do not adequately prepare students for success. Students of color also face harsher disciplinary penalties in school. Black students are three-and-a-half times more likely to be suspended or expelled for the same behavior as white students, which often leads to trouble with the law and jail.

Between 1970-2005, a 700 percent increase in incarceration has disproportionately impacted communities of color with 1 in 15 Black males 18 years or older in prison today, compared to 1 in 106 for white males of the same age. A criminal record prevents access to housing, employment, education, and public benefits, leaving families and communities broken, increasing the chances of recidivism.

When the cards are stacked against you, the notion of simply working harder or making better choices carries little weight. In *The Case for Reparations*, Ta-Nehisi Coates illustrates this point, "It is as though we have run up a credit-card bill and, having pledged to charge no more, remain befuddled that the balance does not disappear. The effects of that balance, interest accruing daily, are all around us."

There are things that we can do each day that may seem small, but can have a profound impact on removing the stain of racism, inequality, and injustice:

- **Learn about privilege.** Understand the differences between individual and institutional racism, and the ways that we take our possessions and positions of power and influence for granted.

- **Spend responsibly.** Financially support minority-owned businesses and organizations that have a commitment to diversity.

- **Evaluate the diversity around you.** Choose jobs, schools, and places of worship that are diverse and value different cultures. Use your positions of power and influence to apply pressure and offer leadership where it does not already exist.

- **Elect leaders who work collaboratively.** Vote for leaders who will work to overhaul broken programs and invest in education and rehabilitation for the marginalized, the left behind, and the forgotten.

- **Build authentic relationships.** Reach out to people of color and ask them about their life experiences – listen and learn. It may feel awkward or uncomfortable at first, but keep trying. *Remember, it is not their responsibility to educate us about racism.*

Perhaps most importantly:

- **Discuss race and injustice openly.** Join people of color in discussing issues of gender, race, and class across generations so that we become more aware of the injustices and work to end them.

It is not enough to say we disagree with racist practices or rhetoric. We must raise the next generation of Americans to be actively anti-racist and committed to reconciliation. We must reject the notion that equality is oppressive to white people. We must reject hateful speech or violence. We must stand with all who face discrimination or injustice. We must speak out against all forms of inequality and injustice. We must teach our children to have compassion and empathy for people who are different from them. We must prove through words and actions that Black lives matter, too.

We are called to put the needs and pain of others before our own, fight for all of God's children, and help the poor and marginalized without condition or judgment. We can end racism, but it is up to us to raise our consciousness and lead the movement. It is up to us to cultivate a new generation of leaders committed to serving others and doing the hard work of creating lasting, positive social change for all.

Rebecca Wiggins leads a nonprofit that supports financial counselors and educators, working to improve financial security for all people. She lives in Columbus, Ohio with her husband and two children and is active in the community around issues of justice and equality. Rebecca can be reached at: hoosierbec27@yahoo.com.

Mary Canty Merrill, Ph.D.

Fair Treatment of All

By Anthony M. Wiley

When I decided to enlist in the United States Navy in October of 2012, before I was shipped off to boot camp and issued my seabag, I was tasked with the responsibility of learning and memorizing the Sailor's Creed. With this creed we vow to defend the Constitution of the United States of America, pledge unquestioning obedience to superiors, and we make a commitment to excellence and the fair treatment of all.

I was bright-eyed, bushy-tailed, and eager to show my ability to take orders and accomplish tasks—and I did. Adjusting to life in the military was simple, it didn't require much thinking. We are given clothes to wear, told where to be, what time to be there, and what to do when we get there. In fact, they have an instruction for almost anything that you can think of. But, no instruction could prepare me for some of the most difficult, emotionally and psychologically draining years in my life. My first year was a piece of evenly sliced homemade red velvet cake. I had graduated from boot camp, A-school (the technical school the Navy sends us to so that we can learn our job), and was just awaiting orders to my first duty station so that I could begin my career in the fleet.

During this limbo stage I met a Chief Petty Officer who was about to retire after completing 20 years of service. He insisted that I become his apprentice so that he could train me in my profession and "kick some knowledge" before he retired—his words, not mine. Between his daily, "the Navy sure has changed since I came in" rants and the occasional, "this generation don't know nothing bout the meaning of hard work" lectures, he held true to his word and decided to pour his full serving of wisdom into my cup. Many of the gems of wisdom that he passed on were very valuable. He often emphasized the importance of saving money, taking advantage of the Navy's benefits, and staying in shape—he was a committed runner and a proud "Drunken Sailor", so it balanced out. On the day before his retirement ceremony and coincidentally the same day that I received my orders to Patrol Squadron TEN stationed in Jacksonville, FL, he stormed in the office and slammed the door shut. It was clear that he was upset about something, but I couldn't imagine what it was, considering he was only a day away from receiving his DD-214, aka his "freedom papers." Then, before I could even ask what was wrong, he called my name with authority, "Wiley!" and when he was sure he had my attention he looked me dead in the eyes and said, "If you want to make it 20 years in the Navy, you gotta learn how to play the game." He did not have to explain himself; I knew exactly what he meant. That was my indoctrination and it became abundantly clear throughout the next few years.

The "game," was learning how to function and navigate in a white-male-dominated institution to avoid ruffling any feathers and meeting opposition. I was learning well, too. My salutes were sharp, my military bearing was impeccable, shoot I even smiled when they questioned my intelligence, "Wow, Wiley that's a big word." I was playing the game and becoming very proficient at it. That is, until Eric Garner was murdered, then Mike Brown, then Akai Gurley, then Tamir Rice, and then Sandra Bland. I couldn't do it anymore. There I was smiling and pretending, trying to prove that I was worthy of being treated fairly, worthy of being present; and not demanding that they prove that they were worthy of my presence. When the Black Lives Matter movement launched, that was the first time in my life that I felt worthy. My voice was being heard, my thoughts were valuable, my presence was felt; I mattered. You probably won't believe this, but being in the military amplifies the experience of living in a racist society. Yeah, I said it! Here we are in 2016, fighting for freedom, fighting for protection under the Constitution, fighting for equality and demanding that America stay committed to the fair treatment of all. It has become very difficult repeating those words everyday, knowing that whether I am in uniform or not I will still be treated unfairly because I am Black.

Unlike most Black males in the military, I came to the realization that there could be no real progress unless we spoke out about our experiences. I transgressed, and made the decision not to play the game. For me, to play the game meant to betray my own soul on a daily basis, which eventually would psychologically destroy me. So in order to remedy the damage that was already done, I requested to have a mental health assessment done by a psychologist contracted by the military. She was a middle-aged white woman, about 5'3" and 135-pounds, max. Before my session, I was asked to complete paperwork and explain the reason that I was there. "Poor coping strategies due to existing in a racist society, stress, and trauma," I wrote candidly.

When she invited me in her office, I could sense that she was not going to be very receptive and would take much of what I was saying as an attack on her and not a critique of white supremacy. Much to my delight, I was wrong. There were many terms and phrases that we use in the social justice movement that she didn't know like "micro-aggressions", but she tried her best to understand. Ironically, she had spent time working in prisons and was very knowledgeable on the subject of corruption in the criminal justice system and how it targets men of color. She affirmed my belief that using my voice was one of the best ways to deliver truth to power and challenge a stubborn system. It has become important to me to exercise my power and raise my voice to challenge other Black men and women in the military to not play the game, but to emphasize that when we make our commitment to excellence and the fair treatment of all, we make sure that we are included—because Black lives matter, too.

Anthony Wiley is a native of Chattanooga, TN. He currently resides in Jacksonville, FL and is active duty in the United States Navy. When he isn't fighting for freedom and democracy, you'll likely find him fighting for social justice and equality, playing the piano, or trying very hard not to think while meditating. He is currently trying to hold on to what sanity he has left before separating from the military. Anthony can be reached at: anthony.m.wiley@outlook.com.

Mary Canty Merrill, Ph.D.

The Evolution of a Cacophony: Why Black Lives Matter

By Denise M. Wisdom

Once upon a clear night in February, I settled down to do my usual cyberspace perusing. As I ventured into one of my favorite local Facebook page "haunts," lo and behold, I was bombarded with a multitude of comments. What, I wondered to myself, "in the world" issue could have generated these many back-to-back comments on the Voices for Equality group page? Thanks to a forward thinking revolutionary (my words not hers), Sistah of psychology and the Catalyst of more (just more), the Voices for Equality Facebook page was birthed to stimulate dialogue, generate understanding, and create action around the issues of diversity, inclusion, justice, freedom, and humanity.

I never witnessed the original posted statement that preceded the round of comments, due to the author deleting it after the firestorm of "voices" rose to a level of discordance that normally is in stark contrast to the usual mellow discussions of outrage and insight focused on racism, discrimination, police brutality and inequalities. So I "followed" the comments on the second post which adhered to the original post. It only took a few seconds to know and understand what issue created the "cacophony of a hundred voices." Three Three words—ALL LIVES MATTER—ramped up and presented, during Black History Month, when the Voices for Equality group had already consensually deemed it sufficient and significant to acknowledge that another three words—BLACK LIVES MATTER—automatically were elevated in status and outranked the meaning/interpretation of the previous statement. I compare the level of discordance to the noise generated when playing the card game of spades when suddenly someone falsely blurts out that the four of clubs "trumps" the ace of spades. Oh the uproar!! The game comes to a screeching halt and usually someone had better be ready to face a "cursing out" or as I say in my "politically correct" voice, a "call to the truth."

As I continued to meander through the comments, so many statements flew past my eyes: *"I am not a racist"*; *"I am not a bad person"*; *"I don't fear words-I also don't like folk putting them in my mouth"*; *"I don't need to be educated"*; *"We are informing you that your choice of words are reinforcing a very harmful rhetoric"*; *"Let go of the defensiveness and learn"*; *"Don't ask a person of color to vouch for you, to defend your fragility"*; *"Why the lynch mob"*; *"White feelings have to take a backseat to Black pain"*; *"I think you just hate All White People"*.

Wow, a cacophonic discussion emblazoned with statements of a "remnants past," a past where progress was slow; where many words and sentiments were unheard, feelings ignored, and communication broken. Did this just happen right here in one of my favorite local Facebook "haunts"? Immediately my mind took me to another place in time; a time when the evolution of a cacophony took the American nation by storm. I transported back to a time of lynchings, protests via African American newspapers and journals to combat racism and discrimination, Ku Klux Klan operations across the country, and inaccurate stereotypical portrayals of Black people. A time of race riots, wicked acts of segregation, and legal fights made to halt social, political, and economic terrorism.

Just like the words on the before-mentioned Facebook page, I reverted back to "seeing" words of activists, through eras of time, fling themselves at me. These words – many grouped together in threes and fours: *"Free at Last"*, *"And Still I Rise"*, *"I'm Black and I'm*

Proud", "Fight the Powers that Be", "I Never Thought I Would See the Day", "Fight the Good Fight", "Am I Not a Man", "I Have a Dream", "Reach Out and Touch Somebody's Hand", "Young, Gifted, and Black", and *"I am Somebody"*; on and on the words flowed in and out of my vision, causing my eyes to water and my ears to ring. These words; true cacophonic disruptions designed to spark movement, elicit shared understanding, and deliver a platform of an equal and level playing field. Some did not enjoy the cacophony; others welcomed it. Words spoken by the likes of Frederick Douglass, Dred Scott, Phillis Wheatley, Paul Robeson, William Edward Burghardt (W.E.B.) Du Bois, Thurgood Marshall, Rev. Martin Luther King, Jr., Sojourner Truth, Maya Angelou, Malcolm X, Audre Lorde, Huey P. Newton, Minister Louis Farrakhan, Booker T. Washington, Gabriel Prosser, Denmark Vesey, and Marcus Garvey.

Jolted back into the present time by a different Facebook post on another page, I began to wonder if the "voices of cacophony" I had witnessed on the Voices for Equality page were "worth it." Did the voices rise up to create a shift? Did the voices spark progress in some shape or form? Did the voices just "let it go," move on and "forget the fuss" of the matter? Why do Black Lives Matter? Will the discussion generate an evolution of comprehension, action, and harmony of discovering ways to "free" people literally and figuratively from the chains of injustice, implicit biases, and institutions?

As these new "whirls of thinking" entered my mind, a new vision entered the atmosphere of my cyberspace connection. I share this vision with you. A vision of a 106-year-old woman, lively in her step, virtuously dancing toward the leader of the free world, in his house... the White House. Upon seeing him and his wife, she shouts for joy in the Oval Office. She reaches out for him; he for her. He introduces her to his wife, the First Lady. All three of them share in the perpetual motion of unity. The cacophony of pure joy and happiness, where some would consider quite unsettling in a room historically occupied by elite white men... three Black people, embracing one another in the White House. One, a man, America's first Black President, Barack Obama; the other, a woman, America's first Black First Lady, Michelle Obama. And another first, a 106-year-old Black woman's, Ms. Virginia McLaurin, first visit to the White House. Think about it... what was the experience of Black people in America, 106 years ago, when Ms. Virginia McLaurin was born? From oppression, racism, systemic discrimination, minority overrepresentation, prejudice, implicit bias, brutality, inferiority, inequality to where we want to be... freedom, emancipation, human rights, marches, movement, triumph, acknowledgment, awareness, diversity, inclusion, equality, multiculturalism. Are we there yet?

Harriet Tubman once said "Every great dream begins with a dreamer. Always remember, you have within you the strength, the patience, and the passion to reach for the stars to change the world." I am glad and grateful that my fellow "cacophonists for equality" did not fall silent when viewing the All Lives Matter post. I don't know about you, but I am willing to "pick my battles," to rise up and let the joyous, cacophonic disruption of the Black Lives Matter evolution continue to change the world. Why? Because I want to dance a "jig" and shout in authentic joy, like Ms. Virginia McLaurin, when I am 106 years old – with a little wink in my eye – knowing that there is a reason why Black lives matter, too.

Denise M. Wisdom serves as a college professor at two educational institutions in the Denver Metro Area. She facilitates curriculum in the Nonprofit

Mary Canty Merrill, Ph.D.

Management, Criminal Justice, and Human Services departments. Ms. Wisdom's professional and civic involvement includes past participation and leadership in: the Urban League; Girl Scouts; Alpha Kappa Alpha Sorority, Inc.; El Pomar Foundation's Multicultural Youth Leadership Initiative; Martin Luther King, Jr. Holiday Committee;, and the Colorado Springs Diversity Forum. She is an avid reader and aspires to become a writer when she "grows up." Denise can be reached at: <u>denwisdom@msn.com</u>.

Chapter 6

A Call to Action

*The master's tools will never dismantle the master's house.
They may allow us to beat him at his own game,
but they will never allow us to bring about genuine change.*
– Audre Lorde

What White People Can Do to Help Dismantle Racism

Few conversations elicit strong feelings and emotions as that of dehumanizing slavery and racism. It's an important social issue, but rarely does anyone want to talk about it, especially white people whose ancestry makes them complicit. It evokes feelings of shame, guilt and embarrassment to be associated with a system that widely diverges from the ideals upon which this country was founded. Nonetheless, the U.S. is expected to become more racially and ethnically diverse in the coming years—a minority-majority nation. The demography of America is changing and we are experiencing a significant shift in the racial and ethnic make-up of this country that affects the once-predominant white population.

Immigration is high and interracial relationships are on the rise. According to the U.S. Census Bureau, for the first time in America's history racial and ethnic minorities now comprise more than half of the under-5 age group. In 2014 there were more than 20 million children under 5 years of age living in the U.S., and 50.2 percent of them were minorities. The Bureau also projects that by 2020, minorities will make up more than half of children under 18 years old. This shift underscores how young people are at the vanguard of sweeping changes by race and class. Non-Hispanic white Americans are expected to become a minority group over the next three decades. By 2044, more than half of all Americans are expected to belong to a minority group (any group other than non-Hispanic white alone); and by 2060, nearly one in five of the nation's total population is projected to be foreign born. The U.S. Census considers Hispanic not a race but an ethnicity. Hispanics can be of any race, and Hispanic origin is determined on Census forms in a question separate from the one regarding race.

These demographic changes have outpaced the change in cultural norms and perspectives necessary to accommodate this level of diversity. Many white people have traditionally chosen to remain ignorant on the topic of diversity and racism, which is a luxury given their privilege, whereas Blacks' and other people of color's lives depend on having knowledge of mainstream white America. Such privilege creates an invisibility that causes whites to remain out of touch with the daily realities of racism and discrimination endured by people of color. Given these demographical shifts, white people can no longer afford to dismiss diversity or ignore issues surrounding race or the treatment of race in our larger society.

Cognitive dissonance, the mental discomfort that an individual experiences when they hold two or more contradictory values, beliefs or ideas, is one of the factors that create resistance among many white Americans when it comes down to acknowledging and confronting racism. To reduce this internal inconsistency, the individual will do whatever is necessary, including turning a blind eye to existing conditions of prejudice and discrimination.

Racism impacts us all, so *no one* is free until we are *all* free. The following quote by an Aboriginal activist sister underscores this fact: *"If you have come to help me you are wasting your time. But if you have come because your liberation is bound up with mine, then let us work together."* Black people do not need to be "saved" by white people. We want you to approach us from a place of equality and mutual respect. Positioning white people as saviors or placing the protection of white feelings and emotions at the center of conversations about racism in America puts us on a counter-productive path. White people must be willing to confront their own internal discomfort and privilege and change the narrative in order for any real social progress to take place. This requires every white person to recognize that they benefit from privilege in order to move the conversation forward.

In this Information Age, there is no excuse for ignorance. Technological advancements have brought dramatic changes to our access to information and our options for obtaining that information. This digital revolution enables people of all ages to access a full range of educational resources and learn on their own terms—*what* they want to learn, *when* they want to learn, and *how* they want to learn it.

Silence is not only complicity in wrong doing, but a betrayal of truth. If you want to be an effective ally (I'll support you as you go through the fire) or accomplice (I'll go through the fire with you), you must first acknowledge your position of privilege, educate yourself, and then take meaningful action. Don't simply believe and embrace everything that you hear or read. Things are not always as they appear at the outset. Knowledge really is power, so here are some concrete ways to nurture a spirit of curiosity, learn about cultures outside of your own, and take intentional steps to help dismantle racism.

UNDERSTAND THE CONCEPT AND TYPES OF DIVERSITY

The concept of diversity comprises acceptance and respect. It means understanding that each individual is unique and moving beyond tolerance to embrace and celebrate the rich dimensions of our humanity.

Diversity comes in many forms. The more prominent ones are: race, ethnicity, nationality, native language, gender, sexual orientation, physical and mental ability, spiritual beliefs and practices and social class. The less salient ones include: age, family status, health status, educational status, occupational status, socioeconomic status, knowledge, skills and talents, ideologies, geographical location, style, military experience and customs.

Diversity presents both challenges and opportunities. Learning to respect and appreciate cultural and stylistic differences and becoming aware of unconscious assumptions and behaviors that influence your interactions will enable you to minimize challenges and maximize opportunities.

Acknowledge That Privilege And Oppression Do Exist

As we've already discussed, racism—a form of oppression—is a persistent social problem in 21st century America. One of the reasons it has been difficult to dismantle is the perpetual denial that it and white privilege exist.

Denial comes in many forms (personal, general, situational, and group-based) and is a defense mechanism that arises as a result of positive self-presentation and impression management: few people, if any, want to be viewed negatively or perceived as a stalwart to social progress. Here are some examples of denial that you have likely uttered at some point:

I have nothing against Blacks.
I have a Black friend(s).
I'm not a bad person.
I'm not a racist.
I'm a decent citizen.
I'm not privileged, because I've never had it easy.
Racism and oppression ended years ago.

Understanding how privilege and oppression operate and how you participate—consciously or unconsciously—is the first step in the process of change. For white people, privilege evokes a psychological and emotional dependence on the rewards of power and dominance. It also yields choices, and one is to opt for the sanity of anti-racist thoughts and acts. Becoming an ally in the fight against racism, discrimination and oppression, whites must commit to a lifetime of intention and active recovery work to support their progress. This self-work is ongoing, so you can never assume that you have "finished" or "arrived."

BE WILLING TO CHALLENGE YOUR CORE BELIEFS

Each person views the world differently. Core beliefs are the thoughts that individuals have—originating from early life experiences—that determine how they interpret their experiences. For example, if you have a core belief that "people of color are inherently bad," you will believe that any person of color who conveys kindness to you has an ulterior motive—they are somehow out to "get" you.

Challenging core beliefs that bolster your prejudicial attitudes, stereotypes and behaviors helps you develop a healthier understanding of yourself and those around you. Before you can challenge core beliefs, you must first identify and understand them by getting down to the hidden beliefs residing in the unconscious. For instance, if you have a fear of public speaking, that fear is not a core belief, but an emotional reaction to a belief—not what others think of you, but what you think of yourself. To identify core beliefs, you must look beyond your thoughts and reactions. When you choose to view a core belief as an opportunity, you are much more likely to transcend and transform any negative beliefs—or those that do not serve you well—into learning experiences that can lead to healthier choices and a more fulfilling existence.

The death toll, suffering and displacement induced by large-scale conflicts engaging groups defined by race, ethnicity, religion and other social identities in this country have reached epic proportions. Eidelson and Eidelson (2003) state:

> *"The power of beliefs to influence perception and behavior has long been recognized, not only in the realm of individual psychology but also in relation to groups large and small. Indeed, beyond the realistic conflict elements of competition over resources and territory, large-scale intergroup hostilities are often driven, in part, by deeply held partisan convictions."*

The authors propose that certain beliefs underlie intergroup conflicts because they operate simultaneously as core beliefs fundamental to the daily and lived experiences of individuals. Within this framework, they identify and describe five domains that are fundamental to the individual pursuits and essential to the predominant concerns and shared narratives of groups: *superiority, injustice, vulnerability, distrust,* and *helplessness.*

Superiority beliefs rest on the conviction of being better than others. The injustice domain involves the perception of being the victim of mistreatment by others. The vulnerability domain is characterized by the view that the world is a dangerous and risky place, where safety and security are elusive. The distrust domain focuses on the presumed hostility and malicious intent of others. Helplessness beliefs involve the perceived inability to influence or control events and outcomes. Each domain signals a lack of empathy and the inclination to understand diverse experiences and points of view emerging from the tendency to harshly judge others, especially when they fail to behave in accordance with one's own inflated self-image.

While some white people will refuse to see the light, others are silent because they either don't know what to say or are concerned about backlash from other whites. Silence is no longer an option when so many lives are being lost and communities destroyed. White people have a role in undoing racism, because white people created it. There *are* tangible ways for you to take an active role in the fight against racism, injustice and inequality to help create a better America.

INCREASE YOUR CULTURAL COMPETENCE

Many, if not most, white people grow up with few significant or intimate interactions with African Americans. Some may have had contact with Black domestic or yard workers, fleeting contact with store clerks or a few Black employees in the workplace. Others have had no contact at all. Consequently, the perceptions that whites have about African Americans stem from what they are taught by parents and other family members, friends, teachers, social institutions and the mass media. Nevertheless, white stereotypes and prejudices can change with more frequent interactions with Blacks beyond the roles of unequal status such as that between an employee and a servant.

One might ask: *Why is it important to build cultural competence?* Diversity is reality. We live in a multicultural society that is comprised of people representing many nationalities and a broad range of cultural experiences. Many factors can affect cross-cultural interactions. Increasing mutual understanding and respect, building trust, and engaging in collaboration require moving through four levels of cultural competence: *cultural knowledge*, *cultural awareness*, *cultural sensitivity*, and *cultural competence*.

Cultural knowledge means that you know the history, characteristics, values, beliefs and behaviors of another cultural group. *Cultural awareness* is being open to changing your cultural attitudes after gaining cultural knowledge. *Cultural sensitivity* means understanding that differences exist among different cultures, but not assigning any values of good, bad, right or wrong. *Cultural competence* integrates the previous stages and translates into operational effectiveness which allows you to validate people for who they are, without judgment.

The benefits of cultural competence include, but are not limited to:

- Increased mutual understanding and respect;
- Increased trust and cooperation;
- Increased problem-solving through new perspectives, ideas and strategies;
- Increased participation and involvement in other cultural groups;
- Decreased fear of mistakes, conflict and competition among other cultural groups; and
- Greater inclusion, justice and equality.

STOP TALKING AND ACTIVELY LISTEN

People of color have every right to be angry and frustrated about the history of racism in this country. And although the conversation implicates whites as a part of the dominant race, it is not about you personally. Therefore, as a white person who daily benefits from privilege, you do not get to silence our pain or police our conversations or our tone. You also do not get to make yourself the center of attention by comparing your own experiences to those of people of color whenever we share our pain.

For example, there is a long history of white women being unable or unwilling to hear Black women's words. This privileged dismissal has erected a fortified barrier in terms of maintaining meaningful dialogue and building any trust. Think before you act. Stop becoming angry and defensive and actively listen to what is being said. Then make a sincere attempt to understand the dynamics of difference and how these racial differences have unfolded throughout American history to bring Black people to the point of even having to say that "Black lives matter" at all.

It is my hope that this old dynamic is shifting—albeit slowly—as we Black women begin speaking our truth and sharing our lived experiences, as white women (and men) open their hearts and minds to not just hear our words, but LISTEN to, REFLECT on, and seek to UNDERSTAND our words... then REACH OUT to us in solidarity if you truly wish to establish meaningful connection that will move us forward. Perhaps this may begin to shatter old relational patterns and narrow the chasm that currently separates us.

As a white person in a privileged position, it is your responsibility to understand and take ownership for the ways in which you unconsciously or consciously perpetuate racism and discrimination. Simply "doing good" for Blacks is not equality. We don't need your pity, we need your privilege. Now *that's* equality.

Mary Canty Merrill, Ph.D.

UNCOVER YOUR HIDDEN BIASES

Blatant racism is easy to recognize, and easy for conscious white people to separate themselves from. But it's those covert and no less insidious slights that continue to exist 153 years after Black people were emancipated from slavery. A hidden—or implicit—bias is an unconscious preference for or against a person, thing, or group. Research tells us that in spite of the best intentions, most people harbor deep-seated resistance to those who are different, whether that difference shows up in the form of race, ethnicity, gender, age, physical characteristics, background, personality or experiences. Bias can also exist in a positive sense relative to favoring family, community and people with whom one feels a shared connection based on shared characteristics and/or experiences. These hidden biases are not conscious or intentional, nor are they a sign of a bad person or a moral failing. They are products of what our brain considers normal, positive or acceptable, and shaped by numerous factors from past experiences to cultural environment to the influence of the community or social media.

An important first step in uncovering hidden biases is identifying and understanding the roots of stereotypes and prejudice, surfacing blind spots and uncovering covert racism. This can be accomplished through a self-assessment—there are a number of free and well-respected online assessments—or through a more in-depth intervention that allows you to examine your personal racial biases. There's nothing to be ashamed or embarrassed about as long as you are intentionally working to identify and overcome unconscious attitudes and make behavioral changes that foster opportunity and growth. Race is socially constructed. Social injustice and inequality will persist until racism and race-based discrimination are completely annihilated and whites no longer derive benefits from their racial status.

Acknowledge That Colorblindness Is Not The Answer

The different life experiences on either side of the color divide significantly contribute to divergent perceptions about racism. Whites tend to locate racism in color-consciousness so view colorblindness as a solution. Conversely, Blacks generally perceive racism as a system of power and privilege and consider racial identity as a core element of their historical and current experience.

At face value, colorblindness might seem like a noble approach, but upon deeper examination, this ideology is actually a form of racism. Colorblindness is not sufficient to heal racial wounds, and considerable research shows that it actually perpetuates group inequalities. This is because colorblindness translates into "I don't see you and I reject your cultural heritage, deny your negative racial experiences and invalidate your uniqueness as a human being." When you say that you don't see color, you are ignoring and perpetuating *aversive racism*—consciously supporting the principle of racial equality while—consciously or unconsciously—harboring negative beliefs, feelings and attitudes about and avoiding interactions with Blacks and other people of color.

Be Aware Of Stereotypical Terminology

Be mindful and socially aware of language. Observe how mainstream media use specific terms that reinforce Black stereotypes: "thug", "riot", "looting", "aggressive", "angry Black woman" and other derogatory terms. Diversify your media to gain broader perspectives and understanding of race-related issues. Avoid using divisive terms that perpetuate stereotypes. Call people out whenever they veer into derogatory terminology and speak the truth about the rampant racism, discrimination and oppression occurring in and destroying Black communities across the country.

Understand The Dynamics Of Cultural Differences

Each of us belongs to a collection of cultures—national cultures, subcultures, organizational cultures, professional cultures, industry cultures or functional cultures. For this reason, we can define culture as a shared system of values, beliefs and attitudes. Our culture affects the way in which we distinguish the actions of others. Many factors can affect cross-cultural interactions; and bias, as a result of cultural and historical experiences, can explain current attitudes as well as how we express ourselves as part of a group and as individuals.

The concept of culture has several layers. First, culture is an iceberg in which only the tip is visible on the surface. This can be referred to as explicit culture, which encompasses observable differences such as physical attributes, public display of emotions, language, artistic expression, and lifestyle behaviors. Second, culture is an onion with multiple layers that must be peeled away in order to reach the core of implicit culture—the truth of who we are as individuals. Third, culture is a mirror image that reflects back to us our values, beliefs, assumptions and norms. Regardless of background, every individual is extremely likely to encounter dynamics of difference in a rapidly and demographically changing society. Thus, it becomes important to carefully consider your own thoughts, feelings and experiences in which you identify and those that you find challenging. This can help you to more effectively understand and appreciate the rich diversity that characterizes all of humanity.

STAY IN YOUR LANE

Sometimes, white allies will get confused, believing that someone has anointed you omniscient ruler over the Black experience. Here are some valuable tips to help prevent you from swerving out of your lane and colliding with Black people:

- If the Black Lives Matter movement has become all about YOU, you're in the wrong lane.

- If you are so focused on advancing your own agenda that you discount or forget what the Black Lives Matter movement even stands for, you're in the wrong lane.

- If you become defensive when a person of color checks you on your viewpoint about Black issues, you're in the wrong lane.

- If you profess to know all about racism, rather than white privilege, you're in the wrong lane.

- If you only speak up about Black lives whenever it's convenient for you, you're in the wrong lane.

- If you talk a good talk, but don't walk the walk, you're in the wrong lane.

- If you claim to know more about being Black than Black people themselves, you're in the wrong lane.

- If you discount the feelings of people of color whenever they express concerns about your behavior and actions, you're in the wrong lane.

- If you are seeking validation, a pat on the back or a trophy from people of color because you're willing to speak out against social injustice and inequality, you're in the wrong lane.

- If you think that you know everything there is to know about racism and discrimination against people of color, you're in the wrong lane.

- If you think that having a Black person in your inner circle qualifies you to fully understand and speak on the depth of the Black experience, you're in the wrong lane.

- If you are now feeling pissed after reading these tips, you're in the wrong lane.

Before you ever profess to be an ally or an accomplice for Black lives or any other lives of color, know your lane… and stay in it.

Take Small Risks To Make A Difference

Learning about and overcoming racism, discrimination and oppression require you to take risks to generate new ways of thinking, doing and being. In *On Matters of Race, Power and Privilege*, Brantley, Frost, Pfeffer, Buccigrossi, and Robinson (2003) share additional ways for whites to make further progress:

1. Recognize that you are also members of a group with distinct patterns of behavior.

2. Track those behaviors and do better to understand their impact on others.

3. Become more aware of the group patterns identified by subordinated group members that negatively impede their access to generally available resources and opportunities.

4. Adjust your behavior to reduce the negative impact of your group membership on all others.

5. Work to influence other members of your group to become more aware and to reduce the overall negative impact of your dominant group membership on all others.

6. Learn to partner and collaborate with people of color.

These tips bring to mind a quote that I recently read in a July 16, 2013 *Huffington Post* article regarding Trayvon Martin (the Black teen fatally shot by a self-appointed neighborhood watchman in Sanford, Florida), and it's in response to the author who wasn't sure what bravery was or how change happened:

> *"Bravery is not a single decision. It's the overall effect of every brave decision you make: every time you do something because it's right, or kind, or honest, rather than because it's convenient or because it's less hard. So do the needful, kind, honest, things, one thing at a time. Then, when something really hard comes up, you'll have the practice you need, and you'll do the needful thing."*

When we ignore our past, we are destined to repeat it. While we cannot change our past, we must not be indifferent to our future. The struggle is *real*... and the struggle continues. Until we're all speaking a common language and sharing a common understanding, it will be virtually impossible to engage in fruitful conversations or enact social change. Saying that Black lives matter does not mean that other lives do not matter. It means that we want to ensure that Black lives matter, too—not just those of whites.

Police brutality and other forms of institutionalized racism will not subside until it becomes a part of the national conversation. Each of us has a sphere of influence. So I am asking you to look deep into your heart, reach out to others and commit to racial healing by doing something—on a large scale or small—that will help win a victory for all of humanity. Let's not wait for others to step up, but step up ourselves and work together to change the status quo and remove the barriers to social justice and equality. Through our collective efforts, change is possible; and I remain hopeful that change will come.

Epilogue

We Are Still Here

By Mary Canty Merrill, Ph.D.

Black people have been through many traumatic experiences. Our hearts have been cut deeply. Our minds have been twisted. Our bodies have been abused. Yet, despite all that we have been through, and though we may be weary at times, **we are *still* here**.

We were kidnapped from our native land—Mother Africa, yet we are still here.

We were shackled in chains, and crammed into the bowels of ships headed for the New World, yet we are still here.

We were forced to sail for weeks, months—and sometimes a year—amid inhumane and diseased conditions, yet we are still here.

We were torn from our families and loved ones, yet we are still here.

We were sold into slavery as property, yet we are still here.

We were raped and sexually abused by slaveholders, yet we are still here.

We were hung and brutally whipped, yet we are still here.

We were branded and mutilated, yet we are still here.

We were hunted down like wild animals, yet we are still here.

We were imprisoned for minor infractions—or no infractions at all—without legal defense or recourse, yet we are still here.

We were spat on, tormented and insulted, yet we are still here.

We were forced into hard labor from sunup to sundown, yet we are still here.

We were devalued as human beings, yet we are still here.

We were used as prizes in lotteries, yet we are still here.

We were used as wagers in card games and horse races, yet we are still here.

We were allotted the bare minimum of food, yet we are still here.

We were given the cast-off clothing of whites, yet we are still here.

We were abused and exploited through medical experimentation, yet we are still here.

We were provided no care for our health, yet we are still here.

We were placed in situations that jeopardized our well-being, yet we are still here.

We were forbidden to buy or sell goods without a permit, yet we are still here.

We were forbidden to own livestock, yet we are still here.

We were subject to nightly curfews, yet we are still here.

We were forced to live in meager shelter with leaky roofs, thin walls and dirt floors, yet we are still here.

We were forbidden to read and write, yet we are still here.

We were forbidden to marry outside of our race, and sometimes forbidden to marry at all, yet we are still here.

We were coerced into nursing white babies, yet we are still here.

We were treated harshly by cruel overseers and made an example to others, yet we are still here.

We were stripped of our freedom, yet we are still here.

We were in physical bondage for 300 years, yet we are still here.

We were subjected to a hard, miserable life that is now difficult to imagine, yet we are still here.

We possessed nothing except our dignity, yet we are still here.

We were forced into segregation, yet we are still here.

We were bitten by vicious dogs, attacked with tear gas and sprayed with fire hoses, yet we are still here.

We were searched at any time and for any reason, yet we are still here.

We were sharecroppers who were cheated and denied land ownership, yet we are still here.

We were robbed of our heritage, history and resources, yet we are still here.

We were denied our constitutional rights, yet we are still here.

We are subject to racial profiling, yet we are still here.

We have been forced into mass incarceration, yet we are still here.

We are still considered an inferior race, yet we are still here.

We have endured modern day genocide, yet we are still here.

We built this country called America with our blood, sweat, and tears, yet we are still here.

We have endured hundreds of years of racism, discrimination and oppression, yet despite everything that we have been through, we are still here.

WE ARE A STRONG, RESILIENT AND NOBLE PEOPLE... AND WE ARE STILL HERE!

In Memory

In memory of the unarmed Black men, women, teens and children who lost their lives at the hands of police or while in police custody between 1999 and early 2016... although you are no longer with us in this physical realm, your spirit remains and we speak your name:

Brian Acton	Cornelius Brown	Norman Cooper
Matthew Ajibade	Darrell Brown	John Crawford III
Carlos Alcis	Denzel Brown	Tyree Crawford
Clinton Allen	Michael Brown, Jr.	Zamiel Crawford
Raymond Allen	Paterson Brown, Jr.	Reynaldo Cuevas
Thomas Allen, Jr.	Raheim Brown	Albert Davis
Wendell Allen	Leroy Browning	Billy Ray Davis
Tanisha Anderson	Aaron Campbell	Richard Gregory Davis
Ross Anthony	Miriam Carey	
Anthony Ashford	James Carney III	Shantel Davis
Alonzo Ashley	Kiwane Carrington	Brian Day
Kevin Bajoie	Chavis Carter	Akiel Denkins*
Jordan Baker	Kenneth Chamberlain	Amadou Diallo
Orlando Barlow		Nehemiah Dillard
Ronald Beasley	Jason Champion	Patrick Dorismond
Lashonda Ruth Belk	William Chapman II	Deontre Dorsey
Sean Bell	Terry Lee Chatman	Reginald Doucet
Jermaine Benjamin	Keith Childress	Samuel Dubose
Sandra Bland	Jamar Clark	Sharmel Edwards
Rekia Boyd	Markus Clark	Salvado Ellswood
Rumain Brisbon	McKenzie Cochran	Miguel Espinal
James Brisette	Rayshaun Cole	

Mary Canty Merrill, Ph.D.

DeAunta Terrel Farrow	Lorenzo Hayes	Sgt. Manuel Loggins, Jr.
David Felix	Alvin Haynes	Andy Lopez
Malcolm Ferguson	Danroy Henry	Ronald Madison
Jonathan Ferrell	Anthony Hill	Asshams Manley
Deion Fludd	Sam Holmes	George Mann
Ezell Ford	Artago Howard	Michael Lee Marshall
Shereese Francis	Donald 'Dontay' Ivy	Kevin Matthews
Shelly Frey	Kris Jackson	Spencer McCain
Darrell Gatewood	Larry Eugene Jackson, Jr.	Kendrec McDade
Eric Garner	Kendra James	Natasha McKenna
Brendon Glenn	Ervin Jefferson	Keith McLeod
Henry Glover	Kathryn Johnson	Tiano Meton
Dajuan Graham	Aiyana Jones	Jason Moland
Ramarley Graham	Bettie Jones	Bernard Moore
Oscar Grant	Brandon Jones	Reginald Moore
Freddie Gray	Derrick Jones	Terrance Moxley
Kimani Gray	Lamontez Jones	Andre Murphy, Sr.
Andre Green	Prince Jones	Earl Murray
Bobby Gross	Curtis Jordan	Roy Nelson
Akai Gurley	Kevin Judson	Bryan Overstreet
Lavall Hall	India Kager	Noel Palanco
Mya Hall	Terrance Kellom	Dante Parker
Wendell Hall	Charly 'Africa' Keunang	Jonathan Paul
Dontre Hamilton	Christopher Kimble	Richard Perkins
Kenneth Harding	Felix Kumi	Brian Pickett
Samuel Harrell	Nuwnah Laroche	Nathaniel Pickett
Darnisha Harris	Victor Larosa III	Kajieme Powell
Eric Harris	Jeremy Lett	Dante Price
Gregory Daquan Harris	Kyam Livingston	Terry Price

Why Black Lives Matter (Too)

Junior Prosper	Alonzo Smith	Shem Walker
Calvon Reid	Yvette Smith	Johnnie Kamahi
Jerame Reid	Alberta Spruill	Warren
Tamir Rice	De'Angelo	Steven E.
Askari Roberts	Stallworth	Washington
Tamon Robinson	Aiyana	Chandra Weaver
Tony Robinson	Stanley-Jones	Wayne Wheeler
Troy Robinson	Timothy Stansbury	Phillip White
Timothy Russell	Victor Steen	Victor White III
Michael Sabbie	Darrius Stewart	Alan Craig Williams
Jonathan Sanders	Christian Taylor	Barrington Williams
Leslie Sapp	Alesia Thomas	Malissa Williams
Walter Scott	Nicholas Thomas	Tarika Wilson
Yvens Seide	Tiara Thomas	Dominick Wise
Frank 'Trey'	Timothy Thomas	Tyree Woodson
Shephard III	Stephen Tooson	Ousmane Zongo
Frank Smart	Naeschylus Vinzant	

*Incident details still sketchy at time of publication

You did not lose your life at the hands of police, but at the hands of a sociopathic, gun-toting, self-appointed neighborhood watch member. Your death was not in vain, but was the catalyst for our modern civil rights movement: **Trayvon Martin**... we speak your name.

#VoicesForEquality

Works Cited

Alexander, M. (2011). *The new Jim Crow: Mass incarceration in the age of colorblindness.* New York: The New Press.

American Civil Liberties Union. (2015). *Racial profiling: definition.* Retrieved from: https://www.aclu.org/racial-profiling-definition

American Heart Association. (2016). *High Blood Pressure and African Americans.* Retrieved from: http://www.heart.org/HEARTORG/Conditions/HighBloodPressure/UnderstandYourRiskforHighBloodPressure/High-Blood-Pressure-and-African-Americans_UCM_301832_Article.jsp#.Vu4V-jF5LdU

Badger, E. (2015). *Black poverty differs from white poverty.* Retrieved from: https://www.washingtonpost.com/news/wonk/wp/2015/08/12/black-poverty-differs-from-white-poverty/

Baptist, E. E. (2014). *The half has never been told: Slavery and the making of American capitalism.* New York: Basic Books.

Bonczar, T. (2003). *Prevalence of imprisonment in the U.S. Population, 1974-2001.* Retrieved from: http://www.bjs.gov/content/pub/pdf/piusp01.pdf

Brantley, C., Frost, D., Pfeffer, C., Buccigrossi, J., & Robinson, M. (2003). *On matters of race, power and privilege.* Rochester, NY: wetWare, Inc.

Coates, T. (2015). The Black family in the age of mass incarceration. *The Atlantic*. Retrieved from: http://www.theatlantic.com/magazine/archive/2015/10/the-black-family-in-the-age-of-mass-incarceration/403246/

Colby, S. L., & Ortman, J. M. (2015). *Projections of the size and composition of the U.S. population: 2014 to 2060*. U.S, Census Bureau. Retrieved from: https://www.census.gov/content/dam/Census/library/publications/2015/demo/p25-1143.pdf

Cook, L. (2015). U.S. education: Still separate and unequal. *U.S. News & World Report*. Retrieved from: http://www.usnews.com/news/blogs/data-mine/2015/01/28/us-education-still-separate-and-unequal

Cooper, B. (2015). *11 major misconceptions about the Black Lives Matter Movement*. Retrieved from: http://www.cosmopolitan.com/politics/a45930/misconceptions-black-lives-matter-movement/

DeGruy, J. (2005). *Post traumatic slave syndrome: America's legacy of enduring injury and healing*. Portland, OR: Joy DeGruy Publications, Inc.

Drake, B. (2013). *Incarceration gap widens between whites and blacks*. Pew Research Center. Retrieved from: http://www.pewresearch.org/fact-tank/2013/09/06/incarceration-gap-between-whites-and-blacks-widens/

Farbota, K. (2016). *Black crime rates: What happens when numbers aren't neutral*. Huffington Post. Retrieved from: http://www.huffingtonpost.com/kim-farbota/black-crime-rates-your-st_b_8078586.html

Gans, H. J. (1995). *The war against the poor: The underclass and antipoverty policy.* New York: Basic Books.

Goffman, A. (2014). *On the run: Fugitive life in an American city.* New York: Picador.

Henry, P. J., Reyna, C., & Weiner, B. (2004). Hate welfare but help the poor: How the attributional content of stereotypes explains the paradox of reactions to the destitute in America. *Journal of Applied Social Psychology 28*(19), 1743-1759.

Jargowsky, P. A. (2015). *Architecture of segregation: Civil unrest, the concentration of poverty, and public policy.* Retrieved from: http://apps.tcf.org/architecture-of-segregation

Johnson, J. (2015). *Flint, Detroit among nation's poorest cities, new Census data show.* Retrieved from: http://www.mlive.com/news/flint/index.ssf/2015/09/flint_detroit_among_nations_po.html

Kerby, S. (2012). *The top 10 most startling facts about people of color and criminal justice in the United States.* Center for American Progress. Retrieved from: https://www.americanprogress.org/issues/race/news/2012/03/13/11351/the-top-10-most-startling-facts-about-people-of-color-and-criminal-justice-in-the-united-states/

Kolodner, M. (2015). *Black students are being shut out of top public colleges.* Huffington Post. Retrieved from: http://www.huffingtonpost.com/entry/black-students-are-being-shut-out-of-top-public-colleges_us_56703e08e4b0e292150f40c4

Loewen, J. W. (2005). *Sundown towns: A hidden dimension of American racism.* New York: Touchstone.

McIntosh, P. (1988). *White privilege and male privilege: A personal account of coming to see correspondences through work in women's studies*. Retrieved from: http://www.collegeart.org/pdf/diversity/white-privilege-and-male-privilege.pdf

Mental Health America (2016). *African American communities and mental health*. Retrieved from: http://www.mentalhealthamerica.net/african-american-mental-health

Mitchell, M., & Leachman, M. (2014). *Changing priorities: State criminal justice reforms and investments in education*. Center on Budget Policy and Priorities. Retrieved from: http://www.cbpp.org/research/changing-priorities-state-criminal-justice-reforms-and-investments-in-education

National Stroke Association. (2016). *Minorities and stroke*. Retrieved from: http://www.stroke.org/understand-stroke/impact-stroke/minorities-and-stroke

Neal, D., & Rick, A. (2014). *The prison boom and the lack of Black progress after Smith and Welch*. University of Chicago NBER Working Paper No. w20283.

Partners Healthcare Asthma Center. (2010). *Poverty and Asthma*. Retrieved from: http://www.asthma.partners.org/NewFiles/BoFAChapter15.html

Pew Research Center (2016). *Wealth inequality has widened along racial, ethnic lines since end of Great Recession*. Retrieved from: http://www.pewresearch.org/fact-tank/2014/12/12/racial-wealth-gaps-great-recession/

Russell, K., Wilson, M., & Hall, R. (2013). *The Color Complex: The Politics of Skin Color in a New Millennium*. New York: Anchor Books.

Sakala, L. (2014) Prison Policy Initiative. *Breaking down mass incarceration in the 2010 Census: State-by-State incarceration rates by race/ethnicity*. Retrieved from:

http://www.prisonpolicy.org/reports/rates.html

Sinha, M. (2016). *The slave's cause: A history of abolition*. New Haven, CT: Yale University Press.

Sue, D. W. (2011). *Microaggressions in everyday life: Race, gender, and sexual orientation*. Hoboken, NJ: Wiley.

Taylor, J. (2015). New DOJ statistics on race and violent crime. *American Renaissance*. Retrieved from: http://www.amren.com/news/2015/07/new-doj-statistics-on-race-and-violent-crime/

The Center for Disease Control and Prevention (2016). *HIV among African Americans*. Retrieved from: http://www.cdc.gov/hiv/group/racialethnic/africanamericans/

The Guardian. (2015). *Young black men killed by US police at highest rate in year of 1,134 deaths*. The Counted. Retrieved from: http://www.theguardian.com/us-news/2015/dec/31/the-counted-police-killings-2015-young-black-men

U.S. Department of Education. (2014). *The condition of education 2014*. IES National Center for Education Statistics. Retrieved from: http://nces.ed.gov/pubs2014/2014083.pdf

U.S. Department of Justice. (2003). *Guidance regarding the use of race by federal law enforcement agencies.* Retrieved from: https://www.justice.gov/sites/default/files/crt/legacy/2010/12/15/guidance_on_race.pdf

U.S. Department of Justice. (2015). *New DOJ statistics on race and violent crime.* Retrieved from: http://www.amren.com/news/2015/07/new-doj-statistics-on-race-and-violent-crime/

Who Leads Us. (2014). *Do America's elected officials reflect our population?* Retrieved from: http://wholeads.us/#

Wilson, V. (2015). *Black unemployment rate dips below 10 percent in 11 of 24 states measured in second quarter.* Economic Policy Institute. Retrieved from: http://www.epi.org/publication/black-unemployment-rate-dips-below-10-percent-in-11-of-24-states-measured-in-second-quarter/

Witters, D., & Liu, D. (2015). *Young Black males' well-being harmed more by unemployment.* Retrieved from: http://www.gallup.com/poll/182507/young-black-males-harmed-unemployment.aspx

YouGov/Huffington Post. (2015). *Poll results: Race.* Retrieved from: https://today.yougov.com/news/2015/06/29/poll-results-race/

Zhao, J. (2015). The plight of black America. *The Chronicle.* Retrieved from http://www.dukechronicle.com/article/2015/05/plight-black-america

CONTRIBUTING WRITER ESSAYS – CHAPTER 5

Laurie Baker:

DeGruy, J. (2005). *Post traumatic slave syndrome: America's legacy of enduring injury and healing.* Portland, OR: Joy DeGruy Publications, Inc.

Constitutional Rights Foundation. (2016). Retrieved from: www.crf-usa.org

Juneteeth.com World Wide Celebration. (n.d.) Retrieved from: www.juneteenth.com

Library of Congress. (n.d.). Retrieved from: https://www.loc.gov/

Shaay Gallagher-Starr:

Bar-Haim, Y., Ziv, T., Lamy, D., & Hodes, R. M. (2006). Nature and nurture in own-race face processing. *Psychological Science, 17*(2), 159-163.

Best, D. L., Smith, S. C., Graves, D. J., & Williams, J. E. (1975). The modification of racial bias in preschool children. *Journal of Experimental Child Psychology, 20*(2), 193-205.

Dore, R. A., Hoffman, K. M., Lillard, A. S., & Trawalter, S. (2014). Children's racial bias in perceptions of others' pain. *British Journal of Developmental Psychology, 32*(2), 218-231.

Elliott, A. M., Alexander, S. C., Mescher, C. A., Mohan, D., & Barnato, A. E. (2016). Differences in physicians' verbal and nonverbal communication with Black and white patients at the end of life. *Journal of Pain and Symptom Management, 51*(1), 1-8.

Sabin, J. A., & Greenwald, A. G. (2012). The influence of implicit bias on treatment recommendations for 4 Common pediatric conditions: Pain, Urinary Tract Infection, Attention Deficit Hyperactivity Disorder, and Asthma. *American Journal of Public Health, 102*(5), 988-995.

Sandi Gordon:

Balkaran, S. (1999). *Mass media and racism.* Yale University *YPQ, 21*(1). Retrieved from: http://www.yale.edu/ypq/articles/oct99/oct99b.html

Blair, I., Steiner, J., & Havranek, E. (2011). Unconscious (implicit) bias and health disparities: Where do we go from here? *Permanente Journal, 15*(2), 71–78. Retrieved from: http://www.ncbi.nlm.nih.gov/pmc/articles/PMC3140753/

Comissiong, S. (2010). Police brutality in America—a hip-hop perspective. *Daily Journal (Opinion).* Retrieved from: http://www.dailycensored.com/police-brutality-in-america-a-hip-hop-perspective/

Griffin, J. (1961). *Black like me.* Boston, MA: Houghton Mifflin.

Indiana University (2004). *Mass media and the African American criminal male stereotype.* Indiana University News Room. Retrieved from: http://newsinfo.iu.edu/news/page/normal/1580.html

Jones, F. (2013). *Black people are targets of the largest media driven psychological warfare campaign in history.* Retrieved from: https://africanpress.wordpress.com/2013/02/27/black-people-are-targets-of-the-largest-media-driven-psychological-warfare-campaign-in-history/

McIntosh, P. (1988). *White privilege and male privilege: A personal account of coming to see correspondences through work in women's studies.* Independent School, Working Paper 189.

The Guardian (2015). *Young Black men killed by U.S. police at highest rate in year of 1,134 deaths.* Retrieved from: http://www.theguardian.com/us-news/2015/dec/31/the-counted-police-killings-2015-young-black-men

Erin Hooton:

Drescher, S. (1999). *From slavery to freedom: Comparative studies in the rise and fall of Atlantic slavery.* New York: New York University Press.

Long, E. (2003). *The history of Jamaica.* McGill-Queen's University Press.

Alexander, M. (2011). *The new Jim Crow: Mass incarceration in the age of colorblindness.* New York: The New Press.

Washington, H. A. (2007). *Medical apartheid: The dark history of medical experimentation on Black Americans from Colonial times to the present.* London: Doubleday.

Krieger, N., Chen, J. T., Waterman, P. D., Kiang, M. V., & Feldman, J. (2015). *Police killings and police deaths are public health data and can be counted.* DOI: 10.1371/journal.pmed.1001915.

Lewis, E. (2013). Civil rights and the changing World. *Humanities, 34*(1.5) Retrieved from: http://www.neh.gov/humanities/2013/januaryfebruary/feature/civil-rights-and-the-changing-world>

Teresa C. Lewis:

Edwards, B. (2016). *Father pens book to explain protest to kids in the time of Black Lives Matter.* Retrieved from: http://www.theroot.com/articles/culture/2016/02/father_pens_book_to_explain_protest_to_kids_in_the_time_of_black_lives_matter.2.html

van Gelder, S. (2016). *The radical work of healing: Fania and Angela Davis on a new kind of civil rights activism.* Retrieved from http://www.yesmagazine.org/issues/life-after-oil/the-radical-work-of-healing-fania-and-angela-davis-on-a-new-kind-of-civil-rights-activism-20160218

Leslie G. Nelson:

ABC News. (2007). *Race in medical care: Skin color matters with patient care.* Retrieved from: http://abcnews.go.com/GMA/Health/story?id=3401076

Hughes, J. (2014). *What Black parents tell their sons about the police.* Retrieved from: http://gawker.com/what-black-parents-tell-their-sons-about-the-police-1624412625.

Kearney, M. S., & Harris, B. H. (2014). *Ten economic facts about crime and incarceration in the United States.* Retrieved from: http://www.brookings.edu/research/reports/2014/05/10-crime-facts.

Adams, C., Robelen, E., & Shaw, N. (2012). *Civil rights data show detention disparities.* Retrieved from: http://www.edweek.org/ew/articles/2012/03/07/23data_ep.h31.html?tkn=RNRFpTpIviHSEInUrVg%2BbNsoHrUv6d7QWbPa&cmp=clp-edweek&utm_source=fb&utm_medium=rss&utm_campaign=mrss

Sharp, G. (2015). *Race, criminal background, and employment.* Retrieved from: https://thesocietypages.org/socimages/2015/04/03/race-criminal-background-and-employment/

Crystal Combs White:

Budget Committee Democrats. (2016). *FACT SHEET: Republican Budget Cuts Education.* Retrieved from: http://democrats.budget.house.gov/fact-sheet/fact-sheet-republican-budget-cuts-education

Cook, L. (2015). *U.S. education: Still separate and unequal.* Retrieved from: http://www.usnews.com/news/blogs/data-mine/2015/01/28/us-education-still-separate-and-unequal

Kids Count Data Center. (2015). *Children in poverty by race and ethnicity.* Retrieved from: http://datacenter.kidscount.org/data/tables/44-children-in-poverty-by-race-and-ethnicity#detailed/1/any/false/869,36,868,867,133/10,11,9,12,1,185,13/324,323

NYU Steinhardt. (2015). *Education and mortality study finds association between high school and college education and life expectancy.* Retrieved from: http://steinhardt.nyu.edu/site/ataglance/2015/07/education-and-mortality-study-finds-less-education-reduces-life-expectancy.html

Schott Foundation for Public Education. (n.d.). *Black lives matter: The Schott 50 State report on public education and black males.* Retrieved from: http://blackboysreport.org/states/?state=Michigan

Rebecca Wiggins:

Alexander, M. (2011). *The new Jim Crow: Mass incarceration in the age of colorblindness.* New York: The New Press.

American Civil Liberties Union. (2015). *Combating mass incarceration.* Retrieved from: https://www.aclu.org/issues/mass-incarceration

American Civil Liberties Union. (2015). *What is the school-to-prison pipeline?* Retrieved from: https://www.aclu.org/fact-sheet/what-school-prison-pipeline

Coates, T. (2014). *The case for reparations.* Retrieved from: http://www.theatlantic.com/magazine/archive/2014/06/the-case-for-reparations/361631/

Davis, A. (1983). *Women, race & class.* New York: Vintage.

DeNavas-Walt, C., Proctor, B. D., & Smith, J. C. (2012). *Income, poverty, and health insurance coverage in the United States.* Retrieved from: http://www.census.gov/prod/2012pubs/p60-243.pdf

Hill, C. (2016). *The simple truth about the gender pay gap.* Retrieved from: http://www.aauw.org/research/the-simple-truth-about-the-gender-pay-gap/

Kochhar, R., & Fry, R. (2014). *Wealth inequality has widened along racial, ethnic lines since end of Great Recession.* Retrieved from: http://www.pewresearch.org/fact-tank/2014/12/12/racial-wealth-gaps-great-recession/

PBS. (2000). *Roots in the sand.* Retrieved from: http://www.pbs.org/rootsinthesand/

About the Author and Editor

Dr. Mary Canty Merrill has spent more than twenty-five years motivating and inspiring clients and audiences across the country to step out of their comfort zone and into their personal power. She began her career in corporate America and today is the president and chief operating officer of Merrill Consulting Associates, LLC an organizational consulting firm based in Denver, Colorado. In addition to being an entrepreneur, Mary serves humanity in a variety of roles—as a psychologist, educator, facilitator, speaker, author, life strategist, human rights advocate, and provocateur—and she is known for her thought-provoking messages, high-energy delivery, and dynamic work in unleashing human potential. She partners with Fortune 500 companies, government and nonprofit agencies, educational institutions, individuals, groups and communities to inspire new levels of confidence, productivity, performance, and success. Her professional blog, *The Inside Out with Dr. Mary Canty Merrill* (www.mcantymerrill.wordpress.com) provides engaging commentary on a broad range of topics that encourage dynamic thinking and transform individual experiences. In addition to *Why Black Lives Matter (Too)*, Mary has coauthored two books: *The Daughters and Spirit of Harriet* and *Miracles, Momentum and Manifestation*. She has penned the introduction and foreword for several other books and is currently writing her fourth book, *Realm of Revelation*, which releases late 2016. Mary can be reached by e-mail at: mcanty@merrillca.com or via her author website at: www.marycantymerrillauthor.com.